Great Songwriting Techniques

Great Songwriting Techniques

Jack Perricone

OXFORD
UNIVERSITY PRESS

OXFORD
UNIVERSITY PRESS

Oxford University Press is a department of the University of Oxford. It furthers
the University's objective of excellence in research, scholarship, and education
by publishing worldwide. Oxford is a registered trade mark of Oxford University
Press in the UK and certain other countries.

Published in the United States of America by Oxford University Press
198 Madison Avenue, New York, NY 10016, United States of America.

Library of Congress Cataloging-in-Publication Data
Names: Perricone, Jack, author.
Title: Great songwriting techniques / Jack Perricone.
Description: New York, NY : Oxford University Press, [2018] | Includes bibliographical references and index.
Identifiers: LCCN 2017038738| ISBN 9780199967650 (cloth : alk. paper) | ISBN 9780199967674 (pbk. : alk. paper) |
ISBN 9780190874032 (companion website)
Subjects: LCSH: Popular music—Writing and publishing.
Classification: LCC MT67 .P46 2018 | DDC 782.42/13—dc23
LC record available at https://lccn.loc.gov/2017038738

9 8 7 6 5 4 3 2 1

Paperback printed by Webcom, Inc., Canada
Hardback printed by Bridgeport National Bindery, Inc., United States of America

CONTENTS

Contents

ACKNOWLEDGMENTS

Patience is not only a virtue but also a gift, a gift that I have experienced from my wife, Rebecca, during the years it has taken to write this book. Our daughter Sonya Rae Taylor, a talented vocalist, guitarist, and songwriter, contributed astute and helpful comments during the many rewrites this book has undergone. She also contributed the vocals on most of the audio samples in the book. My colleagues at Berklee College of Music, Pat Pattison, Mark Simos, and Ben Camp contributed helpful information and feedback. Ben Camp also co- produced the recording of my song "Goodbye Again" that appears on the companion Oxford website containing audio examples. Tanja Utunen, a Berklee alumna, after reading a couple of chapters early on, helped set me on a path that proved to be better and more direct than the one I had initially begun, and Mike Rexford, an entertainment lawyer, gave me some very helpful tips not only on law but also on formatting the book. My lawyer, Paul Sennott, gave me great legal advice and, since he is also a musician, shared his enthusiasm for the book. I also thank Bill Brinkley and Steve Kirby for helping me with the Finale graphics that are such an important part of this book.

Thanks to the two vocalists, both graduates of Berklee College of Music, Emma White and Frank Maroney, who gave excellent, authentic performances of the two original songs that are used to demonstrate the process of songwriting. My wife, Rebecca, aka Labek, is the evocative vocalist on my song "Love Provides" found on the companion website.

I am forever grateful to Norman Hirschy, editor at Oxford University Press, who believes, as I do, that this is a book that needed to be written.

ABOUT THE COMPANION WEBSITE

http://www.oup.com/us/greatsongwritingtechniques

Included on the Oxford website are audio examples to accompany and enhance your songwriting exploration. Passages with correlating audio examples are indicated with ▶.

Great Songwriting Techniques

Introduction

This book is written for those who are serious about songwriting, for those who believe, as I do, that the rational mind has a definite place in the creative process—that once you become familiar with the tools and techniques of songwriting your freedom to create is greatly increased.

Both major disciplines, lyric writing and composing, are included in this text. However, there is a decided emphasis on music and especially on music's relationship to lyrics. Once you've absorbed the information in this book, it will be available whenever needed, so that when you are in that intuitive place—in the zone—you can remain there for longer periods of time. You will be able to finish more of the songs that you've started, and more of your songs will be keepers. It may take time to absorb a lot of the information in this book, but I believe it will be time well spent.

Some knowledge of music notation and basic theory will be very helpful in fully understanding some of the subjects. Even without a fluent knowledge of notation, you should be able to learn a great deal from this book because many of the examples are from songs you will recognize. All the excerpts are short and are solely meant for educational purposes. Oxford University Press has a dedicated site: www.oup.com/us/greatsongwritingtechniques, containing streaming audio that corresponds to the various examples found in this book. If you find that you are attracted to a particular song, there are many sites where you can purchase the song.

Methodology and song selection

The portions of songs that I've used as examples are mainly from well-known and well-written popular songs, not art songs or musical theater songs (although many of the songs from the *Great American Songbook* did have their origins in the Broadway Theatre).

My method is to, as succinctly as possible, teach you a technique and then show you a number of examples of that technique in well-known popular songs. Songwriters range from Irving Berlin to Taylor Swift, and, because I am teaching technique rather than style, examples from these two great writers may appear next to each other. I've also included a few of my songs to illustrate a particular technique and, especially, to demonstrate the process used in composing a song.

A key ingredient to becoming a successful songwriter is your ability to become your own best teacher. This can be done with the guidance I've provided in this book and in *Melody in Songwriting*, published by Berklee Press, distributed by Hal Leonard, and, most of all, through your own commitment to writing songs every day. I also highly recommend collaboration with other songwriters, because it is a great way to learn the craft of songwriting from another person's perspective and because it can produce extraordinary results.

Study, listen, analyze, and write songs regularly and with your newfound knowledge and experience, you won't have to wait for inspiration to begin your next song; your daily attempts will finally allow the muse to enter your creative life on a regular basis.

My personal experience as a songwriter

I began my career as a professional songwriter at about age thirty, a rather late age to begin any career. When I arrived in New York in 1968 I knew that I would be a professional musician. I already had a couple of degrees in music when I was hired to work music at Belwin/Mills Publishing in New York as an office musician. I had not been hired as a songwriter because at that point in time I had not seriously attempted to be one. At Belwin/Mills I wrote lead sheets and put together demo sessions for the staff songwriters, all of whom had little or no formal training in music. Being in the environment of songwriters inspired me to become one. I, however, experienced seemingly endless frustration as I gradually realized that writing commercial songs was not so easy.

I finally came to the conclusion that I did have the foundation (a bachelor's degree in music theory and a masters degree in composition) to study—really study—popular songs and discover the techniques that were used in making them popular. From that moment on, I began to listen to popular songs in a different way: with more intensity and with more openness. The endless hours of listening, transcribing, asking myself questions, and attempting to write songs on a daily basis, finally produced results. Through the analysis of successful songs, not only did I become more conscious of the vocabulary and techniques that were used, but also I learned a new harmonic and melodic vocabulary that differed from the ones I had been exposed to in the staid halls and classrooms of the music conservatories I had attended.

I discovered that one of the most important missing ingredients in my education was grasping the importance of lyrics in songs. Realizing my shortcomings in that area, I started to collaborate with lyricists. Songs started to emerge, and within five years I had successes as a songwriter: a top 5 pop song that I cowrote and solely arranged, a top 10 R&B song, even a top 20 country song.

In 1986 I became chair of the Songwriting department at the premier contemporary music educational institution, Berklee College of Music, an office I held until I retired in 2013. Early on in my tenure as chair, I wrote *Melody in Songwriting*, a book that exposes some of the songwriting techniques presented in this new book, but unlike this text, contains very few examples from well-known songs. Probably the most innovative thing I've done in my lifetime is to emphasize the importance of melody and create a text that actually teaches melody, a subject that has been ignored by higher education for centuries. Paul Hindemith, the great German composer and theoretician, wrote in his *Craft of Musical Composition* this indictment of music academia: "It is astounding that instruction in composition has never developed a theory of melody." I continue to teach melody and to elaborate on my initial theories with concrete examples from the popular song literature in this book.

The book that you are now reading more closely mirrors the way I taught myself to write songs. That method, to study and analyze hit songs that have something substantial to offer the serious songwriter, is the method I've chosen to use in this book.

My thoughts on professional songwriting

Most of the songs presented in this book are successful not only artistically but also commercially. In my teaching, I've always chosen commercial songs as models for technique because they have proven themselves successful to the masses. The word "commercial" has often been maligned with connotations of "less than" or "selling out." In choosing to use commercially successful songs, I'm not endorsing every commercial song, nor am I stating that every commercially successful song is well written. However, the best commercial songs have an appeal to the masses because they contain an innate truth, a connection that cannot be denied, whether it is a groove that has an immediate physical effect or a lyric so perfectly wedded to music that an emotional reaction invariably occurs. Many of them have great songwriting techniques that I've unearthed for my students and, now, for you.

I've often asked myself: "Why do we continue to write songs and what is the purpose and effect of songwriting on society?" My answer may throw you, but I consider it a great truth: popular songs relieve the pressure of being alive, lighten our load, and help us connect to each other. That is the function of popular songs in our society—and a great function and purpose it serves.

This book will provide you with many techniques that will facilitate your ability to fully express yourself through song. Once you've finished writing a song, ask yourself: *Is the message in my song coming across to the listener so that s/he can feel what I feel?* If your answer to this question is "yes," then you may have helped contribute to our common mental health and to the enjoyment of life.

How to use this book

I've attempted to make this book less academic than my first book, *Melody in Songwriting*, through both its language and its format. Certainly, the many short examples gleaned from well-known songs make this study very real, not simply theoretical. I have included a few exercises or activities at the end of each chapter. For the most part, I rely on you to study the techniques demonstrated and to use the techniques and exercises you feel you need. As you try a particular technique, you may find that it leads you into writing an original song; that would be the very best outcome.

This text has a progression from simple to complex and, as in most disciplines, the foundational elements that appear early on are most important. Without them, much of the subjects that appear later in the text will not be as fully comprehensible.

The first part of the book, "The Basics," chapters 1–6, covers basic concepts and techniques. The second part, "Tonal Environments," chapters 7 and 8, presents fundamental studies of tonality, how tonal materials are organized and function. Since these two chapters also contain fairly detailed information related to music theory, they should be used as reference chapters as questions arise. The third part, "Large Considerations," chapters 9–11 deals with developmental techniques, form, the melodic outline, and the melodic step progression. The fourth part, "Harmonic Considerations," chapters 12–14 covers harmony and the intriguing relationship of melody to harmony, as well as harmony's affect on lyrics. A number of less exposed but highly important songwriting techniques are taught in the fifth part, "Deeper into Technique" chapters 15–16. These include writing to a riff, the use of counterpoint, and a study of tonal and rhythmic strategizing. In the sixth part, "Final Results," some gems of exceptional songwriting are revealed and explored and the actual process of writing a song, a subject rarely broached in most texts, is exposed.

PART I

The Basics

1

Beginning A Song

The act of writing a song is a gift to yourself. The moment you decide to write a song, you are exhibiting the courage to create. I use the term "courage" because songwriting is a challenge to your creativity, to your fortitude and, therefore, can be a little scary. And, like most acts that demand courage, the payoff is usually greater than most other endeavors. Luckily, there are many ways that you can begin a song; if one road leads to a dead end, there are many other roads you may try.

Since writing can be and usually is such an intense personal experience, it is best if you shut out the outside world. Turn off your phone and any other intrusive devices, so that you can enter the interior of your being.

Beginning with a title

One of the most direct ways to begin a song is by starting with a title. A title may simply be an indexing device, i.e., a fast way to recollect a song, but it also can be a powerful catalyst for the idea and treatment of a song. Titles are everywhere, and fortunately titles are not copyrightable, so you needn't concern yourself about using a title that has been used before.

What is important is the way in which you treat the title. For example, the title "You Belong To Me" has meant different things to different generations. In the 1940s, the subject of the hit song "You Belong To Me," sung by Jo Stafford, was centered on possessiveness, but its possessiveness was couched in ultraromantic language.

"You Belong To Me"   lyrics by Chilton Price, Pee Wee King, Redd Stewart

Fly the ocean in a silver plane
See the jungle when it's wet with rain
But remember, darling, till you're home again
That you belong to me

In the seventies, at that time of personal confessionals, Carly Simon wrote and sang the same title in much more direct language and with more than a tinge of jealousy.

"You Belong To Me"   by Carly Simon, Michael McDonald

You belong to me;
Tell her you were fooling.
You don't even know her,
Tell her that I love you.

What if you wanted to write a song that uses that same title, but one that doesn't perpetuate the theme of possessiveness—a theme that seems to be built into it? The following is my attempt to do just that, and I hope that in sharing this process it will help guide you in how to conceptualize a lyric. To begin, I simply jot down the main idea without concerning myself about whether the rhythms work in the context of a song.

> I don't want to possess you
> but I can't seem to live without you.
> You belong to me in the same way
> that the air I breathe and the water I drink belong to me.

Now that I can see and hear these thoughts, my task is to make them work as a lyric. I need to find substitute phrases and words that have rhythm and rhyme and can function with music within a song form. To do that, I need to establish a steady beat as a basic guide—to find a *groove*: a rhythmic underpinning that establishes the meter and allows the rhythms of the melody to move and flow naturally.

The first two lines, "I don't want to possess you / but I can't seem to live without you," might work as a beginning verse, but since I realize that those two lines are part of a declaration or conclusion, they are best kept for material that will appear just before the title and the chorus. I need to create a section to set up that declaration. With that thought in mind, I write:

> When I say that, "you're mine"
> I know those words
> make you wonder.
> And when I say, "you're a part of me,"
> I don't mean
> you're under my control.
> You're my life, my heart, my soul,

Now I feel that I can make a declaration and I write:

> And **you belong to me**
> Like the river belongs to the sea
> Like the ocean belongs to the shore
> Like the air that we breathe
> You're my deepest need
> **You belong to me**
> Like I belong to you.

In a sense, I've explained myself to my lover and in doing so I've come up with a way to make the phrase "You belong to me" not as possessive as it initially sounds but, instead, as an outcome of nature and love. I've also found rhythms and rhymes that work within a musical setting and a song form (verse/chorus) in which to express the concept of the song.

The process that I've just taken you through: first coming up with a title that leads to an idea/feeling and concept that you want to express, and then quickly writing in prose some of what you want the lyric to encapsulate, is a an empowering approach to lyric writing. It will furnish you with ideas and some usable phrases but, more than anything, it will help keep your lyric on track.

Interestingly enough, the title "You Belong To Me"—with one word change—was a big hit in 2010 by Taylor Swift. She changed "to" to "with" and with that, "You Belong **To** Me" became "You Belong **With** Me," and the former title lost its negatively possessive connotation. Proof, once again, that one word, even a preposition, can make a huge difference.

Beginning with a lyric concept

Many professional songwriters begin the songwriting process with a title but, in addition, do not proceed until they have a clear idea of how they treat that title; they only proceed when they have a lyric concept. My concept in writing to the title "You Belong To Me" was to make the song as loving and nonpossessive as possible. Concepts are potent sources for inspiration because they often come with an assortment of images and feelings that help flesh out a song.

It doesn't matter if an idea, i.e., an intellectual, objective construct, or a feeling comes first in the writing process, because ultimately these two (idea/feeling; feeling/idea) must meld together into a song concept. Often these two entities must be further tied to an important phrase, usually the title of the song.

For example, a writer might have a desire to write a song about making the world a better place. This lofty goal may, after a short time, bring up feelings of inadequacy on the writer's part. The writer may conclude that the best he can do to change the world is to change his own behavior. This thought might lead to thoughts of closely examining himself—which might lead to a title, e.g., "Man In the Mirror." This might have been part of the psychological process that took place for the writers of "Man In the Mirror," the gigantic Michael Jackson hit written by Siedah Garrett and Glen Ballard.

This lyric is written from the point of view (POV) of an internal monologue, but one meant to be shared with everyone. The formal name of this POV is *first person narrative*.

"Man In The Mirror"   Siedah Garrett, Glen Ballard

I'm starting with the man in the mirror
I'm asking him to change his ways

The notion of making the world a better place has occurred to many writers, but few have succeeded as well as John Lennon in his song, "Imagine."

"Imagine"   by John Lennon

You may say that I'm a dreamer
But I'm not the only one

John Lennon expressed his belief that the world's ills are often caused by nationalism and religion. His concept was to share these thoughts with his listeners. Because he did not preach to us, but instead, invited us to share with him—to imagine a world without boundaries—the song was embraced by all.

One of the first decisions that you must make when you begin a lyric is choosing its perspective, its POV: Who is the singer addressing? "Imagine" is sung in the first person to all of humanity. When the singer addresses the audience directly, as he does here, it is called *direct address*. This is the most immediate and intimate point of view. Since POV is a subject demanding more attention and, therefore, more space than this book allows, I highly recommend you study Pat Pattison's excellent book *Writing Better Lyrics*, which covers this important subject in detail.

A title or general theme for a song is not the same as a song concept. A concept is narrower in focus and more powerful because of it. Once you have a concept for your song, your songwriting process will assume more clarity and directness.

The importance of having a central idea

Everything in your song revolves around and assumes direction from the main idea of the song, what I am calling the *central idea*, which is often encapsulated in the title. The central idea of a song can be presented its first couple of phrases.

Think of Stevie Wonder's "You Are the Sunshine Of My Life":

You are the sunshine of my life
That's why I'll always be around.

or Joni Mitchell's "Help Me":

Help me
I think I'm falling
in love again.

The title and central idea for both songs appear in the first two or three lines.

If the central idea appears at the beginning of your song, both the music and the lyrics must be substantial enough to generate the rest of the song.

There are other songs that have their central idea at the end or final cadence of the first verse or the second verse or at the end of the A section of an AABA song. If your song does not begin with the central idea, but instead begins with a verse that ends with the title, the verse material must continually supply information that leads logically to that culminating line called a *refrain*. Examples abound, e.g., Billy Joel's "Just The Way You Are" ("I love you just the way you are"), and "Movin' Out," Paul Simon's "Still Crazy After All These Years" and "I Do It For Your Love," Bob Dylan's "Blowin' In The Wind" and "Tangled Up In Blue."

If your verse does not contain the central idea, either at its beginning or ending, the central idea will most likely show up in the next section, the chorus. If your narrative requires it, two verses may be necessary before reaching your central idea in the chorus. Many songs contain a verse and an added shorter section called a prechorus. Its function is to create a need in the listener to hear the central idea by building tension and increasing the forward motion to the chorus.

The most popular placement of the title in a verse/chorus song is either in the first line or within the first couple of lines of the chorus. Some choruses contain the title at the beginning of the chorus and at its ending as well. Here are some opening lines of hit choruses:

"Un-break My Heart"   by Diane Warren

Un-break my heart;
Say you'll love me again.

"I Run To You"   by Hillary Scott, Charles Kelly, Dave Haywood, Tom Douglas

This world keeps spinning faster
Into a new disaster,
so I run to you.

"I Can't Make You Love Me"   by Mike Reid and Alan Shamblin

'Cause I can't make you love me if you don't
You can't make your heart feel something it won't.

There are also some verse/chorus songs, much fewer in number, that hold off the statement of the title/central idea until the very end of the chorus.

No matter where it appears, having a central idea in your song is an essential element to your potential success as a songwriter. If you are not able to say what your song is about in one or, at most, two sentences, you probably don't have a central idea.

In the writing process, it helps if your central idea is encapsulated in a title, but if you don't have a title yet, try to formulate a thought that you can hang on to that keeps your lyric on track. I've seen too many student lyrics wander into areas that are totally incomprehensible because they either didn't have a central idea or they got sidetracked along the way.

If you are writing a verse/refrain or a verse/chorus song, the momentum of your verse should progress as directly as possible toward your central idea. Think of yourself as an archer and the verse of your song as an arrow aimed straight at your central idea. When your arrow arrives at the target, your central idea should explode with the main feeling of the song.

Does this mean that you should write lyrics that are always linear, that only give information and contain no metaphors or colorful language? No, of course not. In fact, just the opposite of that occurs when your writing has taken on its own flow. You should know what your song is about and choose to write it in an original way with language that is evocative, that makes your listener feel what you are feeling. The materials of your song, as they emerge, often lead the song in interesting and sometimes surprising directions, just as a character in a novel can lead the author to interesting dialogue or plot development. If this begins to occur, let it happen, but do remind yourself of the central idea of your song and ask yourself if you are veering too far from it. Allowing your song to sometimes lead you is not contradictory to the recommendation that you never lose tract of the central idea of the song; you simply must be able to do both.

Beginning with a musical idea

Many songwriters like to begin with a musical idea and to develop that idea into an entire section before thinking too much about what the lyric may be. It is one of my favorite ways of beginning a song. Music gives form, rhythm, and gesture to a song, and if it feels and sounds good, and is composed for the voice, it aches to have the right words set to it. To realize that your music is giving you hints at the lyrical meaning of the song is a part of the process of songwriting that invites an intriguing and exciting journey of exploration. Since music is abstract, knowing music theory can help you find some of the answers to the question "What is the music saying?" But if you listen closely and are sensitive to each musical gesture, to the kinesthetic qualities of tone, rhythm, and phrase — the rhetorical gestures found in your music that tie it to verbalization—you will find what the music is saying to you.

After composing a section of music, listen to it in various ways with sensitivity to tempo, groove, tone, and melodic rhythm. How does the music make you feel?

- Does the music sound *stable*: calm, contemplative, etc., or *unstable*: agitated, questioning, etc.?
- Are the melodic rhythms conversational, or are they declarative?
- How does the music feel to your body? Does it have a groove? Is it balanced or unbalanced? (Where is it balanced or unbalanced?)
- Does it leave you feeling fulfilled or wanting more? (If the latter is true, it may indicate to you that the music you've created is not substantial enough to contain the central idea).
- Is it atmospheric, capable of capturing a state of mind, or is it more suited to a narrative that leads to a goal area? If so, where are the melodic/harmonic goals located in the music you've composed?

Since words not only have meaning, but are also made up of sounds, your job is to listen for sounds that work with your music. As you listen to your music, try singing words that may be the actual words that you will use in the song, or they may be simply words that sound right but may have no meaning attached. This latter result is called a "dummy lyric," one that uses sounds, nonsense syllables, words you assume will not be the final ones, but that sonically resonate with your music. Listen to the sound of the words in each phrase, especially on important notes such as long notes or arrival points. Listen for places where rhyme is necessary or desired. Ask yourself if an "oo" would sound better than an "ah," or if the pinched sound of an "ee" would sound better than an "i." Sing entire phrases, even though some of the words may seem nonsensical. In doing so, you will probably find a line or two that you will keep in the final lyric.

I consciously look for areas in the song where a title might appear. Often, I find a title or important phrase in my song at cadences and at beginnings of sections because these are areas that attract attention. Once I have a title, I start thinking of ways to treat that title, to have a concept, and gradually my lyrics emerge. A lyric might appear almost immediately, but sometimes it may take much longer and will have to undergo numerous rewrites. Patience and the need to tell the truth in the song should guide you.

Beginning with a melodic idea

Usually a musical idea is a melody not heard in its entirety but heard as a phrase or even part of a phrase or as a rhythm that somehow has enough originality and potential to interest or excite you. Sometimes it may appear with a harmony and groove, or only as a naked melody needing to find a harmony or groove before it comes fully to life.

Here is a melody that appeared without harmony in my aural imagination (Ex. 1.01). The most interesting component of this idea is its rhythm; it seems to have urgency, a need to speak. The pitches are simply the back and forth movement of a minor third, either in the key of D minor or F major. Even that information is suspect, because these notes are available in a few different keys, so it may be too soon to determine the key. The rhythm is full of energy caused by a number of factors: it starts

on the second beat and contains anticipations of the first beats of measures 2 and 3
(▶ AUDIO 1.01).

Ex. 1.01

Moderately fast

Here's a lyric that occurred to me as I listened to the music I had just created (Ex. 1.02)
(▶ AUDIO 1.02).

Ex. 1.02

Moderately fast

I got to — tell — you, I've been up all night ——

I didn't have to think about what the song was going to be about because the music's character (it felt a little nervous) dictated the lyric idea to me. From this incomplete idea, I might ruminate on what had possibly transpired between the singer, (the person singing) and the *singee*, (the person being sung to). I might use this musical and lyric idea to continue the music, leaving the lyric writing process alone for a while, but using the urgency of the music to develop the music more completely. I would then spend some time trying to develop a more complete scenario for the lyric: a possible crisis caused by an argument, a confession, or first date jitters, or the end of an affair, etc. I would try to see the singer and the singee in a particular setting and try to see some visual images of the scenario, so that I could make them available in my lyrics. I would then try to tie the lyric ideas to the melodic rhythms and accents in music I composed. But whatever next step is decided on, a song has begun—and that is what is important.

Sometimes a melody comes with a harmony. That is how the following melody came to me, presenting itself as a more lyrical and complete musical idea (Ex. 1.03). Its main strengths and interest are its shape or contour and the intervals within it. It is more contemplative, less urgent, due to both the slower tempo and less rhythmic activity than in the previous example (▶ AUDIO 1.03).

Ex. 1.03

Moderately

This idea produced my song called "Out Of My Dream," one into which I delve deeply in chapter 18, "Process." The lyric emerged naturally from the music, without a great deal of effort. Coinciding with the nature of the music, the lyric is contemplative (Ex. 1.04) (▶ AUDIO 1.04).

Ex. 1.04 *"Out Of My Dream" with lyric, Jack Perricone*

These two examples indicate a process that I recommend you try. You may not even need an instrument; you simply need your aural imagination and your voice. Imagine a melody—a phrase, short or long. Sing it again and again; now try to find some words to match it . . . and you've begun.

Beginning with a chord progression

Musical ideas can stem from a chord progression. Chord progressions can be evocative and provide a tonal environment in which other more vital elements of the songwriting process—melody and lyrics—can thrive. Combined with a rhythmic groove, chords can generate melodic ideas that would not otherwise occur to a writer.

If a chord progression is played without a rhythmic groove, it may not inspire much (Ex. 1.05) (▶ AUDIO 1.05).

Ex. 1.05

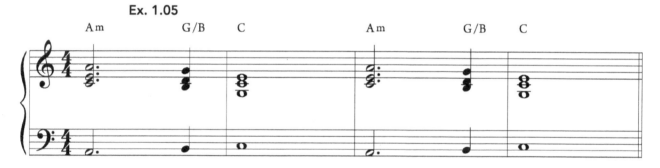

However, once a rhythmic groove is created, it may be the genesis of a song (Ex. 1.06) (▶ AUDIO 1.06).

Ex. 1.06

Emeli Sandé was probably inspired by both the sound of this progression and the rhythmic groove she created at the keyboard. It permeates her gigantic hit "Next To Me" (Ex. 1.07)

Ex. 1.07 "Next To Me" Emeli Sandé

Writing to riffs and tracks

An accompaniment figure provided by a guitar, a piano, or a synthesizer, often produces interesting music that can generate melodic or lyric ideas. You may choose to create an entire song around a repeating rhythmic figure called a *riff* or an *ostinato* (a riff-like figure that appears at various pitch levels) that you've discovered while jamming or experimenting on your instrument. Riff-based musical ideas rely on counterpoint, i.e., the movement of one melody (the riff) interacting with another melody (the vocal melody) to create interest. A riff can be repeated verbatim throughout a section or it can be transposed as the harmonies change.

Two or more people are often involved in the writing of riff-based songs. It is the guitarist or bassist in a group who usually creates a riff and the lead vocalist, using the riff as a fulcrum, who then creates the vocal melody. Many of rock's greatest hits were created from guitar riffs, songs such as The Rolling Stone's "Satisfaction" and "Brown Sugar" or Aerosmith's "Walk This Way." The necessity of two or more people to create a riff-based song has been eliminated with technology. Computers, MIDI, and DAWS have allowed anyone who has basic keyboard knowledge and technology skills to write a riff-based song by simply recording the riff and writing or singing to it. I devote chapter 15, "Riff-Based Songwriting," to this study.

Collaboration

Collaboration is another way to begin writing a song. Play to your strengths. If you know that your strong suit is music and you can use some help with lyrics, do your best to find a good lyricist. Or vice versa, if you are a good lyricist but not much of a musician, do your best to find a good composer. The act of collaboration is challenging but can also be empowering and lead to great success. The most common pairing in traditional songwriting has been that of composer and lyricist: Rodgers and Hart, Dietz and Schwartz, Arlen and Mercer, Goffin and King, Lennon and McCartney, Taupin and John, etc.

Many of today's hits are written by groups of people, four or five writers per song, each an expert in one part of the whole mix of elements and skills involved in making a hit. The track producer concentrates on what audiences like to move to, creating the groove and the basic harmonic movement; another tech type, a sound designer, concentrates on electronic sounds meant to entice the public with novel sounds; the top line writer (formerly known as the songwriter), writes or cowrites the lyric and melody, crafting the type of language and lyric phrases that the artist's audience expects to hear. In this age of specialization, it is no wonder that in commercial songwriting there are so many specialists involved in making the product.

Summary

There are many ways to begin a song: with a title, a lyrical concept, a melodic idea, a chord progression, a groove, or a riff. Beginning a song often occurs in a rush of inspiration. If inspiration dwindles or if it's not fueled by real knowledge, then the song often goes unfinished. My hope is that the rest of this book helps to supply you with the tools, techniques, and the knowledge it takes to for you to finish the song.

Activities

• Seek titles. Find three titles per day for a week. Look to newspapers, magazines, books, movies, and Broadway shows and titles from songs of the last century. At the end of a week, choose four titles out of the group that you have collected and write fresh concepts for each of them. Always have your antennae out seeking song ideas, catchy phrases, etc. Listen for common phrases that can be made to be unique by a change of a word ("I Second That Emotion") or by a change in its usual context ("Poker Face"). Many outstanding titles have already been used but, luckily, titles cannot be copyrighted so they are available to you (e.g., John Legend had a huge hit in 2014 with "All Of Me," a title usually associated with the jazz standard written in 1931).

• Actively seek out ideas/concepts. Practice thinking conceptually; a title alone will not be enough to get your creative juices flowing or captivate an audience; you'll need to find a unique way of treating that title.

• Develop a strong aural imagination. How often do you think music (not think about music, but actually hear it in your aural imagination)? Get away from an instrument and try to hear a musical phrase that could be used in a song. Once you find one you like, try coming up with a lyrical phrase that matches it—and you'll be on your way to writing a song.

• Compose a melodic idea; record and notate it. Write two different, yet viable lyrics that work with it.

- Find a chord pattern with a groove that appeals to you. Repeat it, record it, or loop it using a sequencer. Write a melody and lyric to it.

- Use music technology to get started. Naturally, if you can play an instrument well and if you have a good voice, you may not need to use a sequencer or DAW. Technology, however, does furnish you with a great way to spark a musical idea by providing novel sounds and textures and, most importantly, rhythmic grooves that can act as the underpinning for your song.

- Read as much as possible; take note of colorful language, interesting figures of speech, details that help you to perceive a picture of the events. Be cognizant of the clarity or lack of clarity in the writing, whether it's within a newspaper article, a magazine article, a short story, or a novel.

- Write every day. Whether you attempt to write an entire song, music without words, or words without music, do write something every day. Write, write, write, and actively listen to what is current; in this way, you will begin to grasp both the musical gestures, grooves, and forms that are being used. Remember that John Lennon and Paul McCartney had written over 100 songs before they met George Martin, and yet that great producer was not happy with what they initially showed him and the Beatles were forced to sing someone else's song for their first recording.

- Try different approaches to beginning a song: start with a title, a lyric idea, a concept; start with a groove, a chord pattern, or a melodic idea. Do not get stuck by always beginning a song the same way; have courage and free your imagination.

- Examine your strengths as a songwriter and your weaknesses. If you feel the need, begin a search for a collaborator who has strengths where you have weaknesses. No matter where you live, you are bound to find a local songwriter's club or workshop, but if you can't find one locally, try the Internet.

2

Introduction to Melody

In this chapter, you will be provided with an overview of melody that will help guide you in the more detailed study that occurs in the following chapters.

Melody: pitch and rhythm

The study of melody writing is wide ranging, involving not only an examination of the individual components of melody such as pitch, rhythm, phrase length, contour, etc., but also melody's relationship to lyric, to the tonal center, to harmony, and to song form. Melody is made up of both pitch and rhythm; therefore, a thorough study of melody must include both of these elements. When one of these two elements is missing or is minimally used, the demeanor of the music is radically affected. For example, Gregorian chant contains a rhythmic component that is minimal in order to transport us away from bodily pleasures and allow us to enter into the realm of the spiritual (Ex. 2.01).

Ex. 2.01 Gregorian chant

At the other end of the spectrum, rap eschews pitch for the most part, and its rhythms tie us to bodily movement (Ex. 2.02).

Ex. 2.02 "Super Bass" Onika Minaj, Daniel Johnson, Ester Dean, Roahn Hylt

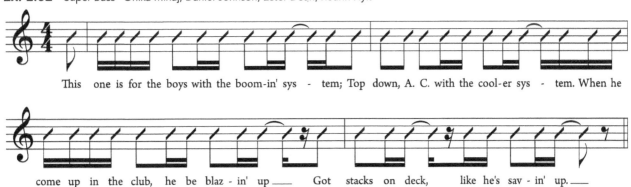

Songwriting demands that you consider the attributes and the limitations of the human voice. No matter how interesting a melody may sound when played on an instrument, it may not work when sung. You must consider the range of the voice within the context of

the type of voices that sing popular songs. Vocal ranges vary with each individual artist, but if you are writing without a specific artist in mind, it is best to be fairly conservative and keep the song within a range of an octave and a fifth. Female vocals are written where they sound, and male vocals are notated in the treble clef one octave above where they sound.

No matter how poor you may think your voice is, it is vital to the creation of a song for you, the songwriter, to feel and hear the sounds that emanate from the human instrument. Sing your song as you write it, and it will inform you and most likely, inspire you.

Conceiving a melody: melody's connection to lyrics

Melody, including most instrumental melody, is derived from vocal gestures: conversational speech, exclamations, guttural utterances, and verbal gestures—the entire panoply of how we orally communicate with each other. A verbal gesture includes, e.g., a question, an exhortation, an exclamation, a whisper, and many more subtle gestures that occur naturally, depending on our state of mind or the state of mind we are trying to project. Verbal gestures involve both rhythm and pitch. (Although pitch is most often associated with exact musical pitch, here I am referring to a heightening of the frequency range when, e.g., we ask a question.) Certainly, you would intone the words "I love you" to your beloved in a completely different way than you would say, "I'm going to the store to buy a quart of milk."

Melody, when used in song, is an extension of speech that not only encapsulates the literal meaning of the words and gestures but also enhances their meaning. If, as a songwriter, you accept this definition of how melody should function, you have a way to judge whether your melody succeeds or fails.

Study the following four very different melodies; sing them and notice how each of them successfully captures a state of mind and a genuine expression of feeling.

Ex. 2.03 "You've Got A Friend" Carole King

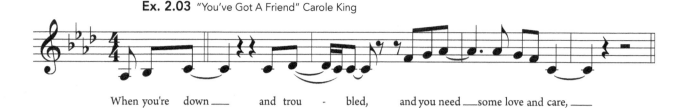

When you're   down____   and   trou - bled,   and you need ____some love and care, ____

Whether you use a major scale, a minor pentatonic scale, a modal scale, or any number of other scales available to you as the basis for your melody, the choice you make will greatly influence the effect it will have. The melody in the verse of "You've Got A Friend" (Ex. 2.03) begins in minor, and by doing so, reinforces the perception of the needs of the person addressed, while the chorus of this song, in A♭ major, the relative major key to the key of F minor, positively reinforces the availability of a friend.

The tempo you choose for your song is also a major factor in its effect. The melody of "You've Got A Friend" is in a medium ballad tempo. The melody presents itself in broken rhythms—the pauses after the words "down" and "troubled" are an indication of the thoughtfulness and care that the singer is extending to the singee. The melody slowly rises to the word "need," the most important word and the climax of the phrase. "Need" occurs on the longest held note of the phrase and connects to "some love and care," completely capturing the gesture of reaching out to express sympathy for someone.

"War" is an exhortation, a cry for sanity in an insane world (Ex. 2.04).

Ex. 2.04 "War" Norman Whitfield, Barrett Strong

This song is a protest against man's inhumanity to man, sung by both the lead singer and by a backup group in the African tradition of call and response, a perfect way to present a subject that involves all of us. Exclamations, guttural reactions, the bare-bones sound of the minor pentatonic scale, and strong rhythms followed by rests force us to the truth of this extraordinary musical and lyrical statement.

The romantic purity and ardent romanticism of Oscar Hammerstein's lyric has a counterpart in Kern's lyrical melody that is based around a major scale that slowly descends, with occasional leaps of perfect fourths or diminished fifths up and down that add intensity and shape to it (Ex. 2.05). The melody includes chromaticism, the language of romantic composers such as Schumann and Tchaikovsky. It is full of lovingly held notes, and is sung in long legato phrases. This melody, written in 1939, like all melodies and all music, is an indication of its time, the state of mind not only of individuals but also of an entire society.

Ex. 2.05 "All The Things You Are" Oscar Hammerstein, Jerome Kern

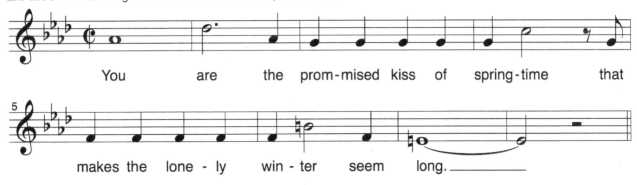

An antipode to the Kern/Hammerstein paean to love and romance, Taylor Swift's "Bad Blood" is a lover's commentary on a failed relationship (Ex. 2.06).

Ex. 2.06 "Bad Blood" Taylor Swift, Max Martin, Shellback

Since the singer wants the singee to feel the pain he has inflicted on her, she attacks him with machine-gun-like rhythms. In contrast to "All The Things You Are," this melody

has shorter phrases with many repeated notes and repeated melodic phrases that underline the complaint and expression of hurt.

Through this look at melodies of four diverse songs from different styles and eras of songwriting, we are able to realize that melodies must be judged in their proper context, a context that is tempered by style, and the era in which the song was written, but most of all by the relationship of words to music in the service of feeling. This understanding is necessary before we delve deeper into the techniques that evolve from this relationship. There are excellent songwriting techniques, valid in all styles, in each of these examples—and those techniques will be explored in detail in the ensuing chapters.

Melodic rhythm

Melodic rhythm is one of the most important elements used in constructing a song—and one of the most overlooked by songwriting novices. It has an intimate connection to words, especially to rhyme. Once words are attached to the notes of a melody, the importance of rhythmic placement becomes apparent. When you hold out a note, you emphasize the importance of the word that is being sung; when you use slow-moving notes or fast-moving notes in telling your story or in projecting thoughts, you are communicating not only the words but also the feeling behind the words.

Consider how you might speak the following lyric:

Take my hand
Let's run away
To a sun-drenched wonderland.

Try speaking it in time with an underlying steady beat. Infuse the lyric with personal involvement. Speak it in a steady tempo, and then try speeding up or slowing down the tempo until you've achieved the right tempo for the lyric. Choose rhythms that best communicate the meaning of the lyric. Have you highlighted the important words in the lyric?

Here are four different rhythmic settings (Exs. 2.07–2.10) using the same pitches at the same tempo that demonstrate how a rhythmic setting can affect the listener's reaction to it.

The first setting is simply not credible. The words are sung practically at a somnambulant rhythmic pace (▶ AUDIO 2.07).

Ex. 2.07

The second setting, although better than the first, makes the singer sound rather too formal, because of the number of notes that fall on downbeats (▶ AUDIO 2.08).

Ex. 2.08

Take   my   hand,   let's   run   a-way   to   a   sun-drenched   won-der-land.

The third setting is acceptable, with a more natural rhythm (the longer held note on "take," the shorter held note on "my"), with a slight sense of urgency (the syncopations on "away" and "wonderland") (▶ AUDIO 2.09).

Ex. 2.09

Take   my   hand,   let's   run   a-way___   to   a   sun-drenched won-der-land. ___

The last rhythmic setting begins after the first beat and enlivens the lyric with syncopations, indications of a high degree of enthusiasm (▶ AUDIO 2.10).

Ex. 2.10

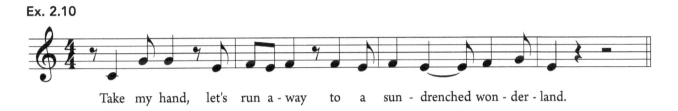

Take   my   hand,   let's   run   a-way   to   a   sun-drenched won-der-land.

Rhythm is physical, and physicality is a vital part of what makes a popular song popular. Tempo plays an important part in how your song is perceived, but the groove—the rhythmic pattern occurring in the accompaniment—the underlying "feel" of the song, is equally important because melodic rhythm is generated from it.

Memorable melodic rhythms

Once you've written or conceived of a melody for a song, one of the most important questions to ask yourself is, "Is this melody rhythmically interesting and engaging?" The following two examples contain interesting and memorable melodic rhythms.

"Happy," a hit by Pharrell Williams in 2013–2014 is infectious due to its groove, its melodic rhythms that are full of syncopations, and the call-and-response activity between the lead vocal and instrumental riff (Ex. 2.11). The time in between vocal phrases helps listeners take in what has been sung and to feel the infectious groove, practically inviting dance.

23

Ex. 2.11 "Happy" Pharrell Williams

It may sound cra - zy, ___ what I'm 'bout to say

(Instrumental)

Sun-shine, she's here; ___ you can take a break.

(Instrumental)

If you were to speak the lyric to "Crazy Thing Called Love" (Ex. 2.12) in a conversational manner, you would not pause between, e.g. "thing" and "called," nor would you speak those words in such discrete rhythms. But this lyric statement is beyond conversational; it is an outpouring of emotion that produces this slightly fragmented but effusive statement. The underlying groove of this song is what propels all this song's vocal rhythms, causing it to be physicalized well beyond the rhythms used in ordinary speech. Because of this, it connects us to our bodies as well as our emotions, reinforcing the physical attraction, the joy, and the confusion of being in love that underscores this entire song.

Ex. 2.12 "Crazy Little Thing Called Love" Freddie Mercury

This thing   called love, ___   I just ___   can't han-dle it. ___ This thing

___   called love, ___   I must ___   get round to it. ___ I ain't

The placement of the phrase in time—the beginning and ending of a musical phrase—is especially important. If a melodic phrase begins after (Ex. 2.11) or before (Ex. 2.12) the downbeat of a measure, the impetus for movement is there from the very beginning. As listeners, we are drawn into a conversation or thought that is already in motion.

However, when you begin a phrase on the first beat of a measure, it has a sense of stability, best suited for making a statement or declaration like the one in Example 2.13.

Ex. 2.13 "Fly Like An Eagle" Steve Miller

A m

Time keeps on slip-pin', slip-pin', slip - pin' in-to the fu - ture.

Conversational and declarative melodies

In order to understand what causes a melody to have its effect on the listener, it must be examined in a number of different ways: by itself, in relationship to the tonal center, in relationship to the chords, and especially, in relationship to the lyric as well as in the context of the entire song.

Not all melodies are meant to be memorable. What initially may seem to be a rather dull melody, in fact, may be a setup or a perfect foil for the main melody that occurs in the next section of the song. We need some melodies to simply be functional or conversational in nature, so that when the main idea of the song appears, more unique rhythms and pitches can accentuate it. *Conversational rhythms* are those that are found in ordinary speech containing rhythms that flow and breathe naturally to form the syntax for the subject at hand. Characteristics of *conversational type melodies* are the preponderance of conjunct intervals, mainly seconds with an occasional interval of a third, with very few intervallic leaps, and rhythms that begin before or after the downbeat.

Adele's verses are usually conversational, often intimate in their tone with rhythms that invite listeners in to share personal secrets. The length of phrases and the space in between phrases are completely naturalistic (Ex. 2.14).

Ex. 2.14 "Hello" Adele Adkins, Greg Kurstin

Hel - lo, it's me I was won-der-ing if af-ter all these years you'd like to meet

Notice how the rhythmical setting of "Hello, it's me" feels at the outset of the song. The hesitations between "Hello" and "it's me" and the next phrase signals to the listener that this is not an ebullient greeting, but one fraught with fear of intrusion.

Characteristics of *declarative melodies* are larger intervals, longer notes, repetitive phrases, and an emphasis on the downbeat position.

The verse preceding the declarative chorus of Sam Smith's hit is full of sixteenth notes (Ex. 2.15). The downbeat at the beginning of this chorus contains a dramatic silence before the important question is completed, an example of how silence can be more dynamic than sound. The high, long held note on the syncopated second beat expresses the ardor and serious intent of the singer, forcing us to listen more intensely than if it had appeared on the downbeat.

Ex. 2.15 "Stay With Me" chorus, Sam Smith, James Napier, William Philips, Tom Petty, Jeff Lynne

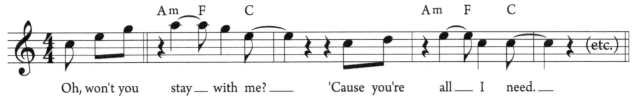

Oh, won't you stay — with me? —— 'Cause you're all — I need. ——

Conversational type melodies are most often found in the verse sections of songs, while more declarative type melodies are often found in choruses and refrains. The verse and chorus sections of the 2014 hit, "Let It Go," from the movie *Frozen* exemplifies these characteristics (Ex. 2.16).

The verse begins with a description of a wintry scene sung in the calm rhythms of a storyteller that are attached to a melody with no interval larger than a third.

Ex. 2.16 "Let It Go" verse, Kristen Anderson Lopez, Robert Lopez

The   snow glows white on the moun-tain to-night;   not a   foot-print __ to be seen. ____

In contrast to the verse, the chorus begins with two exhortations that lead to the downbeats of the first and second measures, including a leap of an ascending P5th in measure 2 (Ex. 2.17).

Ex. 2.17 "Let It Go" chorus

Let it go, ____   let it go; ____   can't __ hold it back an-y more. ____

The rhythms of ordinary conversation and a melody mainly made up of conjunct intervals form the verse of Cyndi Lauper's mammoth hit from 1979, "Girls Just Want To Have Fun" (Ex. 2.18).

Ex. 2.18 "Girls Just Want To Have Fun" verse, Robert Hazzard

I   come home in the morn-ing light. My moth - er says,"When you gon-na live your life right?"

The title line arrives on the downbeat of the chorus, reinforced by its eighth-note pickup (Ex. 2.19). The melody of the title or refrain line contains longer pauses between phrases and larger intervals—a P5th down, a M7th up—and interesting rhythms, making it more declarative and memorable than the verse that leads to it. The title line also repeats with a slight melodic variation that allows the melody to cadence on the tonic note on the downbeat, a tonal statement that reinforces the lyrical one.

Ex. 2.19 "Girl Just Want To Have Fun" chorus

And girls just want to have f - un,   Oh,   girls just want to have   fun. ____

The choice of where your lyrics are placed causes listeners to hear the lyric as conversational or declarative. Joni Mitchell cries out for help in a persuasive, declarative way by beginning the first phrase of her song on the downbeat. The pause in the middle of the phrase heightens the double meaning of the phrase and captures the sense of losing oneself to another (Ex. 2.20).

Ex. 2.20 "Help Me" Joni Mitchell

The placement of the phrase within the meter—whether it begins before, after, or on the downbeat of a measure—has an impact on the song's form and, most importantly, on the listener by providing contrast from one section of a song to another.

Bill Withers establishes a serious tone in his great song by making a statement that begins his verse on a downbeat (Ex. 2.21).

Ex. 2.21 "Lean On Me" verse, Bill Withers

His chorus is made more personal by having the phrase begin as a pickup (Ex. 2.22). Imagine the chorus of "Lean On Me" beginning on a downbeat instead of before the downbeat. It would come off as more of a directive than as the loving gesture that reaches out to us and is the essence of this song.

Ex. 2.22 "Lean On Me" chorus

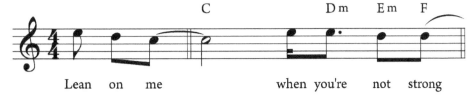

Arpeggiated melodies

Although most melodies mainly contain conjunct intervals with fewer disjunct intervals interspersed, there are some melodies that mainly consist of broken chords called arpeggios. Melodies made up of arpeggiated chords are fairly easy to sing and provide the listener a simple pathway to follow, like evenly spaced rocks in a stream that allow you to hop from one to another.

Hank Williams, the extraordinary country singer/songwriter, wrote a number of hit songs based mainly on melodies that arpeggiate the underlying harmonies (Ex. 2.23).

Ex. 2.23 "I Can't Get You Off Of My Mind" Hank Williams

George Gershwin also wrote some memorable songs based on chordal arpeggiation, but he often employed the upper extensions of the harmonies (7ths, 9ths, 11ths, 13ths) to achieve this in a jazz style (Ex. 2.24).

Ex. 2.24 "I Loves You, Porgy" music by George Gershwin, lyrics by DuBose Heyward

A hit in 2014, "Bang Bang" contains an arpeggiated melody built from the C7 chord tones with one added tone, A, for its entire chorus (Ex. 2.25). The contrast in *tessitura* (the particular vocal range used in a section of a song) between the two phrases, the first sung by the lead vocalist, the second, a conjunct melody sung by background vocalists, helps make this melody work.

Ex. 2.25 "Bang Bang" Max Martin, Savan Kotecha, Richard Görransson, Nicki Minaj

Melodic shape and direction

One of the first ways humans attempted to symbolize music through notation (c. 9th century) was to indicate the direction and contour of the melody. Whether notes rise, fall, or stay in the same place, is basic to grasping a melody. Just like our normal speech patterns, melody tends to rise with expressions of exuberance and to fall with expressions of depression or sadness. A simple statement like "It's a beautiful day" set melodically in a scalewise movement upward feels authentic, but seems a little less credible when set in a downward direction (Ex. 2.26).

Ex. 2.26

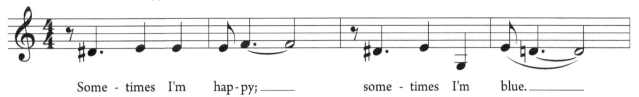

It's a beau - ti - ful day.   It's a bea - ti - ful day.

The melody of the standard "Sometimes I'm Happy" indicates directionally what the lyrics are stating (Ex. 2.27).

Ex. 2.27 "Sometimes I'm Happy" Victor Youmans, Irving Caesar

Some - times I'm hap - py; _____   some - times I'm blue. _____

But be warned: there are no rules, nor should there be, for setting emotional states to music; simply be sensitive to them. Trying to musically parallel every word can easily turn into "Mickey Mousing," the term used for matching every move in a cartoon with a musical equivalent; it cheapens rather than heightens expression.

Characteristics of memorable melodies

The most obvious and important element in making anything memorable in song is repetition. Given that fact, what makes a melody uniquely memorable? In some memorable melodies, it is the element of rhythm that defines the melody; in others, it is the intervals and shapes of the melody. In most, it is a combination of both interesting rhythms and pitches combined with a lyric that perfectly fits the melody. Placement of the phrase—either at the beginning or ending of a section—is equally important.

Most melodies are built in conjunct intervals: whole steps or half steps or intervals no larger than a third. However, when an intervallic leap larger than a third occurs, it calls attention to itself and helps define the melody. If a melody contains nothing but whole steps and half steps, it may grow monotonous; if it contains too many leaps, it may become too difficult to follow. A memorable melody usually contains an interesting rhythm combined with a few well-placed leaps (Ex. 2.28).

Ex. 2.28 "Sweet Caroline" Neil Diamond

Sweet Car-o-line, ___ good times nev-er seemed so good.

The interval of a major 6th down (soon followed by a memorable horn fill), followed by an upward leap of a minor 6th set in a memorable rhythm gives this melody an extra dose of personality.

The same characteristics, an interesting rhythm combined with a few well-placed leaps, show up in this Duke Ellington standard (Ex. 2.29).

Ex. 2.29 "I Got It Bad (And That Ain't Good)" lyrics by Paul Daniel Webster, music by Duke Ellington

Ne-ver treats me sweet and gen - tle the way he should.

Duke Ellington took a common melodic ornament called an *inverted turn* (an elaboration of the main note by beginning the figure with a note below it and following it with a note above it), and did a slight variation on it by leaping up a major 9th (D_4–E_5) instead of simply moving up an adjacent second (D_4–E_4)—this is called an *octave displacement*—and created a melody that has lasted at least fifty years and possibly one that will last throughout many centuries (Ex. 2.30).

Ex. 2.30

Inverted turn

interpreted as   transformed into

"I'm With You," a hit in 2002 by Avril Lavigne, also displaces a note by an octave in order to create an interesting and memorable melody. Instead of the C♯ moving up a half step to the D, which would have been expected, it moves down a major 7th, creating a unique melody that underscores the sentiment expressed in the lyric (Ex. 2.31).

Ex. 2.31 "I'm With You" Avril Lavigne, Lauren Christy, Scott Spock, Graham Edwards

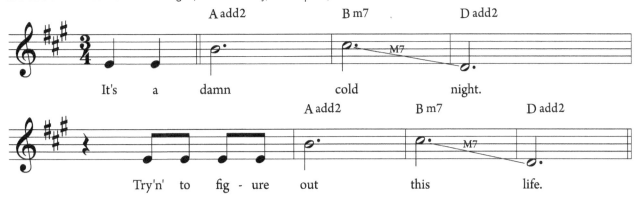

A song "hook"

A song "hook" is meant to be memorable: the part of a song that gets stuck in your head and hooks the listener. A hook has the same elements contained in most memorable melodies: a compelling rhythm and an interesting shape.

This 2014 hit by Maroon 5 begins with the song's chorus that contains a strong hook. The hook highlights the sound of lead singer Adam Levine's extraordinary vocal range and unique sound (Ex. 2.32).

Ex. 2.32 "Animals" Adam Levine, Shellback, Benjamin Levin

As important as a hook is in the writing of a hit song, it is often the placement of the hook within the song and how the song builds up to the hook that causes it to have the kind of impact that it does. Simply isolating the hook of a song and showing it as the be-all, end-all makes as much sense as isolating the punch line in a joke: it simply has little impact unless you hear it in context. Some present-day songs have as many as three, four, or more hooks contained within them. A hook may also be an instrumental melody, an unusual or exotic sound or textural gesture that is memorable.

The hook to Justin Bieber's 2015 hit "Sorry" is made up of a combination of a synthesized vocal sample of his voice and his actual voice singing the title phrase (Ex. 2.33).

Ex. 2.33 "Sorry" Justin Bieber, Julia Michaels, Justin Tranter, Sunny Moore, Michael Tucker

Summary

In the process of writing a song, you must be able to zoom in to deal with the details of lyrics, melody, and harmony and to zoom out to hear the overall form and impact of what you've created. Likewise, this chapter zooms out to give you a good idea of how to conceptualize writing a melody for a song without giving you all of the details of the techniques involved. That is what the rest of the book hopes to do.

Activities

- Listen to songs, especially melodies, intently and with purpose.
- Study the lyrics from a favorite song, then listen to how the melody heightens the feeling the words generate.
- Listen to verse/chorus songs. Notice how verse melodies are usually more conversational, while chorus melodies are more declarative.
- Make a list of your favorite and most memorable melodies. Ask yourself why these melodies stay with you; do they contain the characteristics of memorable melodies listed in this chapter?
- Study songs that you have written; do the characteristics of memorable melodies appear in them? If not, using my guidelines for creating memorable melodies, try rewriting them.

3

Rhythm and Rhyme

Rhythm

Rhythm is the element in music that has the most influence on form. Like the bones in our bodies, it provides the skeleton that gives melody its structure. Many budding songwriters concern themselves first with other musical elements, e.g., melodic pitch, harmony, etc., and ignore the importance of melodic rhythm, to the detriment of their ability to become better and more successful songwriters. Rhyme is language's strongest connective to melodic rhythm. That is why these two subjects, rhythm and rhyme, are grouped together and the reason this chapter appears so early in this book.

A lyric is an aural experience that takes place in musical time with rhythms that exist in relationship to a steady beat (or meter) and with phrases that have a direct and visceral relationship to one another in which words, rhythms, and pitches bond with meaning. This is one of the main differences between a lyric and a poem: a lyric exists in musical time while a poem exists in a more amorphous subjective time. You can examine a poem, scan or reread various sections of it at your leisure, and enjoy it in many ways, but you don't have to hear it in relationship to a steady beat. A lyric, however, is almost always heard in relationship to a steady beat with rhythms that have a direct relationship to that beat and are, therefore, much more visceral.

Rhyme

A word that rhymes is a word that is similar to, but not the same as, the word with which it is rhymed. A *perfect rhyme* is defined as two words that contain the same vowel sound and the same ending consonant sound but have a different consonant sound that precedes the vowel. Examples: host/boast, ring/thing, hazy/lazy. Other rhyme types will be discussed later in the text.

Rhyme is a very powerful songwriting tool, because rhyme uses the sound of the word itself in order to make a connection to music. Sheila Davis, in her groundbreaking book, *The Craft of Lyric Writing*, indicates that a music that *chimes* asks for a word that *rhymes*. What she did not state is that the *chiming* element of music is not produced by pitch but by rhythm. The correspondence between melodic rhythm and rhyme, although not always one-to-one, is intimate and is a cornerstone of songwriting.

Matched phrases

Matched phrases are melodic phrases that have the same or similar length and the same or very similar rhythmic ending with the same rhythmic emphasis (i.e., containing the same poetic foot, e.g., an *iamb, - /,* or *trochee, / -*). The end position of a lyric line is important because that is where rhyme usually occurs. Matched phrases call for rhyme. Songwriters who have a good song-sense automatically hear this and accommodate this natural union. Matched musical phrases are symbolically designated with the same letter: a/a, b/b, c/c, etc. Rhymes in this book are symbolically designated by the use of the same letter surrounded by parentheses (a) (a), (b) (b), etc.

Here's a little ditty I wrote in order to demonstrate this bond between rhythm and rhyme (Ex. 3.01; ▶ AUDIO 3.01).

Ex. 3.01

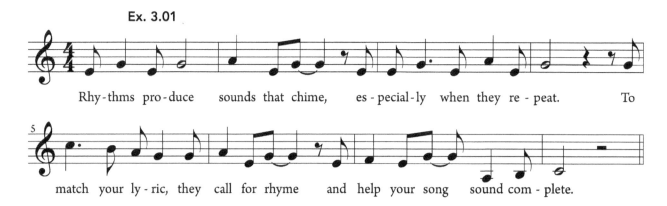

The connection between rhythm and rhyme is more easily recognized once pitch is removed from melody. The first phrase ends on the anticipation of beat 3 in measure 2 and is marked a; the second phrase ends on the downbeat of measure 2 and is marked b. These two phrases are followed by a nearly exact repetition of the same rhythms, rendering a set of matched phrases. The correspondence between the melodic phrase structure and the rhyme scheme is one-to-one, with each a-phrase producing an (a) rhyme and each b-phrase producing a (b) rhyme (Ex. 3.02; ▶ AUDIO 3.02).

Ex. 3.02

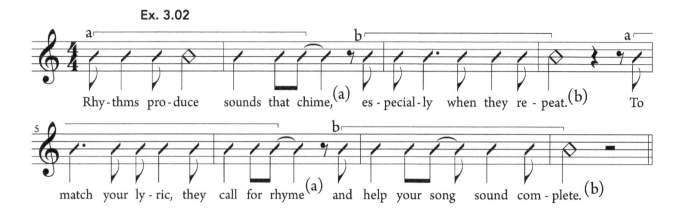

Smokey Robinson, a premier songwriter from Motown Records, chose to parallel the melodic rhythm with rhyme in "The Way You Do The Things You Do" (Ex. 3.03).

Ex. 3.03 "The Way You Do The Things You Do" William "Smokey" Robinson, Robert Rogers

A melodic phrase order of a, b, a, b doesn't have to use a parallel a, b, a, b rhyme scheme. In fact, it often uses an x, a, x, a, rhyme scheme in order to avoid using too many rhymes.

Music	Rhyme
a	x
b	a
a	x
b	a

The second phrase in a four-line lyric is important, because it is in the balancing position. When the fourth phrase in a four-phrase structure echoes the second phrase, it asks for a rhyme. (The balancing position is the halfway mark within the structure. In a four-line structure, it would be the end of the second line: in a six-bar structure, it would be the end of the third line.)

Irving Berlin's "How Deep Is The Ocean" (Ex. 3.04) begins with an a, b, a, b phrase order with a rhyme scheme of (x), (a), (x), (a).

Ex. 3.04 "How Deep Is The Ocean" Irving Berlin

Four matched phases, a, a, a, a, allow for many choices of rhyme schemes, ranging from (a) (a) (a) (a) to (a) (b) (a) (b) to (x) (a) (x) (a) to (a) (a) (b) (b). The verse of "Stuck In the Middle With You" (Ex. 3.05) contains four matched phrases: a, a, a,

a. The writers chose to use rhymed couplets: (a), (a), (b), (b). The rhymed words found at the ends of phrases in the verse of "Stuck In The Middle With You": "night," "right," "chair," and "stairs" all fall on downbeats, or more accurately, on the anticipation of downbeats. (An *anticipation* is a type of syncopation that produces an accent to the beat it anticipates.)

Ex. 3.05 "Stuck In The Middle With You" Joe Egan, Gerry Raffert

Well, I don't __ know why I came here to-night. ____ I got a feel-ing that some-thing ain't right.

__ I'm so scared ___ in case I fall off my chair, ____ and I'm won - drin' how I'll get down the stairs.

Inexactly matched phrases

If a phrase is approximately the same length as a previous phrase, has the same rhythmic ending, but contains different internal rhythms, it is still considered a matched phrase. In order to differentiate it from a matched phrase that uses the exact same rhythms, it is referenced as an *inexactly matched phrase*.

The first and second phrases in "Grenade" end on the same beat: beat three of the second measure of the two-measure phrases (Ex. 3.06). Except for the four eighth notes that lead to the last articulated note on beat 3 in measure 2 and measure 4, the two phrases have markedly different rhythms. Nonetheless, these are matched phrases. I've designated them as *inexactly matched phrases*. For analysis purposes, the letter followed by the prime symbol a', b', etc., designates inexactly matched phrases.

Ex. 3.06 "Grenade" Bruno Mars, Philip Lawrence, Ari Levine, Brody Brown, Claude Kelly, Andrew Wyett

Eas-y come, eas-y go that's the way you live. Oh, take, take, take it all, but you nev-er give.

The use of inexactly matched phrases provides some variety to your internal rhythms, allowing your lyrics to gain more freedom while retaining a structurally matched status.

The Bee-Gees hit "Stayin' Alive" is an example of the use of inexactly matched phrases, with both phrases ending on the sixteenth-note anticipation of the fourth beat (Ex. 3.07).

Ex. 3.07 "Stayin' Alive" Barry Gibb, Maurice Gibb, Robin Gibb

Well, you can tell __ by the way I use __ my walk, I'm a wo - man's man, no time to talk.

37

Using inexactly matched phrases can provide enough variety so that only one or two phrases need be used throughout an entire song. This is the strong unifying element that Cole Porter used extensively in the choruses of some of his biggest hits, including "What Is This Thing Called Love" and "At Long Last Love" (Ex. 3.08). John Lennon also used this technique throughout two of his best-known songs, "Imagine" and "In My Life."

Ex. 3.08 "At Long Last Love" Cole Porter

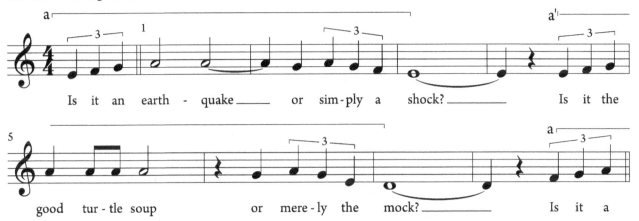

Is it an earth - quake _____ or sim - ply a shock? _____ Is it the

good tur - tle soup or mere - ly the mock? _____ Is it a

Each melodic phrase in the entire chorus of "At Long Last Love" ends on the first beat of the third measure of a four-measure harmonic phrase.

Note: Since there is little need to differentiate *inexactly matched phrases* from exactly *matched phrases* except for what has already been observed, henceforth, both inexactly and exactly matched phrases will simply be referred to and analyzed as *matched phrases*.

Masculine and feminine rhymes

Rhymes found on a downbeat or anticipated downbeat positions (and by downbeat, I mean any beat within the measure, not just the first beat) are referred to as *masculine rhymes*. *Masculine* rhymes always end on a stressed syllable (Ex. 3.09).

Ex. 3.09

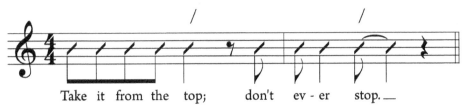

Take it from the top; don't ev - er stop. __

The other type of rhyme, one that is not as frequently employed as an end rhyme but is equally as important, is called a *feminine rhyme*. The less frequent use of feminine rhymes in the end rhyme position is due to the fact that it is sometimes difficult to find feminine rhymes that do not call undo attention to themselves. A feminine rhyme is a rhyme in which the stress is on the penultimate (second from last) syllable of the word and ends on an unstressed syllable, the musical equivalent of the upbeat position (Ex. 3.10).

Ex. 3.10

Stephen Sondheim uses a lot of feminine rhymes in his lyric setting of Leonard Bernstein's music for "I Feel Pretty." The first line, "I feel pret-ty, oh, so pret-ty", sets the rhythmical impulse for most of the song and ends with a feminine ending. Notice, however, that at the end of the two lines in the balancing position (lines 2 and 4), where rhyme is called for, he uses a masculine rhyme.

"I Feel Pretty" (line endings)   lyrics by Stephen Sondheim,
                                                 music by Leonard Bernstein

                  / -
Line 1: Oh, so pret-ty
                     - /
Line 2: witty and bright
                  / -
Line3: And I pi-ty
                    - /
Line 4: is-n't me to-night.

Internal rhymes

Rhymes found at the end of phrases are, logically enough, called *end rhymes*. Rhymes used within a phrase are called *internal rhymes*. As used by Paul Simon in his delightful "50 Ways To Lose Your Lover," *internal rhymes* can be subtle (as found in its verse) or dynamic (as found in its chorus). Internal rhymes bind the lyric and melody together, provide an additional emphasis, and produce acceleration because rhyme acts as a subtle form of accentuation. In the verse, there is a fairly subtle use of internal rhyme (Ex. 3.11).

Ex. 3.11 *"50 Ways To Leave Your Lover" verse, Paul Simon*

The prob-lem is all in-side your **head,** she **said** to me

In the chorus the internal rhymes are more obvious and add immensely to its rhyth-mic punch (Ex. 3.12).

Ex. 3.12 *"50 Ways To Leave Your Lover" chorus*

Just slip out the **back, Jack,** Make a new **plan, Stan.** You don't need to be **coy, Roy,** Just lis-ten to me.

The rhyme placement in "50 Ways To Leave You Lover" is so much a part of the song that it is impossible to imagine any other words or any other rhyme scheme working as well.

Rhyme as a catalyst to creation

Rhyme can and often does serve as a catalyst for the creation of music. This is because the sound of words that resonate with one another is very much like music. Words not only have meaning but also, like music, are made of sounds that suggest rhythms. Rhyme allows words to be as close to music as words can be. You can imagine the music of this magical Joni Mitchell song as soon as you hear the mellifluous rhymes within this sublime lyric:

> "Both Sides Now"   Joni Mitchell
>
> Rows and flows of angel hair
> And ice cream castles in the air
> And feather canyons everywhere,
> I've looked at clouds that way.

It is important to remember that although words carry meaning, they are also sounds, colorful, intriguing sounds with implied rhythms that, when transmuted into melodic rhythms and pitch, form the foundation of songwriting.

The order of the phrases

Joni Mitchell uses an (a)(a)(a)(x) order of rhymes in "Both Sides Now." This particular order, three lines that end in rhyme followed by a fourth line that doesn't rhyme, is found in numerous songs in many diverse styles. The music for this phrase order follows the same scheme: three matching melodic phrases a, a, a, followed by a phrase that usually contains the same number of measures as the previous phrases, but a different number of stresses, and— most important—ends in a different metric area (x). Because the last phrase is different and therefore calls attention to itself, it often serves as the perfect place to house the title of the song, as demonstrated in the end rhymes in Paul Simon's "I Do It For Your Love" and Bob Dylan's "Make You Feel My Love."

"I Do It For Your Love" (end of lines)   Paul Simon

Line 1: on a rainy day   a
Line 2: the grass was gray   a
Line 3: we drove away   a
Line 4: I do it for your love   x

"Make You Feel My Love"   Bob Dylan

Line 1: in your face   a
Line 2: is on your case   a
Line 3: a warm embrace   a
Line 4: To make you feel my love.   x

Ira Gershwin's lyric for "How Long Has This Been Going On" does a variation of this scheme. He initially uses the combined first two one-measures phrases as one unit (a) but uses the short break within the phrase—a kind of musical comma—to split the third line lyrically, so that an internal rhyme, (b) (b), can be enjoyed.

Here, he was reacting to the matched rhythms (b, b) found within the larger phrase.

"How Long Has This Been Going On"   George and Ira Gershwin

	Rhyme	Music
I could cry salty tears	(a)	a
Where have I been all these years?	(a)	a
Little wow, tell me now	(b)(b)	a
How long has this been going on?	(x)	x

The above lyric is shown in its rhythmic setting (Ex. 3.13).

Ex. 3.13

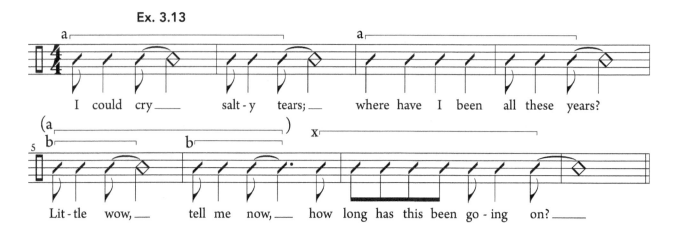

This particular order of the phrases (a, a, a, x) is so satisfying because, as much as we enjoy the three rhymes in a row, we really do not need to hear a fourth one. The fourth line, because it is different, calls attention to itself and, therefore, is a ideal place to highlight a title.

To rhyme or not to rhyme

Although rhyme is an essential part of popular songwriting, there are a few commercially successful songs that eschew rhyme completely. Two that I'm aware of are Paul Simon's "America" and the standard "Moonlight In Vermont" by John Blackburn and Karl Suessdorf. Both of those songs have music that is not highly rhythmic and that contains quite a lot of space between phrases, and both have lyrics that are powerfully visual. Although these songs prove that songs without rhyme can succeed, rhyme is, nonetheless, one of the most powerful tools in a songwriter's toolbox.

As already stated, not all matched phrases should garner rhymes. To do so might make the lyric sound trite. Matched phrases in the main balancing positions, however, usually call for rhyme. In Billy Joel's "Just The Way You Are" the balancing position occurs at the end of the third phrase that ends on the anticipation of measure 7 and on the sixth phrase that ends on the anticipation of measure 15. They are the only phrases that demand rhyme and receive it (far/are) (Ex. 3.14).

Ex. 3.14 "Just The Way You Are" melodic rhythm Billy Joel

Although too many rhymes can have a negative, cheapening effect that can sometimes be disastrous to a song, if you use perfect rhyme and rhyme substitutes as intelligently as Diane Warren does in "Because You Loved Me," the effect can be breathtaking. The first six melodic phrases of the chorus of this gigantic hit song are matched or inexactly matched and help build the chorus into an emotional crescendo (Ex. 3.15).

The lyric in the chorus of "Because You Loved Me" uses perfect rhymes in its first four lines (weak/speak, see/me) and then uses an imperfect rhyme that employs the long "e" vowel sound to make a sonic connection in its next two lines, (reach, believed). This is an example of the use of *assonance*, the repetition of the same vowel sound in different words, a device often found in imperfect rhymes. The use of assonance is found in many of today's songs and provides today's songwriter with many more choices.

Ex. 3.15 "Because You Loved Me" chorus, Diane Warren

The six matched a-phrases in a row in the chorus of "Because You Love Me" are paired with the following rhymed couplets:

weak
speak
see
me
reach
believed

Only the last melodic phrase is not a matched phrase, one that ends with a feminine ending and, because of that, spotlights the title:

I'm everything I am
Because you loved me.

Perfect rhyme, imperfect rhyme, assonance, and consonance

Since rhyme itself is a structural musical device, in that it adds one more sonic element to the closure of a phrase, a hierarchal grouping—from strongest to weakest—of rhyme closures looks like this:

- *Told* and *sold* is a **perfect rhyme** because the two words have a different beginning consonant with the same vowel and same ending consonant.
- *Told* and *moat* is an **imperfect rhyme** that uses **assonance.** Both words contain the same vowel sound but a different ending consonant.
- *Crunch and branch* is an **imperfect rhyme** that uses **consonance.** The two words have different vowel sounds but use the same ending consonants.

Since this book centers on music and prosody, not lyrics alone, for further study of rhyme I recommend Pat Pattison's book, "The Essential Guide To Rhyming, 2ⁿᵈ Edition."

Balance, the norm

Rhythm can be examined at the micro level, e.g., what the rhythm of each melodic phrase contains, or at the macro level, e.g., the relationship between each section of a song. Most sections of music are balanced. Balance in music is determined by how many measures are in each section or subsection, e.g., a two-measure phrase followed by a two-measure phrase is balanced. Those two phrases could be balanced by, e.g., a four-measure phrase, or balanced by a three-measure phrase followed by a one-measure phrase. The thirty-two-measure AABA form (sectionalized 8+8+8+8) found in the majority of the songs in the *Great American Songbook* and the sixteen-measure rap form are two prime examples of balance as the norm in song form.

Confusion often occurs in defining the difference between balance and symmetry. A balanced section does not have to be symmetric. Any symmetric structure is, by definition, balanced—but symmetry is more exacting: symmetry means that the second part duplicates the first part. One element in a section of music, e.g., the harmony, may be symmetric (the same four chords may repeat in the same rhythm throughout) but the melodic rhythm and melodic phrase lengths may vary. This means that one element of music, the melody, may be asymmetric while another element, the harmony, may be symmetric.

The first four measures of John Legend's "All Of Me" is a balanced section of music, but is not totally symmetric. The chords move in steady half notes to form a symmetric pattern, while the melodic phrases vary in length and rhythm. Meanwhile, rhyme employing assonance and internal rhyme supply the glue that help hold it all together (Ex. 3.16).

Ex. 3.16 "All Of Me" John Stephens, Toby Gad

This microcosm of diverse activity—the way the elements of a song do different things at the same time, yet are beautifully unified—provides the listener with a satisfying experience. Creating songs that do this is one of the great joys experienced in the act of writing a song.

Rhyme as a unifying factor

Rhyme can also be used to knit together musical phrases that are not matched. Rhyme acts as a unifying element in "Ready To Take A Chance Again," a hit for Barry Manilow in 1971 (Ex. 3.17).

Ex. 3.17 "Ready To Take A Chance Again" music by Charles Fox, lyrics by Norman Gimbel

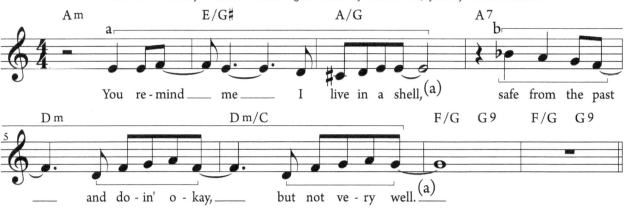

This beautifully written song has melodic phrases that do not match each other: the a-phrase begins on the third beat of measure 1 and ends on the anticipation of beat 3 of measure 3; the b-phrase begins on the second beat of the fourth measure and ends on the anticipation of beat 1 of the seventh measure, but the rhymes felicitously connect the disparate phrases and help to unify the verse. Notice, too, how the three matched rhythms (bracketed in the example) that are housed in the b-phrase do not elicit rhymes. Employing rhyme there most likely would have sounded trite. However, there are sonic connections: the ā sound of "sāfe" does resonate with the sound of "o-kāy." Notice how the perfect rhyme (shell/well) is used as a counterpoint to the unmatched phrases, helping to unify the entire section. This is also a good example of a balanced structure (4+4 measure harmonic phrase structure) housing an asymmetric melody.

Hugh Prestwood, a wonderful songwriter, also uses rhyme to connect disparate rhythmic phrases.

Here is the beginning of his lyric in the chorus of "Ghost In This House":

I'm **just** a **ghost** in this **house**	(3-stressed line)
I'm **just** a **sha**dow up**on** these **walls**	(4-stressed line)
As **quie**tly as a **mouse**	(3-stressed line)
I **haunt** these **halls**	(2- stressed line)

After the third line, we expect to hear another 4-stressed line like, "I **choose** to **live** here and **haunt** these **halls**," placed metrically in a matched position to the second line, but instead are immediately presented with a 2-stressed line: "I **haunt** these

halls." This phrase is both unexpected and very satisfying. Rhyme helps make this asymmetric phrase structure sound completely natural (Ex. 3.18).

Ex. 3.18 "Ghost In This House" Hugh Prestwood

The strategic use of rhyme

Bob Dylan is a rhymester who has no equal. He is also an amazingly adept strategist. "Like A Rolling Stone" has a rhetorical style that draws the listener in and, like any great orator, Dylan keeps his listener involved by his use of space, time, and repetition. Dylan's combination of intriguing rhymes, syncopated rhythms, and phrases that are packed full of information—followed by vocal silences that demand that you to listen for the next words—is irresistible.

> "Like A Rolling Stone"   Bob Dylan
>
> Once upon a time you dressed so fine,
> Threw the bums a dime in your prime, didn't you?
> People'd call, say "Beware doll, you're bound to fall,"
> You thought they were all a'kiddin' you.

Words that are read from a page and words that are heard in musical time, with melodic rhythms set against a beat, are two very different conditions that often produce totally different results. "Like A Rolling Stone" provides us with a great example of how musical time affects the perception of a lyric.

Try reading the lyric without hearing the music and then listen to the lyric in Dylan's musical setting and pay attention to the syncopations, the way rhymed words shake hands with one another; feel how the long pauses build tension and call attention to the meaning of the anticipated phrase. Notice how Dylan's jeering accusations are heightened by metrically isolating "didn't you?" and "a'kiddin' you." Now notice that the second part of the song (not included in this text but available at any number of Internet sites) beginning with "You used to laugh about" uses twice as much time—two measures—to say what it has to say as the previous section that began "Once upon a time you dressed so fine"—a phrase that was sung in one measure's time. Finish singing that section to yourself, feeling the beat and how each two-measure phrase balances the last two-measure phrase until you reach the last word "proud," which rhymes perfectly with "loud." That seems like the end of a perfectly balanced section consisting of four two-measure phrases, and should provide us with closure. Instead, we get another phrase: "About having to be scrounging your next meal," a phrase that lasts four measures and that ends with "**meal**," a word that rhymes with nothing that came before it! This is a moment of genius in the song, because of the way it sets up the chorus. How satisfying it is to finally hear the rhyme, "How does it **feel**," at the end of the first line of the chorus.

The way Bob Dylan uses rhythm, especially the spaces between phrases, makes those spaces as important as the words themselves. I'm reminded of the rhetorical gestures of the great orator Martin Luther King, or the prodigiously talented jazz musician Miles Davis, who completely understood and used the power of space between phrases.

The element of surprise

"Like A Rolling Stone" uses the element of surprise to both delight listeners and to shine a very bright spotlight on the chorus. Most songs don't use the element of surprise to manipulate their audiences as well as it is used in this song. The usual route professional songwriters take is to set up musical and lyrical expectations in their listeners—and then satisfy them. Billy Joel's "Just The Way You Are" does exactly that: the musical phrases are all balanced and rhyme occurs where we expect to hear rhyme. When the music and lyric are as tasty as they are in Billy Joel's song, there is no need for further manipulation.

This is how the element of surprise works: expectations are based on hearing a pattern; once a pattern is established, we expect the pattern to continue. After hearing an established pattern—e.g., an a-phrase followed by a b-phrase; if the next a-phrase is not followed by a b-phrase we tend to be intrigued and pulled into the song. If, on the other hand, our expectations are continually thwarted, or no expectations are set up, we tend to stop listening altogether. Therefore, the choices you have are: (1) set up expectations in order to satisfy them, or (2) set up expectations in order to surprise your listeners. If you do not set up any expectations or continually thwart your listeners' expectations, you most likely will lose your audience.

Surprise in songwriting is almost always a subtle surprise, one that the listener is only vaguely aware of. Nonetheless, small surprises are very powerful because they keep people listening.

Bruno Mars's song "Grenade" stayed on the top of the pop charts for an inordinately long time due to a number of factors. Among those factors, the surprise element was indispensible. Expectations for what will occur in the second section of the verse 1 are set up in the first section, since both sections begin with very similar music. Since the first two melodic phrases are similarly matched, we expect the next two melodic phrases to also match its a, b, a, b structure and rhyme scheme (x), (a), (x), (a), as demonstrated below.

The first part of verse 1 starts out as a complaint by the singer to his lover concerning his lover's inability to reciprocate the strong feelings he has for her.

"Grenade" verse 1, end of lines and rhyme scheme,

> Bruno Mars, Philip Lawrence, Ari Levine,
> Brody Brown, Andrew Wyatt

	End of line	Music
Line 1: easy go	(x)	a
Line 2: you live,	(a)	b
Line 3: take it all,	(x)	a
Line 4: never give	(a)	b

We expect something like:

	End of line	Music
Line 1: was trouble	(x)	a
Line 2: first kiss,	(b)	b
Now I'm hurt, hurt so bad	(x)	a
Won't get over this.	(b)	b

Instead, the second part of the first verse contains a powerful surprise:

	End of line	Music
Line 1: was trouble	(x)	a
Line 2: first kiss,	(x)	b
Had your eyes wide open	(x)	x
Why were they open?	(x)	x

We are completely bamboozled by this lyric writing move, because not only did our rhyme expectations get thwarted but also we are given an unlikely—but brilliant—lyric: "Had your eyes wide open. Why were they open?"

We can't help but be drawn into the song at this juncture, because the writers have turned the table on us and, at the same time, turned on a very large spotlight. They were aware of, and made excellent use of, the fact that when we listen, whether we are conscious of it or not, we have expectations. They also knew how powerful it is to not always satisfy every expectation and that more pleasure can be derived from a surprise. "Why were they open?" is more than an intriguing question (the fact that this is a question is important because when a singer addresses a singee, the ultimate receptor is you, the person listening). It is an indication that the girl's character is suspect; she is someone who doesn't make commitments and does not take this kiss as seriously as the love-besotted singer of the song obviously does. In this one line, the songwriters have begun to hold us captive. *Once you understand how to set up listener expectations, you may choose to either fulfill those expectations or give your listeners something that is even better: surprise and delight.*

Summary

The connection of rhythm and rhyme is the most basic and powerful connection that exists in songwriting. With rhyme, music and words dance beautifully together. Without rhyme, music and words may conflict with each other, especially when music asks for rhyme and the words refuse to cooperate. Rhyme, imperfect rhyme, and assonance are all useful ways to have words produce a concordance with music that is very powerful. When a song's melodic phrase structure is rather complex, rhyme can be used as a way to help the diverse phrases connect to one another. Rhyme, however, should not be over-used, because doing so can make your song sound trite. Nor should rhyme be used simply because it provides the right sound. It is almost always wiser to choose a meaningful word rather than a word that doesn't quite mean what you want it to say—even if it rhymes. It is best to satisfy both sonic demands and meaning. This usually requires rewriting and rewriting and rewriting until—finally—you have it.

Rhyme can:

- parallel your music with sounds that have meaning
- provide delightful connections within a phrase
- accelerate or decelerate your phrase
- provide closure
- spotlight a title or other important phrases
- knit together disparate melodic phrases
- enable your listeners to remember your song
- be used or omitted strategically to produce the element of surprise

Activities

I believe that one of the best ways to achieve a strong song-sense is to fully realize the connectivity and power of rhythm and rhyme in the creation of a song. Doing the following activities will involve you in ways that simply reading about technique will never fully achieve.

Use my examples (Exs. 3.19–3.22) as models in order to create an eight-measure section of a song (▶ AUDIO EXS. 3.19–3.22).

- Create a two-measure rhythmic phrase and repeat it three times. Begin your rhythm before, after, or on the first beat. Try to include some syncopation. The structure is made up of an a, a, a, a, phrase order. In my example, I altered some of the *matched phrases* into *inexactly matched phrases* in order to provide some variety and also to connect the third and fourth phrases.

Ex. 3.19

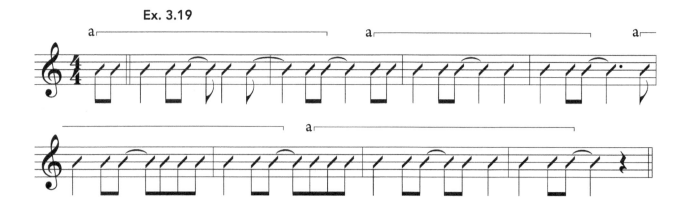

Once you have composed an eight-measure section that you believe will work with a lyric, note where the important stresses fall and begin exploring various subjects for your lyrical ideas. Let the rhythms guide you and let the lyric involve your feelings as soon as possible. Allow your creativity to be guided by your feelings, not only your intellect. Use one of the following rhyme schemes: a, a, a, a; a, a, b, b; a, b, a, b; x, a, x, a.

Here is my example with lyrics containing an a, a, b, b rhyme scheme.

Ex. 3.20

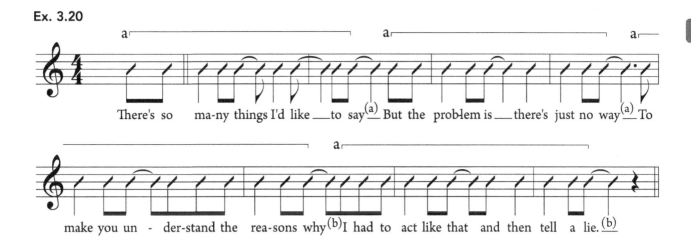

• Add melodic pitch to the given rhythms.

Ex. 3.21

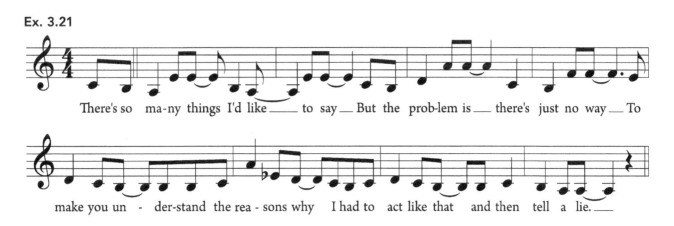

The lyric expresses an apology filled with regret. This caused me to write a melody in the minor mode, including a blues note on the word "reasons."

• Add chords to your melody.

Ex. 3.22

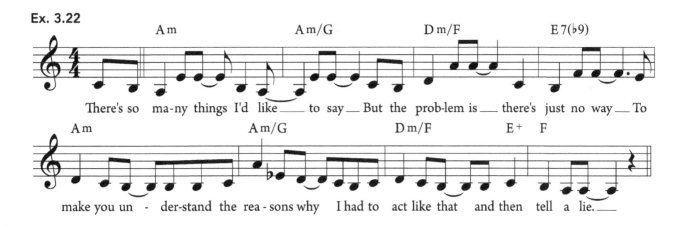

I ended my section on a <flat>VI chord because I wanted to keep the section open, so that I could easily move into the next verse, or possibly add a phrase.

Try writing your own rhythmic phrases and use this method with various phrase orders: a, b, a, b; a, a, a, x; or vary the length of your phrases, for example, make the length of your a-phrases one measure and the length of your b-phrases two measures and use an a, a, b/a, a, b phrase structure in order to create an interesting eight-measure section.

This method has proven to be one of the fastest and most efficient ways to approach the creation of a song. However, because it starts with body (rhythm) and mind (order), it demands that your emotional-self become involved as soon as possible. Create lyrics that generate something that involves you emotionally and then allow your lyrics and your feelings to drive the rest of your song.

• Create a verse section that is a balanced section of music, add a line that doesn't rhyme with anything in the verse, and rhyme the first line of your chorus to the last (added) line in your verse (use "Like A Rolling Stone" as a model). Attempt to surprise and delight yourself and you will, no doubt, do the same for your listeners.

Tone Tendencies

The most natural thing for a songwriter to do when beginning a song is to start strumming chords on a guitar or laying down some changes on a keyboard in a rhythm that feels good to the body and then to begin singing something that fits with that chord pattern, and voilà, you have the beginning of a song! There is nothing wrong with this approach—in fact, there is much to recommend it. This approach, however, often causes melodies to be too completely tied to the chords and does not inspire much melodic independence.

Another and more basic approach to creating a melody is to establish a key either by playing or singing a scale and internalizing the relationship of the notes to one another. Then, without reference to harmony, create a melody. This can be achieved intuitively, but having real knowledge of how tone tendencies work can help you immensely in having better control of your melodic choices.

Understanding melody's relationship to the tonal center is crucial to your understanding melody's relationship to chords. The relationship of the melody to the tonal center is a primary relationship, whereas the relationship of the melody to the harmony is a secondary relationship. In order to more fully understand both of these relationships, we must look further into the nature of tonality itself.

The importance of tonality

Tonality is essential to our enjoyment of popular music. The reason for this is simple—we have been given few clues as to the nature of the universe, but nature has provided us with the *harmonic series*. Unlike many subjects that must be studied deeply to be understood, music speaks to practically everyone because there is a universal language—and that language, no matter how many dialects it assumes, is determined to a large extent by the harmonic series (Ex. 4.01).

Ex. 4.01 Harmonic series

The *harmonic series* or *overtone series* is a ratio of sound vibrations present in every musical note. A sounding note produces a series of tones that are not heard as separate notes but are absorbed into it. The main note is called the *fundamental* (the note on which the series of overtones is based; in example 4.01, the note is C) and contains within it all the notes that appear in the harmonic series. The ratios of those notes decreases in amplitude as the series moves further away from the fundamental. The first overtones, those closest to the fundamental, that have the most power are the perfect fifth and major third, producing a major triad. This accounts for the universal acceptance of the sound of a major triad as euphonious by everyone on this planet. The power of tonality affects everyone—musician and layperson alike.

Tonality

If the harmonic series is given by nature, then why isn't it adhered to in a more exacting way by us? Why have we tempered the scale? Why have we created scales that do not adhere to the tones given in the harmonic series? (E.g., *fa* and *ti*, notes that are in a major scale, do not appear in the harmonic series.) These questions are easily answered by understanding that we are both creatures of nature and creatures of culture. The scales we use are reflections of our need to express ourselves fully, to express the consonances and the dissonances that we encounter in life. Music is a symbolic language, therefore, the symbols we choose must represent who we are, how we act, and how we feel, reflecting both the consonances and the dissonances of our existence.

Major scale in relationship to the harmonic series—stable and unstable tones

The major scale contains the very consonant tones *do*, *sol*, and *mi*, found at the beginning of the harmonic series, as well as very dissonant tones that are found at a great distance from the fundamental or that seemingly have no relationship to that fundamental. I've designated the tones that are consonant to the fundamental (the fundamental corresponds to the tonic of any given key) as "stable" (symbol: *st*) and the tones that are dissonant to the fundamental as "unstable" (symbol: *ust*) (Ex. 4.02).

Ex. 4.02 Stable and unstable tones in the major scale or Ionian mode

Example 4.03 shows the hierarchy of tonal stability found in the major scale, from the most stable to the least stable. The stability or instability of each tone is measured by each of the tones' place in the harmonic series. Those closest to the fundamental are the most stable.

Ex. 4.03 Most stable to least stable tones in the major scale or Ionian mode

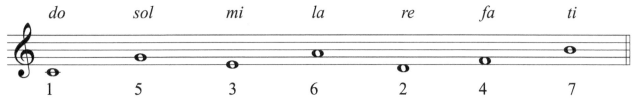

The stable tones in a major scale and in all of the commonly used scales are 1, 5, and 3—*do*, *sol*, and *mi* (in that order of consonance) in major tonalities and *do*, *sol*, and *me* (in that order of consonance) in minor tonalities; all other tones will tend toward these three columns of tonal stability. *Fa* and *ti* are one half step away from their stable neighboring notes, *mi* and *do*, and because of this proximity have an increased tendency to resolve to them (Ex. 4.04).

Ex. 4.04 Tone tendencies in the major scale or Ionian mode. An unbroken arrow indicates movement of an unstable tone to its primary resolution. A broken arrow indicates movement of an unstable tone to its secondary resolution.

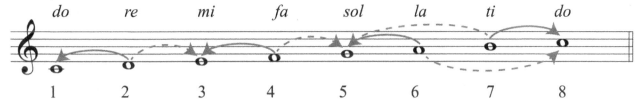

Tone tendency, the natural tendency of a tone to either stay where it is because it is consonant or stable in a scale, or to move because it is dissonant or unstable, affects all aspects of a song.

If you are one of those musicians who only consider your melody in relationship to the chord that supports it, I ask that you try a new approach to composing a melody, one that will ultimately give you more freedom and control over both your melodic and harmonic materials. Try singing the melodies in the examples while holding down the tonic in the lower register of your instrument. A keyboard works best, especially any keyboard that can sustain a note—like an organ or a synthesizer patch with a long release. If using a piano or guitar, you'll simply have to activate the note more often.

Melodic progression

When an unstable tone appears in a melody in any prominent way—a beginning note of a phrase, a high note, a low note, a held note, and especially, the ending note of a phrase—it calls attention to itself, becomes kinetic and beckons for resolution to a stable tone. This event produces a tension/release activity that generates *melodic progression*. The term "melodic progression" is seldom used in teaching music (much more common is the term, *harmonic progression*). But melodies do progress, and your recognition of tone tendencies empowers you to use their tendencies strategically in order to create melodies that progress in logical and satisfying ways.

53

Play or sing the following melody (Ex. 4.05) while you hold C, the tonic note, in the bass. There are three points of tension in the melody, the D (*re*) and B (*ti*), that appear in the second measure and again, B (*ti*), the last note. Ending a phrase on a dissonant note such as *ti* sets up expectations, causing interest to occur (▶ AUDIO 4.05).

Ex. 4.05 Melody ending on *ti*

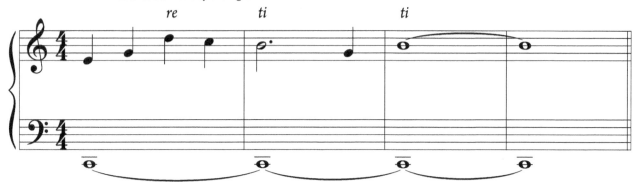

In Example 4.06 *ti* in the second measure resolves to *do* in the third measure. We feel both a sense of progression as *ti* finds it way to *do* and a sense of resolution when it reaches its goal. This simple need of a note with tension to resolve to a note with less tension is the basis for melodic interest and melodic progression (▶ AUDIO 4.06).

Ex. 4.06 Melodic resolution

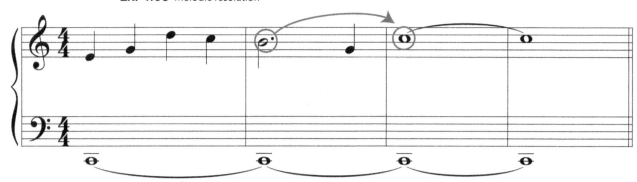

Tone tendencies and form

The relationship of the melody to the tonal center has deep reverberations on every aspect of a song, including its form. Like a mild call for help or a dropped handkerchief, an unstable note at the end of a phrase asks for resolution. If a phrase or a section ends unresolved on an unstable note, it sets up expectations that a resolution of the unstable note will eventually arrive.

A strategic use of tone tendencies in demarcating form is found in many folk songs that cadence on an unstable pitch midway through a section of music. *Re*, the note that often ends the first half of the section (the first circled note in the examples below), asks that the second half of the section furnish the resolution to *do* (the second circled note in the examples below). This delayed resolution holds the listener's attention until resolution is achieved and is an example of how tone tendencies produce melodic progression.

Examples are abundant in folk music literature; here are three recognizable ones (Exs. 4.07–4.09).

Ex. 4.07 *"Oh, My Darling Clementine"*

Ex. 4.08 *"Tom Dooley"*

Ex. 4.09 *"Home On The Range"*

The symmetric form (i.e., the melodic rhythms in the first half are duplicated in the second half) found in the above folk songs doesn't appear very often in contemporary popular songs, which are usually more structurally complex. However, the strategic use of tone tendencies does remain a major factor in creating expectations and then satisfying them, as in Example 4.10, where the first three phrases end on *re*, which finally resolves to *do* at the end of phrase 4.

Ex. 4.10 "I Wanna Dance With Somebody" George Merrill, Shannon Rubicam

Oh,— I wan-na dance —with some-bo - dy.   I wan-na feel the heat   with some-bo - dy.

Yeah, ___ I wan-na dance ___with some-bo - dy,   with some - bo-dy who loves __ me.

Immediate and delayed resolutions

There is no rule that states that an unstable tone *must* resolve to a stable tone, nor is there a rule that states *when* an unstable tone should resolve to a stable tone; there are simply implications and tendencies. Unstable tones either resolve immediately to the next note (*immediate resolution*) or to a note much further from it (*delayed resolution*).

In Example 4.11, each unstable tone resolves immediately—*re* moves to *do, ti* moves to *do,* and *la* moves to *sol* (▶ AUDIO 4.11).

Ex. 4.11 Immediate resolution

In Example 4.12, *fa* does not resolve to *mi* for nearly two measures, producing a delayed resolution (▶ AUDIO 4.12).

Ex. 4.12 Delayed resolution

"Blue Bayou" contains many immediate resolutions, but also contains a number of important delayed resolutions. *Re* immediately resolves to *do* in measure 1, but *re* also ends the second melodic phrase, leaving it unresolved or *open. Do,* the final note of the melody in measure 7, provides the delayed resolution (Ex. 4.13).

Ex. 4.13 "Blue Bayou" Roy Orbison, Joe Melson

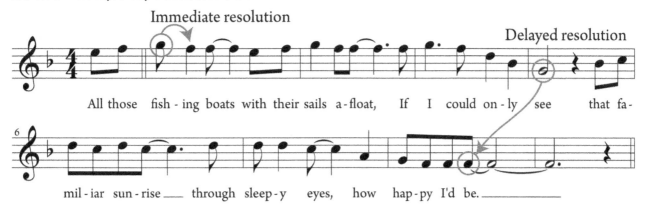

57

Dependent and independent melodies

Melodies that are tonally and rhythmically interesting enough to exist on their own, and don't need the element of harmony to prop them up, are called *independent melodies*. Melodies that are dependent on either harmony or on another melody happening simultaneously, such as a riff or some other counterline are called *dependent melodies*. Neither of these two types of melodies (independent or dependent) prevails; in fact, most melodies have parts that are independent and parts that are dependent.

Independent melody

"Yankee Doodle" is a good example of an independent melody (Ex. 4.14). Fife and drum corps often play it, and no one ever complains about missing the harmonies. You may ask yourself, as I have, why is the melody to this old bastion of American patriotism so satisfying without harmonies?

Ex. 4.14 "Yankee Doodle"

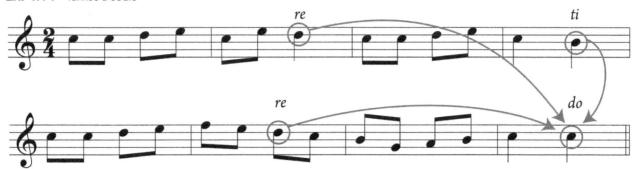

This melody sets up tonal and rhythmic expectations and then satisfies them. The first phrase ends on *re*, the second phrase ends on *ti*, the third phrase ends on *re*, and the last phrase ends on *do*, the note that is the resolution to both *ti* and *re*, the goal that everyone is waiting to hear.

A more contemporary example, P!nk's "Just Give Me A Reason," is a highly melodic song that contains an opening phrase with the characteristics of an independent melody. In this example, the unstable tones immediately resolve to their stable neighbors (Ex. 4.15).

Ex. 4.15 "Just Give Me A Reason" P!nk, Jeff Bhasker, Nate Ruess

Right from the start, ——you were a thief, —— you stole my heart and I, your wil-ling vic - tim.

Notice how *fa* resolves to *mi* in the first phrase and how *la* resolves to *sol* in the second phrase and, in doing so, create interest and progression.

Other well-known independent melodies include "Over The Rainbow" and "Happy Birthday."

Dependent melody

The lack of tonal interest in dependent melodies is caused by too many stable tones and too few unstable tones in the melody.

Once appropriate harmonies are added to a dependent melody, it may become vibrant, much the way a rather bland food comes to life when interesting condiments are added to it. Examples of *dependent melodies* abound. Here are the first eight measures of Antonio Carlos Jobim's "One Note Samba" without chords (Ex. 4.16).

Ex. 4.16 "One Note Samba" Antonio Carlos Jobim

This is just a lit - tle sam - ba built up - on a sin - gle note.—— Oth - er

notes are bound to fol - low, but the root is still— the note.—— Now this

Here is "One Note Samba" with its lush harmonies (Ex. 4.17).

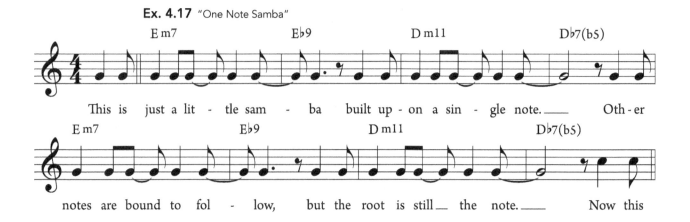

Ex. 4.17 "One Note Samba"

E m7   Eb9   D m11   Db7(b5)

This is just a lit - tle sam - ba built up - on a sin - gle note.—— Oth - er

E m7   Eb9   D m11   Db7(b5)

notes are bound to fol - low, but the root is still— the note.—— Now this

Examples 4.16 and 4.17 alert us to the importance of understanding that both tonal relationships, melody to tonal center and melody to harmony, are at play when composing. It also alerts us to the fact that conscious choices, rather than solely intuitive ones, can be made once you've understood the primary relationship of melody to tonal center. Once accomplished, you can easily hear where your melody needs assistance or buttressing from chords or possibly another melodic line (e.g., a riff) in order to maximize musical interest.

Examine and sing the melody of Dolly Parton's iconic "I Will Always Love You" (Ex. 4.18). Sing the melody as you hold a sustained low A, the tonic in this example, on an instrument, and, as you sing the melody, feel the increased energy caused by the unstable notes within the melody and feel the decreased energy as *re* or *ti* resolve to *do*, the tonic note, A. The waves of energy caused by this basic tension-and-release factor are one of the main means of creating interest and beauty found in all music.

Melody in two tonal relationships

Ex. 4.18 "I Will Always Love You" Dolly Parton

The rhythmic placement of the words and the melodic choices made by Dolly Parton make this declaration of love timeless. The preponderance of the tonic note in the melody—the most stable note—reinforces the message of the song, that of total commitment to the relationship.

This melody is typical of most melodies, in that it is not totally independent nor totally dependent. The melody is centered on *do*, with *do* appearing on the downbeat of every measure. The two notes that embellish and enliven this melody are two unstable notes, *re* and *ti*. Without those two notes this melody loses all of its meaning and memorability. Measures 3–5 are almost an exact repetition of measures 1–3, with the exception of the high C♯ that helps give the melody more interest (Ex. 4.19).

Ex. 4.19 "I Will Always Love You" melodic outline

The music becomes more vibrant with the addition of harmony (Ex. 4.20).

Ex. 4.20 "I Will Always Love You" with harmony

When a melody is full of stable tones and has slight progression, as found in this example, harmony must create forward motion. The tonic note in the melody first appears in relationship to the tonic triad, then in relationship to the VIm chord, and finally, in relationship to the IV chord. The harmonies progress further away from the tonal center with each iteration of the tonic note. The dominant harmony then appears leading back to the tonic and the cycle begins again. Example 4.21 demonstrates how a somewhat dependent melody is enhanced by a chord progression.

Ex. 4.21 Melody in two relationships

Harmony: Secondary relationship

Tonic : Primary relationship

In this one example we can begin to perceive the importance of tone tendencies, the role of dissonance in both melody and in harmony, the importance of harmony in relationship to melody, and the levels of complexity that exist within a seemingly simple music.

Characteristics of each of the unstable pitches in the major scale

Each unstable note in the hierarchy of a scale has its own characteristics; I've isolated each of the four unstable tones, *re, la, fa,* and *ti* in the following examples to demonstrate this. The following examples will give you a good idea of how each of the unstable tones have been used in popular songs.

Re

The 2nd scale degree, *re*, is one of the most potent and strategically useful unstable notes. Placing a highly kinetic note like *re* at the end of a melodic phrase causes the phrase to be unresolved and sets up listener's expectations, as demonstrated in Examples 4.08–4.11. The intrinsic kinetic power of *re* is apparent in John Mayer's masterful "Stop This Train," where it ends each of the phrases in the chorus, except for the last phrase—the phrase that contains the title and the long awaited tonic note. Ending so many phrases on *re* gives the song the sense of forward motion alluded to in the song title (Ex. 4.22).

Ex. 4.22 "Stop This Train" end of the chorus, John Mayer

"Stop This Train" presents us with another excellent example of the power of a delayed resolution.

"Don't Know Much," a great song recorded initially by Barry Manilow, later by Bette Midler, and made into a hit by Linda Ronstadt and Aaron Neville in 1989, is another independent melody whose beauty is apparent without harmony. It contains a verse in which most of the phrases—except the one containing the title—end on *re*. Measure 2 in Example 4.23 does contain a resolution to *do*, but quickly moves to end the phrase on the unstable *fa*. The natural resolution of *fa* is to *mi*, a resolution found in measure 8, where the melody reaches a climax on the word "be" (*mi* is displaced up an octave). The final phrase provides the resolution of *re* to *do*. This example clearly demonstrates the power and directionality contained within unstable tones and how their use as ending notes of phrases has consequences in subsequent phrases.

Ex. 4.23 "Don't Know Much" Barry Mann, Cynthia Weil, Tom Snow

La

The 6th scale degree, *la*, is the least unstable and therefore the least dynamic of the four unstable diatonic tones found in major. Nonetheless, *la* provides just enough tension to mildly ask for resolution to *sol*, the fifth of the key. It is the most dulcet of the unstable tones and plays a big part in making many well-known melodies memorable (Ex. 4.24).

Ex. 4.24 "Crocodile Rock" Music by Elton John, Lyrics by Bernie Taupin

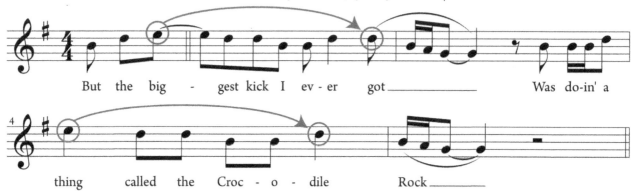

The sweetness of the melody of "Hey Jude" is partially due to the prevalence of *la* (Ex. 4.25).

Ex. 4.25 "Hey Jude" John Lennon, Paul McCartney

We can easily hear the honeyed tone of the 6th scale degree, *la*, in Percy Sledge's evocative song. Notice how *la* initially resolves to *sol*, but then appears again unresolved, providing a sweet dissonance (Ex. 4.26).

Ex. 4.26 "When A Man Loves A Woman" Calvin Lewis, Andrew Wright

Fa

The 4th scale degree, *fa*, can be a very effective tone to heighten tension and interest, as it beckons its resolution to *mi*, the third of the key. This is of strategic importance if it is placed at a cadence, and even more so if that cadence contains the title, as it does in the Taylor Swift/Liz Rose song "You Belong With Me" (Ex. 4.27).

Ex. 4.27 *"You Belong With Me" Taylor Swift, Liz Rose*

Notice that while *fa* initially resolves to *mi* in an immediate resolution in measure 2, it appears again on the first beat of measure 4, again resolving momentarily, only to jump down by a major 7th to the lower octave *fa*, increasing the tension and finally resolving to *mi* on the anticipated downbeat of measure 6. Tone tendencies have a tremendous effect on the lyric; notice how the first phrase containing "you belong with me?" ends in a question. This question is matched tonally by a phrase that ends open on the unstable *fa*. When the next phrase appears, "You belong with me" is made as a statement (almost a demand) with the expected resolution to the stable *mi* providing closure and strengthening the song's message. This is stupendous writing.

The fourth degree's strong tendency to resolve downward probably had a lot to do with the lyric of "When I Fall In Love" that is perfectly linked to this memorable melody. Note that the word "forever" ends open (Ex. 4.28).

Ex. 4.28 *"When I Fall In Love" music by Victor Young, lyrics by Edward Heyman*

Fa is almost as potent an unstable tone as *ti*, making it the perfect choice for the fervent setting of "darling" in this iconic song (Ex. 4.29).

Ex. 4.29 *"Love Me Tender" Elvis Presley, George Poulton, Ken Darby*

Ti

Ti is the most potent unstable tone in major. It is full of yearning because of its proximity to *do*. Stevie Wonder uses the seventh degree, *ti*, (also called the "leading tone" because of its natural tendency to lead to the tonic), to express feelings of love and yearning (Ex. 4.30).

Ex. 4.30 "I Just Called To Say I Love You" Stevie Wonder

I just called to say ____ "I love ____ you",

Jerome Kern knew the emotive power of the leading tone; it is one of the main driving forces in this great melody (Ex. 4.31).

Ex. 4.31 "The Song Is You" music by Jerome Kern, lyrics by Oscar Hammerstein

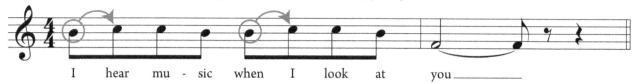

I hear mu - sic when I look at you _____

Anyone singing this great melody, even without the support of a harmonic instrument, will feel the intrinsic tension/release, the passion created by this tonal movement.

Secondary resolutions

It would certainly be boring if every tone tendency were followed by its most natural resolution, if *re* and *ti* always resolved to *do*, or if *fa* always resolved to *mi*, etc. This would certainly limit our choices and our creativity. It is best to keep this fact in mind: tone tendencies are just that, tendencies—not hard and fast rules. Quite frequently *re* will move to *mi*, as *fa* may move to *sol*, or *ti* may move to *la*. These are the secondary resolutions of unstable tones.

If an unstable tone moves to its normal or most natural resolution, for example, when *re* moves to *do*, it is natural but rather uneventful. (Most unstable tones, except for *ti* and sharped chromatic notes, tend to move down.) But when the unstable tone is satisfied by a secondary resolution, for example, when *re* moves up to *mi* instead of down to *do*, a shot of energy is created that can carry a song a long way.

"Need You Now," a huge hit for the group Lady Antebellum, has a chorus melody that begins on *sol*, then leaps to *re*, but *re* does not resolve to *do*. Instead it moves up to a secondary resolution, *mi*, providing a charge of energy that propels the melody forward. At the end of the phrase, *ti* does not resolve to *do*, but moves, instead through *la* to *sol* (Ex. 4.32).

Ex. 4.32 "Need You Now" Hillary Scott, Charles Kelley, Dave Heywood, Josh Kear

It's a quar-ter af-ter one, I'm____ all a - lone and I need____you now.____

In Example 4.33 I've altered the melody of "Need You Now" by having the unstable tones rigidly move to their primary resolutions. With these alterations, the melody loses most of its beauty, just as the lyric loses its unification with the music. Instead of the feeling of expectation and hope that the original chorus produces, my rewrite, with most of the stable tones collapsing into their expected resolutions, causes the listener to hear a rather mournful, hopeless plea that ends with a feeling of resolution, resulting in the exact opposite of what the lyric demands.

Ex. 4.33

It's a quar-ter af-ter one, I'm____ all a - lone and I need____you now. ____

What effect might you imagine would occur when *ti* does not resolve to *do*, but instead moves to *la*? *La* is not a stable tone either, and the result of a very unstable tone moving to a slightly less unstable tone and then finally resolving to its secondary resolution, *sol*, can produce a very poignant effect, one that can be heard in the opening of "La Vie En Rose."

Ex. 4.34 "La Vie En Rose" music by Marguerite Monnot and David Louiguy, lyrics by Edith Piaf

ti   la   ti   la   ti   la   ti   la   sol

Hold me close and hold me   fast, The mag-ic spell you   cast, This is la vi-en   ro - se.

Chromatic notes

All chromatic notes are more dissonant than any of the diatonic notes. Once a diatonic tonal environment has been established, the use of a chromatic note is akin to throwing a pebble into a still pond. Chromatic notes tend to resolve to the nearest diatonic note. Chromatic notes were used extensively in what is referred to as the Romantic Era of music (c. 1825–1900). Songwriters in the United States, influenced by European music, frequently used chromatic notes both in melody and harmony during the era of ragtime music (c. 1880–1918). Chromatic usage is found in the *Great American Songbook*, and appears in traditional R&B, but hardly at all in rock and today's pop songs. Notice that all chromatic notes have two possible names, e.g., C# = D♭; they are either sharp or flat and usually move in the direction that their names indicate. Sharps resolve up a half step to a diatonic note and flats resolve down a half step to a diatonic note (Ex. 4.35).

Ex. 4.35 Chromatic notes

The following two examples are of melodies with chromatic notes that greatly affect the lyrics and the feelings generated by them. *Note: In all examples where chromatic notes appear, numbers instead of solfege syllables are used for analysis.*

Irving Berlin always seemed to be in touch with the sensibility of the masses, and I believe a good part of that connection occurred because Berlin was in touch with his own emotions, and knew how to translate them into musical expression matched by lyrical gems. All the warm feelings of Christmas are generated by his choice of some highly emotionally charged chromatic notes in this memorable melody. Here he uses #2 and #4. #2 moves up to 3 (*mi*) and #4 embraces 5 (*sol*). In the same way that half-step movements found in the diatonic scale, *ti* to *do*, or *fa* to *mi*, resonate with a lyric that has emotional power, chromatic tones heighten feeling and draw us into the song (Ex. 4.36).

Ex. 4.36 "White Christmas" Irving Berlin

I'm   dream - ing   of   a   White   Christ - mas

Richard Rodgers musically conjures up an exotic island by sustaining #4—a tone that is the most dissonant interval to the tonic—for over a measure, finally resolving it to 5, *sol*. He then sequences the melody down a third to another chromatic tone, #2, that finally resolves to 3, *mi*, and with these few notes he magically transports us to a South Sea Island (Ex. 4.37).

Ex. 4.37 "Bali Hai" music by Richard Rodgers, lyrics by Oscar Hammerstein

Ba - li   Hai   may   call you,   a - ny   night,   a - ny   day.   In your

Other scales

Different type scales—i.e., major, minor, modal, blues—have different tone tendencies, although scale degrees 1, 3, and 5, or 1, ♭3, and 5 consistently are the stable tones in each scale. It is beyond the scope of this chapter to include each one of these scales; however, it is important to show some of the most frequently used scales and their tone tendencies.

Tone tendencies in the Aeolian mode (or natural minor)

The scale degrees in the Aeolian (or natural minor) have similar, though not exact, tone tendencies as in major. The 1, ♭3, and 5 are the stable tonal columns to which all other tones gravitate. The fourth degree in minor does not have a half step relationship to the third scale degree, so its tendency to resolve to ♭3 is not as strong as is its counterpart in major. *Re*, now a half step away from ♭3, has a strong tendency to move it. ♭7, *te*, does not have as strong a pull up to the tonic because it is a whole step from it.

Ex. 4.38 Aeolian mode, primary and secondary resolutions

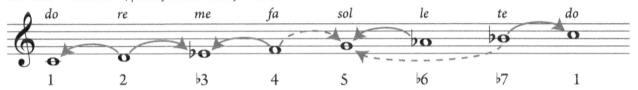

In the Aeolian mode or natural minor, ♭6, *le*, is the most unstable tone since it is a half step away from *sol* and, therefore, has a strong tendency resolve to it. This causes the ♭6 scale degree to take on more melodic significance. The title, "Sober," of this hit for P!nk in 2008, is highlighted by the use of the potent ♭6 resolving to 5 (Ex. 4.39).

Ex. 4.39 "Sober" P!nk, Nate Hills, Kara DioGuardi, Marcella Araica

Bon Jovi's hit "You Give Love A Bad Name," prominently features the ♭6 scale degree on the word "heart" resolving to 5, and 4 on the word "love" resolving to ♭3 in this strong hook (Ex. 4.40).

Ex. 4.40 "You Give Love A Bad Name" Jon Bon Jove, Desmond Child, Richie Sambora

Shot through the heart, and you're to blame. Dar-lin', you give love ____ a bad name.

Tone tendencies in Mixolydian mode

The Mixolydian mode regularly shows up in songs that appear on the Billboard charts in genres as diffuse as folk, rock, country, and dance and pop. This mode often appears in conjunction with another scale. It is closely allied to the blues scale, and it easily morphs into the more familiar and more tonally stable Ionian mode (Ex. 4.41).

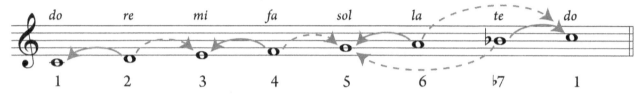

Ex. 4.41 Mixolydian mode, primary and secondary resolutions

Miranda Lambert achieved great success in employing the Mixolydian mode in its pure state with bluegrass-influenced songs such as "White Liar" (Ex. 4.42)

Ex. 4.42 "White Liar" (in F Mixolydian) Natalie Hemby, Miranda Lambert

Hey, ____ white ____ li - ar, ____ the truth comes out a lit - tle at a time. ____

One of the benefits of writing in a mode other than Ionian or Aeolian is that its unique flavor allows the song to have a slightly unusual sound, one that separates it from the many songs that are recorded and released each day. Lordes, e.g., had a tremendous hit, "Royals," in 2013, partially due to her use of the Mixolydian mode in that song.

Tone tendencies in the Dorian mode

Ex. 4.43 Dorian mode, primary and secondary resolutions

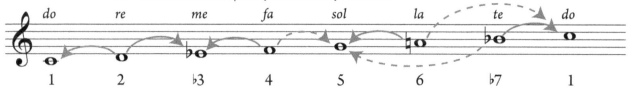

Sting often gravitates to the Dorian mode in his songs, probably because of his earlier immersion in jazz as well as his interest in folk music. "Be Still My Beating Heart" is in the Dorian mode (Ex. 4.44). A tritone exists between the stable third, ♭3, and the unstable sixth degree in this mode, causing this melody to sound so unique. The resolution of *la* is to the fifth of the key, *sol*.

Ex. 4.44 "Be Still My Beating Heart" (in A Dorian) Sting

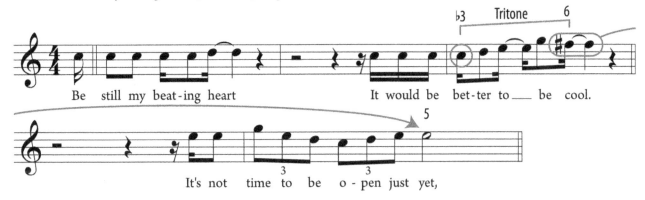

Tone tendencies in the melodic minor ascending

When the melodic minor scale ascends, it uses the major 6th and the major 7th of its parallel major scale, which endow it with more upward thrust (Ex. 4.45).

Ex. 4.45 Melodic minor ascending, primary and secondary resolutions

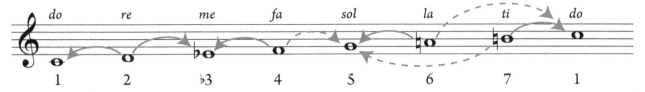

However, when the melodic minor scale descends, it transmutes into the Aeolian mode (natural minor scale), causing a more natural flow in the downward direction to *sol* (Ex. 4.46).

Ex. 4.46 Melodic minor descending (same tone tendencies as the Aeolian mode)

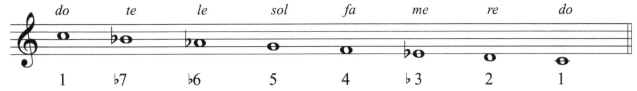

The additional color and variety provided by both the ascending and the descending melodic minor scale is found in the melody of "Beautiful Love" (Ex. 4.47).

Ex. 4.47 "Beautiful Love" Victor Young, Wayne King, Egbert Van Alstine

Beau - ti - ful love, you are a mys - ter - y. Beau - ti - ful love, what have you __ done to

Ascending   Descending   Ascending

me?   I was con - tent - ed 'til you came a - long, thrill - ing my soul with your song

Tone tendencies' relationship to the lyric and to prosody

Your choice of tones, whether stable or unstable, evoke a broad spectrum of possible meanings that help direct lyric choices. If you are sensitive to tone tendencies, your ability to discern your melody's implications to your lyric is tremendously increased.

Broadly defined, the term "prosody" refers to the relationship of words to music. In order to effectively create prosody that highlights the meaning of the lyric, all elements of music are employed: rhythm, pitch, and harmony. Other factors, tempo, choice of tonal environments, and texture broadly define the field in which the song transmits its message. For example, "Happy Birthday" is always sung at a comfortable medium tempo and in a major key. Imagine it being sung at a slow tempo in a minor key! The prosodic power of tone tendencies is apparent in this celebratory tune: think of the two notes in "Happy Birthday" that house the birthday person's name; for example, the name, "Rich-ard" that contains two syllables with stress on the first syllable. Those two notes are meant to highlight the birthday boy's name and for a moment to dangle that name in front of everyone. (Haven't you experienced that moment of slight embarrassment as your name is momentarily exhibited for all to hear?) Both tones, *ti* and *la*, that house the name are unstable and provide the tension that sets up the resolution of the final phrase: "Happy birthday to *ti-la*, happy birthday to you!" Did you notice that there is no immediate resolution to either *ti* or *la*? That is where that sense of dangling or being exposed comes from. And finally, "You" is sung on *do*, leaving everyone with a smile.

As we've just experienced, the use of an unstable tone in the melody not only causes melodic progression, but also may have profound prosodic consequences to the lyric. This is exemplified by Richard Rodgers's sublime setting of Oscar Hammerstein's lyric—a lyric that by itself may be perceived as bland or too sweet—but with the addition of Rodgers music is perfect (Ex. 4.48).

> Oh, what a beautiful morning
> Oh, what a beautiful day
> I got a beautiful feeling
> Everything's going my way.

Ex. 4.48 "Oh, What A Beautiful Morning" music by Richard Rodgers, lyrics by Oscar Hammerstein

Oh, what a beau-ti-ful morn - in', Oh, what a beau-ti-ful day._____

I got a beau-ti-ful feel - in' Ev-'ry-thing's go-in' my way._____

In measure 1, Rodgers places *ti*, scale degree 7, in the melody. This causes the unexpected ♭7 in measure 3 to have an even greater significance on the syllable "morn" of the word "morning," producing a musical gesture that lifts our heads to the glorious sun. After absorbing the sound of the ♭7, the return of the leading tone, 7, in measure 11 on the first syllable of "feel-in'" generates an emotion that can't be duplicated by words or music alone.

"Probably Wouldn't Be This Way," a big country hit for Lee Ann Rimes in 2005, is an unusually introspective song to have achieved such success, a success partially generated by its stunning prosody. The song is reflective of a young girl's inner turmoil. The restless melody in both the verse and prechorus refuses to progress as it winds around itself, providing a perfect musical depiction of a neurotic state of mind (Ex. 4.49).

Ex. 4.49 "Probably Wouldn't Be This Way" John Kennedy, Tammi Kidd

Got a date___ a week from Fri - day with __ the preach - er's son. ___ Ev'-ry-bod-

- y says ___ he's cra - zy I'll have to_____ see I fin

The song is in the key of D, and the phrases in the verse section all end on the unstable C♯, the leading tone, causing the melody to highlight the lyric's tension and create a palpable sense of instability.

"On My Own," a hit in 1986 for Patti LaBelle and Michael McDonald, has a verse that contains phrases ending on stable tones that mirror the singer's memory of a once stable relationship (Ex. 4.50).

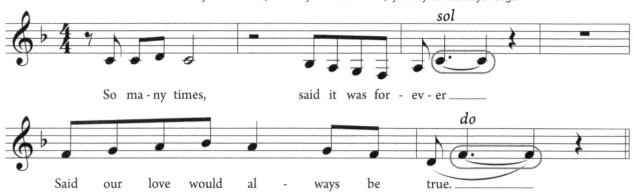

Ex. 4.50 "On My Own" verse, music by Burt Bacharach, lyrics by Carole Bayer Sage

sol

So ma - ny times, said it was for - ev - er_____

do

Said our love would al - ways be true._____

In the chorus, we discover that her lover and she are no longer together, and she, fully realizing what has occurred, states that she is "on my own." Every one of the melodic phrases in the chorus ends on an unstable note, *re*, underlining the fact that the once stable relationship no longer exists (Ex. 4.51).

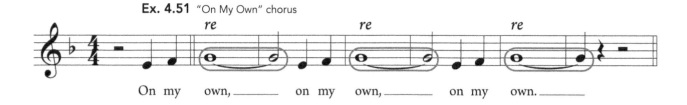

Ex. 4.51 "On My Own" chorus

re   *re*   *re*

On my own, _____ on my own, _____ on my own. _____

Summary

If you are conscious of the natural melodic tendencies inherent in whatever tonal environment your song is in, you will have a very potent tool for creating interesting, meaningful melodies. As you pay close attention to each tone, feeling its consonance or dissonance to the tonal center, you will gain more control of how your melody progresses and mirrors the lyrics' intention. This activity demands a certain kind of quiet in order to allow you to hear deeply, without the distraction of harmony.

This chapter is devoted to melody's relationship to the tonal center—the primary tonal relationship. Other chapters are devoted to melody's relationship to harmony, its important secondary tonal relationship. That relationship, however, cannot be understood at a deep level until melody's relationship to the tonic is absorbed by you. Once you have developed this sensitivity, you will have more control over the melodies you write, the harmonies you choose, and the effect these choices have on your lyric.

Activities

• In order to internalize a deeper sensitivity of melodic tone tendencies, write a melody (a phrase or two will do) that:
  • highlights *fa* and allows *fa* to resolve to *mi* in a delayed resolution.
  • highlights *ti* and allows *ti* to resolve to *do* in a delayed resolution.
  • highlights *la* and allows *la* to resolve to *sol* in a delayed resolution.

- Use *re* in a strategic way to set up *do*. Write a section of music that is eight measures in length that provides interest by cadencing on *re* in its first half and resolving to *do* in its second half. (See Examples 4.07–4.09.)
- Compose an eight- to twelve-measure independent diatonic melody in a major key to the tonal center. You may find it helpful to start with a simple drum groove to aid you in the process of composing your melodic rhythms. Continually remind yourself of the tonal center by playing it as a low bass pedal tone. Be especially aware of the tone tendencies of prominent unstable notes in your melody, resolving some immediately, delaying resolutions in others. The unstable tones that may occur at the end of some of your phrases may sound like they should resolve, but resist the temptation to immediately try to find a harmony for them; save finding the "right" harmonies for your melody once you've completed writing your melody to the tonal center. After completing your melody, ask yourself if you happy with your choices. Did you use any secondary resolutions? If you didn't, try using some. Secondary resolutions can provide a boost of energy or an interesting result.
  - Write lyrics to your melody and make necessary revisions to accommodate how these two elements can optimally function together.
  - Find harmonies that enhance the melody and lyrics.
- Write a melody to the tonal center in the Aeolian mode, making sure to use ♭6.
- Play and sing the Mixolydian mode until you feel you've absorbed its character, and then write a melody to the tonal center using it.
- Play and sing the Dorian mode until you feel you've absorbed its character and then write a melody to the tonal center using it.
- Rewrite your melodies until you are happy with them.

Often, a benefit of doing these and other exercises is that a song will emerge. (The muse is just waiting for a chance to join you.)

5

Setting Lyrics to Music/Setting Music to Lyrics

The art and craft of songwriting is based on the ability to bond music and lyrics perfectly with each other. If you can match musical accent to lyrical accent, determine the right underpinning or groove, and choose a tonal environment and tempo that allow the phrases to fit the ebb and flow of the lyrics' emotion and meaning, you are well on your way to being a fine songwriter. The ultimate goal of this union is to have the lyrics become more than simply words on a page and for the music to be infused with a specificity that it never could have achieved on its own. The combination of the right word with a specific sound and musical gesture transforms the ordinary into the extraordinary.

Writing lyrics to music gives the lyricist the unique pleasure to define, quite specifically, what the music is "saying." I find the greatest joy in songwriting to be this very activity. I am always delighted, after working for however long it takes, to hear my music become a song. The music that was once an abstraction now has a literal component that actually defines what that music means to me. Conversely, writing music to a given lyric allows you to take the lyric's accents and define exactly where they are placed in time, to make the phrases breathe in a defined way. It allows you to choose melodic pitches—consonant or dissonant, high or low—that focus the lyric's meaning, and to find harmonies that refine the feelings that you aim to induce in yourself and your listeners. The mixing of melody, harmony, lyric, and rhythmic underpinning is alchemy—chemistry that goes well beyond science—and is the art of songwriting.

Rhythm and meter—the basics

The rhythms that you choose to propel your lyric are dependent on the basic pulse or meter that you set. Metric groupings and rhythmic groupings use the same basic accents or stress patterns. Any group of 2 is accented: **1**, 2. If the meter is 2/4, the first beat receives the most stress (Ex. 5.01).

Stress symbols that are used in poetry serve us as well:

- $/$ designates primary stress
- $//$ designates secondary stress
- $-$ designates an unstressed beat or syllable.

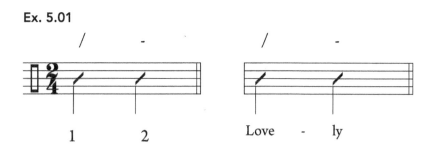

Ex. 5.01

A two-syllable word like "love-ly" has an accent on the first syllable and matches the strong/weak stress pattern.

If there is a grouping of two of any note value, two half notes, two quarter notes, two eighth notes, two sixteenth notes or two thirty-second notes, the first note is stressed, the second is not. Any group of 4 is accented in the following manner: **1**, 2, **3**, 4. In 4/4 time, beat **1** receives slightly more stress than beat 3, while beat 2 and 4 are unstressed.

In example 5.02, the lyric "Give me something" shows more emphasis being placed on the word "give" than on the syllable "some" of the word "something" because of its placement within the measure (Ex. 5.02).

Ex. 5.02 Metric stress in 4/4 time

If eighth notes are employed, they also receive the same stress pattern: strong, weak, medium strong, weak. Since the eighth notes in Example 5.03 are placed in the context of 4/4 meter, they are also subjected to the stress pattern that the meter imposes on them. Therefore, beat 3 still receives slightly less stress than beat one. (Since only three symbols are available to designate stress patterns, there is no easy way to symbolically show the subtle difference in the degrees of stress that occur.)

Ex. 5.03 Combined rhythmic and metric stress

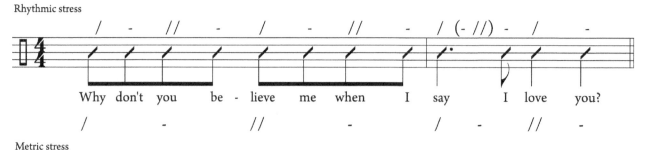

Rhythmic stress

Metric stress

Any group of three is accented in the following manner: **1**, 2, 3; beat **1** is stressed, while beats 2 and 3 are not. Any group of three receives the same stress pattern (/ - -).

This holds true whether it is a group of three eighth notes that occurs in any compound meter such as 6/8, 9/8, or 12/8 time or a group of three that appear as triplets in, e.g., 2/4 or 4/4 (Ex. 5.04).

Ex. 5.04

The rhythms in Example 5.05 are notated in different meters but sound the same.

Ex. 5.05

In R&B ballads,12/8 time is often used; its basic meter is felt both in the four dotted quarter notes and in the three eighth notes within the each of the four dotted quarter notes. 12/8 meter, frequently found in the music of Black churches, is used in the great R&B ballad, "If You Don't Know Me By Now," a song that expresses a heart-felt plea for understanding and trust in a relationship (Ex. 5.06).

Ex. 5.06 "If You Don't Know Me By Now" Kenny Gamble, Leon Huff

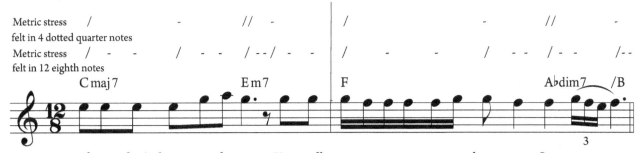

A more complete explanation of stress patterns is to be found in chapter 3 of my book *Melody in Songwriting*.

Syncopation

The use of *syncopation*, the accenting of a beat or part of a beat that normally is not accented, is one of the main characteristics of the American popular song, inclusive of all styles: ragtime, jazz, country, rock, R&B, and hip-hop.

Just to assure that you know what I mean by "syncopation," I'll set the phrase "I'd like to show you how to syncopate" in a completely unsyncopated setting and follow that with a setting that is full of syncopations. Syncopations are marked with an "x" above them (Exs. 5.07–5.08).

Ex. 5.07

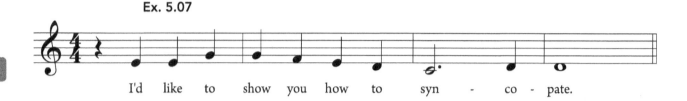

Ex. 5.08

Syncopated rhythms highlight the beat they anticipate, providing that beat with an accent. Syncopations in Example 5.08 highlight the words "like" (anticipation of beat 3 in measure 1), "show" (an anticipation of beat 1, measure 2), "how" (anticipation of beat 3, measure 2), and the syllable "pate" of the word "syncopate" (anticipation of beat 1, measure 4). Syncopation occurs in measure 3, where the "syn" of "syncopate" falls on the normally unaccented second beat and is held over to the fourth beat, making it the most noticeably accented syllable in the phrase.

The first eight measures of Robbie Robertson's great "Up On Cripple Creek," a song that was a big hit for his group, The Band, is all about motion. Syncopation helps in creating that motion (Ex. 5.09).

Ex. 5.09 *"Up On Cripple Creek"* Robbie Robertson

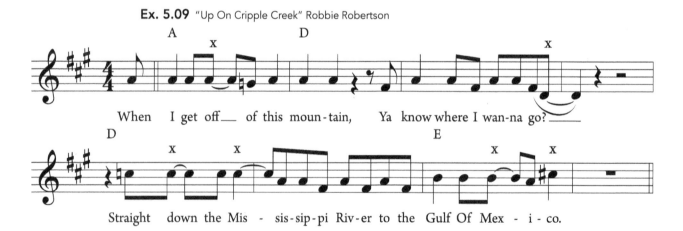

The recording of this classic song is highlighted by an infectious groove and melodic rhythms that are full of syncopations (marked with an x) on the syllables: "off," "go," "straight," "down," "Miss," "Mex," and "co," that give the lyrics their nonstop forward motion.

Sara Bareilles uses syncopation to great advantage in her hit, "Love Song." Notice how it enlivens her song and highlights important words in her lyric (Ex. 5.10).

Ex. 5.10 "Love Song" Sara Bareilles

Beginning with music

Music that sounds good, feels good, and is rhythmically secure provides a structure that invites a lyric. This is the reason why many professional songwriters begin with music. It is often easier to write a song with an instrument in hand, especially a guitar, an instrument that asks that you play rhythms on it over which you can sing your melody. Beat boxes or computer programs like GarageBand are also very useful tools. The best means to achieve creative freedom is to be able hear music internally through your aural imagination and by involving your body in creating a groove. We all have an internal clock that we can adjust to any tempo, and this internal motor aided by your imagination can generate rhythms that groove and propel a melody without any external help.

Once you've composed music for your song, study your music in order to fully realize which notes are the most important ones in each phrase. Listen to which phrases have a great deal of tension or, conversely, are very relaxed. Listening intently for how rhythm and rhyme work in your song will be one of your first concerns, because matched rhythms and matched phrases induce rhymes to occur.

Process

Process, the actual act of composing a song, is intense, intimate, and seldom shared except, possibly, in collaboration. However, sharing may provide a great learning opportunity, so I would like to share the process I used in creating "Love Provides," a song in which the music was written first. My task was to find a lyric that lived up to my music. Here are the first sixteen measures (Ex. 5.11) (⏵ AUDIO 5.11).

Ex. 5.11 "Love Provides" measures 1–16, Jack Perricone

Music helps determine where rhyme is called for and can lead to a choice of a rhyme scheme that provides a perfect concordance between music and lyric. My process is to listen to the rhythms of each phrase and determine where matched phrases exist. The first musical phrase, ending on the second beat, does not have a partner anywhere within this section (hence, the label "x"), so I don't consider rhyming it with anything. However, every other phrase does have a matching phrase and, therefore, is labeled either "a" or "b."

Finding where rhyme can take place is an important analytical tool. Discovering what the actual content of the lyric is involves digging deeper. Questions that I ask myself include: "What is this music making me feel?" "Is the music making a statement or is it more ruminative or conversational?" "Is the music asking for a narrative, or would it work better in capturing a state of mind?"

The music for the song that was to become "Love Provides" moves from a minor tonality to a major tonality within its sixteen measures, a transformation that certainly must be reflected in the content of the lyric. The music feels vulnerable. Even as it cadences in major, there is a sense of quiet pursuance about it. It seems to be exposing a state of mind.

Finding the exact words that have both meaning and accentuation that match the music is usually a difficult undertaking. After many attempts to find a lyric phrase that matched not only the rhythms but also the feeling of the first melodic phrase, I finally came upon "Troubles can seem to last forever." The first line of any song is very important; it must involve the listener and set the tone for the entire piece. "Troubles can seem to last forever" does what a first line should do. It resonates with the music's minor tonality and with its rhythms. And its content is intriguing enough to involve the listener (Ex. 5.12).

Ex. 5.12 "Love Provides" setting of the first line

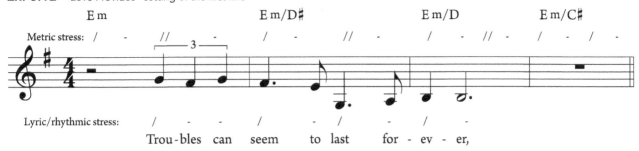

Basic to finding a lyric that works with a given melody is the ability to grasp the syllabic stress in words and the normal accentuation of the spoken language. The first word of my lyric is "troubles," a two-syllable word that is accented heavy, light (/ -). All the other words in the first phrase are one-syllable words except for "forever," a three-syllable word accented: light, heavy, light (- / -).

/　-　-　/　-　/　-　/ -
Trou-bles can seem to last for-ev-er

These words perfectly match the accentuation and flow of the music I composed.

The word "troubles" placed on the third beat (a stressed beat, but not as stressed as the first beat), directs the listener's attention toward "seem," placed on the first beat of the second measure. I put both words in naturally accented positions, thus assuring that both words are given their proper weight.

Notice how the three-syllable word "forever" (- / -) is set rhythmically, with the unaccented "for" placed as an eighth-note pickup to "ev," placed on the stressed downbeat, and the unaccented second beat, "er," placed on the unaccented second beat.

This same process continues throughout the writing of every line until a lyric emerges that possesses both content and poetry, so that the two streams of information, music and words, are heard as emanating from the same source. The lyrics progress from a dark area of the psyche to a lighter one, reflecting the gradual movement of the music from minor to major. Here is the entire A section of the song, with each matched phrase connecting with a rhyme, producing a very satisfying result (Ex. 5.13; ⓟ AUDIO 5.13A).

Ex. 5.13 "Love Provides" first verse

Because this music is balanced but not symmetric, I can repeat the entire structure. This renders an A section that repeats but, of course, with different lyrics. The final song form of "Love Provides" is AABA. This entire song can be heard at www.oup.com/us/greatsongwritingtechniques (▶ AUDIO 5.13B).

If you begin with writing music first, you must study your own music and notice where matched phrases exist, where phrases peak, and where the cadences could possibly house a title or refrain line. Be careful in assuming that because you've written the music, you know your music well enough for a lyric to simply emerge from it. Too often I've made the mistake of loving my music so much that I have accepted words that more or less fit with the music, not because the words and music complemented each other. The result was a lessening in the effect of both the music and the lyric.

The sounds of words

If you haven't got a clue as to what the lyric should be, try singing what is called a "dummy lyric" (the term used for a temporary lyric) to your music. Try singing different vowel sounds to your melody. Remember that *lyrics are sounds as well as a means to communicate information*. Does an "oo" sound work better than an "ee" sound? Is your music full of rhythmic hits that demand consonants? Do you need a guttural "g" or a smoother consonant like an "l" or something in between, possibly an "m" or the slightly harder "n"? Even if your "dummy" lyric makes no sense, it will point your lyric in the right sonic direction.

Paul McCartney's initial title for "Yesterday" was "Scrambled Eggs." We may laugh at that, but in the final lyric he retained the long ā found in "eggs" that helped give him the title we now know. That title probably showed the way for the direction of the entire song. Likewise, Paul Simon once told a group of students at Berklee College of Music that his initial title line for what is now known as "Kodachrome" was "Coming Home." By hanging on to the sound of "om" and conceptually thinking of something more interesting than "coming home," Simon was able to create a uniquely memorable song.

Try singing the Beatles "Let It Be," but instead of singing "Let it be, let it be, let it be, let it be," sing instead, "Let it go, let it go, let it go, let it go." Notice how the guttural "g" gets in the way of a natural flow of one note to another and produces an unwanted sound. Do you notice how the melody loses its edge with the "o" sound? When I sing, "let it be," I feel that the melody is rising, even though I know it is sometimes descending, whereas, when I sing "let it go," I definitely feel the melody's descent.

Vowels work especially well on long held notes. If your melody starts on a long note or is preceded by a few pickup notes that lead to a long note on a downbeat, you will have to assure that the word that falls on the downbeat is a meaningful word in which a vowel sound will not sound strange if held. Here are a couple of examples of songs that successfully do just that. The sound of "love" in "Breaking Up Is Hard To Do" (Ex. 5.14) and the sound of "rule" in Coldplay's "Viva La Vida" (Ex. 5.15) provide the singers with vowel sounds that they and their listeners can enjoy.

Ex. 5.14 "Breaking Up Is Hard To Do" music by Neil Sedaka, lyrics by Howard Greenfield

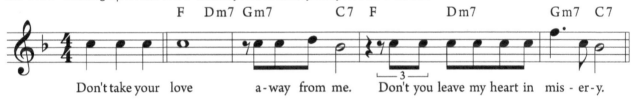

Ex. 5.15 "Viva La Vida" Guy Berryman, Jonny Buckland Will Champion, Chris Martin

Keep this in mind: vowel sounds are excellent for legato singing and for long notes; consonants are excellent for rhythmic attack and for punctuating a phrase, especially at cadences. Songs from the *Great American Songbook* like "You Go To My Head" or "Somewhere Over The Rainbow" are meant to be sung legato and, therefore, emphasize vowel sounds. Songs like "Satisfaction" ("I can't get no sat-is-faction") and "Get Back" emphasize consonants because consonants have the sharp edges needed for the rhythms of rock. I'm reminded of the importance of consonants each time I hear an Otis Redding recording where he uses "got-ta, got-ta, got-ta" to reinforce the rhythms of the song.

The sounds of exclamations and nonsense syllables are very much part of today's songwriting vocabulary, as are words that are repeated simply because they sound wonderful. These are gestures that definitely should be incorporated into your writing lexicon (Ex. 5.16).

Ex. 5.16 "Firework" Katie Perry, Mikkel Eriksen, Tor Hermansen, Sandy Wilhelm, Ester Dean

Make 'em go "Ah, ah,— ah" You're gon-na leave 'em all in awe, awe,— awe _____

Exclamations and nonsense syllables not only sound good but can also indicate an attitude that informs the listener. Paul Simon's "Hey, hey, hey" causes us to realize the irony in his lyrics (Ex. 5.17).

Ex. 5.17 "Mrs. Robinson" Paul Simon

Hea-ven holds a place ___ for those who pray _____ Hey, hey, hey,

Hey, hey, hey. _____

When we feel something deeply or react to an incident that delights us, we make sounds, not sentences that contain information. A "whoa!" to indicate surprise or an "ah!" to indicate joy are usually more effective than any number of descriptive words in a well-formed sentence.

Assonance and alliteration

There was a time when perfect rhyme was the only type of rhyme considered to be acceptable. This was a rule that Broadway writers strictly adhered to and, to a large extent, still do. Perfect rhyme certainly presents intellectual challenges to writers, and often produces clever lyrics that have an appeal to Broadway audiences. But something more visceral than cleverness is usually sought after in a pop song. Rock and roll, Bob Dylan, and more recently, rap, have annihilated the notion that in the realm of popular song perfect rhyme is a necessity or always a better choice than imperfect rhyme and/or the use of assonance or alliteration to make make sonic connections.

Perfect rhyme, however, is one of a number of choices to be considered and is usually the best choice when complete closure is needed. It is often used in end-rhyming positions, because it acts the way a full cadence does in music and is great for highlighting a title or an important lyric.

When you want to have some sonic connection between words, but do not want to call undue attention to them, you have many choices. Imperfect rhyme, assonance, alliteration, and consonance are used extensively in today's lyrics. The bonuses you receive in choosing to look beyond perfect rhymes are (1) the tremendous amount of words you have available, hence, you increase your ability to express yourself more completely (2) use of these substitutes for perfect rhyme act in your lyrics as substitute chords do in a deceptive cadence in music; they stop the motion, but not completely.

You will find assonance, alliteration and perfect rhyme in the last two lines of the chorus lyric of "Wind Beneath My Wings" by Jeff Silbar and Larry Henley.

"**I** can **fly high**er than an **e**agle (perfect rhyme: I/fly) (augmented rhyme: fly/higher)

'Cause you are the **w**ind ben**e**ath my **w**ings." (alliteration: wind/wings) (assonance: be/eagle/ beneath).

The sound of the words within this chorus, the internal rhymes and sonic connections resonate so beautifully with each other that end rhyme, which does not appear in the entire chorus, is not missed at all.

Assonance, alliteration, and imperfect rhyme are used in the opening lines of Taylor Swift's "Red" (Ex. 5.18)

Loving him is like **d**riving a new Maserati

down a **d**ead end str**ee**t. (alliteration: driving, down, dead)

Faster than the w**in**d, passionate as **sin**, (imperfect rhyme: wind/sin)

ending **s**o **s**udden**ly**. (alliteration: sin/so/suddenly) (assonance: street, suddenly)

Ex. 5.18 "Red" Taylor Swift

As astutely as imperfect rhymes, alliteration, and assonance are used, Taylor Swift's musical setting makes their use even more palpable. Hearing "Faster than the wind," "passionate as sin" nearly takes our breath away because Swift doesn't wait for the next downbeat to begin the second phrase but instead begins it on the third beat. The following melodic phrase, "ending so suddenly," does what the lyric says—it ends so suddenly.

85

Collaboration—writing lyrics to a given piece of music

If you were asked to write lyrics to a given piece of music, would you be able to meet the challenge? The phenomenal composer Michel Legrand gave the following music to the lyricists Alan and Marilyn Bergman (Ex. 5.19).

Ex. 5.19 Music by Michel Legrand

As we listen to and examine this music, we can make some observations:

- The rhythms of the melody seem to be conversational, rather than declarative.
- The melody in the first two phrases begins after the first beat, on the upbeat of 1, and the movement is toward the second measure. The first phrase has a feminine ending; the second phrase has a masculine ending.
- The first two phrases end on unstable pitches (*re* and *la*) and on harmonies that do not fully resolve.
- The third phrase "answers" or balances the first two measure phrases by its four-measure phrase length; it also ends on a stable tone and on the tonic chord.

What is this music saying? What it said to the highly sensitive and talented Bergmans was this (Ex. 5.20):

> How do you keep the music playing?
> How do you make it last?
> How do you keep the song from fading too fast?

Ex. 5.20 "How Do You Keep The Music Playing?" lyrics by Alan and Marilyn Bergman, music by Michel Legrand

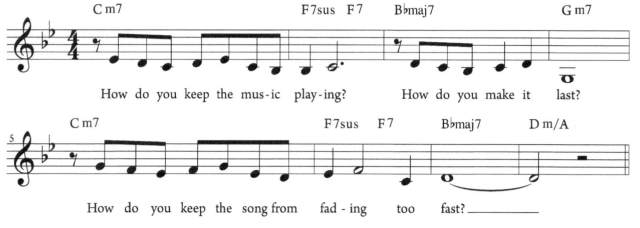

- Since each musical phrase begins with the same rhythms, the Bergmans use an equivalent rhetorical term, *anaphora*, beginning each line with the same word or words; in this case "How do you."
- The first two phrases end on unstable pitches and lead them to make both phrases questions.
- In the third phrase, the Bergmans astoundingly allude to the end of the relationship with "fading too fast." They recognize more stability in this third phrase, caused by the four-measure phrase that balances the first 2 two-measure phrases and cadences on a stable tone as well as the tonic chord. They also answer their own questions by choosing to make that answering phrase itself a question ("How do you keep the song from fading too fast?"). Here, they are also responding to the music, because it is somewhat open structurally. Although the third phrase balances the first two phrases, the entire section is still an asymmetrical three phrases (phrase one: 2 measures; phrase two: 2 measures; phrase three: 4 measures). This may seem too subtle a consideration, but I believe that these very subtleties are what cause a song to be elevated from merely good to great.
- Rhyme and assonance are used effectively. Rhyme, *last/fast*, is used to link diverse phrases together (the first two phrases to the third phrase). Assonance ("plāying," "māke it" and "fāding") is used on a similar melodic figure.

The concept of the song deals with the problem of keeping a romantic relationship alive and well over many years. With music this beautiful, it is not surprising that the Bergman's chose to use the word "music" in the title and that music itself is the metaphor for love.

Beginning with lyrics, process

The first questions to consider when you are given lyrics, or when you've written them yourself, are 1) What feeling or feelings do the lyrics generate? . . . and 2) How may you enhance that feeling with music? Say the lyrics rhythmically; say them over and over again to a beat until you can feel rhythmically where they want to live. Feel how one phrase balances another, or if it doesn't, search for ways to make it feel better to your body. Yes, your body—more than your mind—helps determine the metric and rhythmic setting of your lyric.

There are many ways of beginning a lyric: writing from a title, writing from a phrase, writing from a concept, writing from a rhythm that you have imagined. If you have a lyric idea that you don't initially hear in musical time, jot down your thoughts in prose. Later on you can deal with making the rhythms and rhymes work in the context of a song lyric. For example:

Song idea: *Immediate attraction/love at first sight*

Quick prose improvisation:

Wow! What just hit me? It was like a lightning strike, a thunderbolt, or an earthquake. I love what I just felt and I want to feel more. Where did she come from? Where did she go? I've just got to find her.

Obviously, this is not a lyric, just some related thoughts I jotted down. It is not a lyric because it doesn't have the rhythmic and sonic connections that are needed to work with music. It does, however, contain the ideas that can generate a lyric. It may even contain a line or a phrase or two that can be used in a final lyric.

I now try to hear some of the lines I've jotted down in time, i.e., to a steady beat that contains a groove.

I like the first line I wrote, "Wow, what just hit me?"; it gets your attention and asks you to listen. It also gives me a feel for the tempo and even the groove of the song—a medium up-tempo rock groove. The second line introduces the object of my attention and attraction: the girl. I also used "Where'd she come from? Where'd she go?," dropping the grammatically formal "did."

> Wow, what just hit me?
> I love how she made me feel
> Like a thunderbolt
> A thousand volts
> It's hard to believe she's real
> Where did she come from?
> Where'd she go?
> I gotta find her
> That's one thing I know.
> I'd go around the world to find that girl.

After writing the verse, a title emerges: "Around The World." Notice how I chose only one ("thunderbolt") out of the three descriptive terms that I had initially come up with. I eliminated a few lines and added some because I needed to have rhythms that felt comfortable to my body. I tried to find rhythms that chimed and that provided opportunities to rhyme.

The music and lyrics for this song did not show up in their pristine form. Only through trial and error, through singing various melodies to some rhythms I had jotted down or imagined and playing various chords and chord progressions on a keyboard (this activity is important, because placement of chords helps generate the meter and groove) did I finally come up with a section of music that I could accept. This process is one that most writers experience. Once in a while, if you are lucky, you will hear music and words come together naturally for an entire song or entire section of a song—you will be in the zone. When that happens, just be grateful for it. Otherwise, it's trial and error until you find what you've been seeking.

After experimenting with a traditional major tonal environment that produced a false start, I came to realize that a blues/rock sound was the best style for my lyric (Ex. 5.21; ⊙ AUDIO 5.21).

Ex. 5.21 *"Around the World"* Jack Perricone

The rhythmic setting is meant to reflect and strengthen the emotion that is being experienced. The first line "Wow, what just hit me" demands some time between "Wow" and the rest of that exclamation, and space is also demanded after it. In the next phrase "I love how she made me feel," the two most important words, "love" and "feel" are placed on first beats. Syncopation is used on "thunderbolt" and "thousand volts" to accentuate the heightened reaction the singer experienced in meeting this girl. "Hard," "believe" and "real" are emphasized in the next phrase. Two one-measure phrases "Where'd she come from?" "Where'd she go?" are answered by a two-measure phrase, "I gotta find her, that's one thing I know," allowing matching phrases on the third beats of measures 9 and 11 on the words, "go and "know." The last phrase, "I'd go a-round the world to find that girl," is stretched out producing a four-measure phrase that balances the 1+1+2 measure phrases that preceded it. This also highlights the title.

The pitches chosen for this lyric are mainly from the bluesy, minor pentatonic scale. The harmonies are blues derived, a subject that is explicated in chapter 8.

Learning from the masters

In the following detailed study of two or three lines from two great songs, I hope to show the intimate connections between the words and the music that help elevate these songs into the pinnacle of songwriting (Exs. 5.22–5.23).

"Bridge Over Troubled Water"   by Paul Simon

Like a bridge over troubled water,
I will lay me down.

Ex. 5.22 *"Bridge Over Troubled Water" Paul Simon*

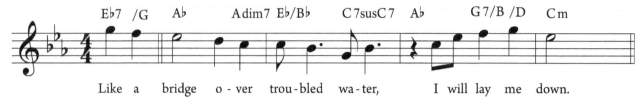

Paul Simon begins his setting of this memorable refrain with two pickup quarter notes on "Like a," leading to the target word, "bridge" on the downbeat of beat one. "Over," a word with syllables that are stressed *heavy-light*, falls perfectly on beat 3 and 4. The important word, "troubled" occurs on beat one. Simon does not set the second syllable of "trou-bled" on the second beat, but sets it the way it is said, without hesitation or undue emphasis, placing the second syllable on the second eighth note of the first beat, an unaccented position. He sets "wa-ter" in a similar way, with the first syllable of the word receiving stress due its position on the strong third beat but with the second syllable set one eighth note after beat 3. The next phrase begins after the downbeat. This allows the singer and listener a chance to breathe—an important consideration when setting a lyric—and this also allows the word "I" to not be unduly accented. The word, "lay" is placed on beat 3, allowing the targeted word "down" to occur on the downbeat of beat 1 of the fourth measure. Paul Simon knew the importance of this statement when he wrote these memorable words, and he chose rhythms in his music that match the dignity that is found in his lyrics. This kind of consideration—adherence to what a lyric is demanding, not only in the words themselves, but in the way those words are stated—communicates at a deep level.

The pitches chosen for the setting of the title to this iconic song begin with notes in a high register that move in a downward scale and then move upward, giving a feeling of positivity. The melody is full of stable tones that reinforce the positive message. Nonetheless, the melody has a lot forward momentum propelled by two pickup notes harmonized with a dynamic secondary dominant, E♭7, that begins the phrase and with a C7, another secondary dominant appearing in the middle of the phrase, creating additional momentum. The melody that ends on *do* reinforces the stability of the statement being made. However, complete closure is avoided, since *do* is supported by VIm, producing a *deceptive cadence* (see chapter 7, Ex. 7.13), an indication that there is more to follow.

"Hey Jude"   John Lennon and Paul McCartney

Hey Jude, don't make it bad
Take a sad song
And make it better

Ex. 5.23 *"Hey Jude"* John Lennon, Paul McCartney

Lennon and McCartney's great song "Hey Jude" begins with its memorable salutation on a quarter-note pickup that helps highlight "Jude," a word that appears on the downbeat and is held for two beats. The phrase, "don't make it bad" has a stress pattern, - //- /, with "make" falling on the unstressed fourth beat and the less stressed "it" leading to the targeted word, "bad," that falls on a strong first beat in measure 2. The word on beat 1 in the next measure is "sad," forming an inner rhyme with "bad." The important word, "song," occurs on beat 2 and is held into beat 3 (the syncopation on beat 2, along with the leap of the interval of a fifth, highlights "song"). Adjectives, like the word "sad," rather than the nouns they are embellishing, are often placed on strong beats. This is due to the specificity that adjectives have (the phrase loses its meaning without the word "sad"). The last word of this first stanza, "better," occurs on beat 1 of measure 4, with its second syllable given two slurred sixteenth notes plus a half note, a musical softening that gives added meaning to the phrase, like a hand placed on the shoulder of a son as fatherly advice is given.

You may be wondering, after my dwelling on the importance of rhythm in lyric setting, if I haven't paid enough attention to pitch as an important way of calling attention to a lyric. Yes, of course, pitch is important. Look at the pitch on the word "song"; both the choice of *do* and the leap to it, highlight it. Notice how *re*, on the downbeat of measure 2 and *fa*, on the downbeat of measure 3, two unstable tones that surround *mi*, the final note of the phrase in measure 4, cause tension to build in the center of the phrase on the words "bad" and sad" that is so satisfyingly resolved at the end on the word "better." That said, I firmly believe that rhythmic placement is the priority in setting a lyric.

This is what we can we learn from this microscopic examination of these settings from two great songs:

- The music coincides with the natural accentuation of the words.
- The natural shape of the language is preserved.
- Important words fall on strong beats.
- Words that are simply functional, such as articles, prepositions, or conjunctions, are assigned to rhythmically weak or unstressed positions.
- Longer note values are designated for words that are most meaningful.
- The lyric setting allows the singer to "breathe"; this also allows time for listeners to take in what has been sung.
- The lyric setting coincides with the rhetorical gesture. If the lyric is conversational, it is set so that it resembles those rhythms that are found in conversation; if the lyric is

making a declarative statement, then the rhythmic gestures correspond to making an important statement. The chorus of "Bridge Over Troubled Water" is declarative, while the beginning of "Hey Jude" is more conversational.

• The lyrics enhance the music.

Too many songwriters misaccent words or emphasize unimportant words when they attempt to set their lyrics to music. Some argue that missetting or misaccenting is part of a style. This actually may be the case in some songs that are highly stylized. But too often this occurs because the writer is too lazy to seek out another word or phrase or is fearful that changing one word might mean a rewrite of a couple of lines. Consider the word "rescue," a two-syllable word that is accented heavy-light (**res**-cue). If it is misaccented as res-**cue**, chances are that it will not be understood or it may pull the listener out of the song while attempting to reconcile the problem. Do not take the easy way out; consider the difficulty involved in hearing words when they are sung.

Attempt to choose words that not only sound good but also have meaning, and never choose a word that has the right meaning but sounds wrong.

Pat Pattison, the amazing lyric-writing teacher at Berklee College of Music, has his students repeat this phrase, "Preserve the natural shape of the language" until it becomes a mantra they carry with them for the rest of their lives. I would like to add to that mantra: "Place the lyric in its most natural musical environment." By that I mean that you should be aware of all the elements of musical setting that enhance the meaning of the lyric: the rhythms, the scales, the harmonies, the tempo, and especially, the groove.

Learning from masters of collaboration

Sir Elton John and Bernie Taupin have enjoyed collaborating with one another for nearly fifty years. Their method of collaborating is initially for Taupin to create an entire lyric and then for Elton John to compose a musical setting for it, often without any further consultation between them. Elton John sets lyrics with an acumen that is rare. I've often read through Taupin's lyrics before listening to Elton John's setting of them and have been amazed upon hearing the beauty, nuances, and delightful surprises that Elton John had found and that I had not imagined occurring. Of all their songs, Elton John's setting of Taupin's lyrics to "Goodbye Yellow Brick Road" is one of his best.

> "Goodbye Yellow Brick Road"   lyrics by Bernie Taupin
>
> You know you can't hold me forever
> I didn't sign up with you
> I'm not a present for your friends to open
> This boy's too young to be singing the blues.

The problem inherent in setting any lyric is finding a way for the lyric to work in musical time. A lyric may look great on a page, but after scanning it and attempting to fit it in to something that feels good to the body, it often has to be edited to make it conform to musical meter and balance. The first two lines of Taupin's lyrics contain three stresses each followed by two lines containing four stresses each.

        /   /   /
    You know you can't hold me for-ev-er
      /   /   /
    I didn't sign up with you
    /   /   /   /
    I'm not a pres-ent for your friends to o-pen
          /   /   /   /
    This boy's too young to be sing-ing the blues.

This lyric structure is balanced with each of its 3-stressed lines and 4-stressed lines matched. The rhyme scheme is x, a, x, a, with the second line, a 3-stressed line, rhyming ("you") with the fourth line, a 4-stressed line ("blues"). Rhyme connects these two rhythmically disparate phrases.

If Elton John adhered to the implied road map that the rhythms of the lyric had outlined, the resulting music would have been balanced as well. The last two lines might have been set in the following way (Ex. 5.24).

Ex. 5.24

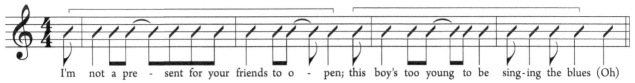

I'm not a pre - sent for your friends to o - pen; this boy's too young to be sing-ing the blues (Oh)

Instead, he created a very original music that captured all of us (Ex. 5.25).

Ex. 5.25 "Goodbye Yellow Brick Road" music by Elton John, lyrics by Bernie Taupin

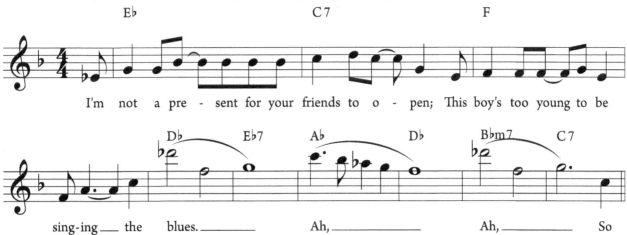

I'm not a pre - sent for your friends to o - pen; This boy's too young to be

sing-ing — the blues. _____ Ah, _____ Ah, _____ So

Once he decided to expand the phrase length, he did so with a child's delight and a genius's hand. No one except Sir Elton John would have set the word "blues" with those ecstatic "ahs" for an added six measures.

Suggested study

One of the best exercises you can do by yourself, where you are both teacher and student, is to find a lyric of a song you have never heard before. This is easy to do, especially now, with so many websites dedicated to lyrics. Try setting a lyric of a song that you've never heard before. Refrain from referring to the original musical setting of it until you've set it first yourself. I suggest any number of fine lyricists' works, e.g., Bernie Taupin, Jackson Browne, etc.—the choices are vast. Once you have written your own music to their lyrics, listen to the music actually written for those lyrics by the original composers. How does your lyric setting compare? Did you capture the emotion that you were hoping to capture? Are your groove, rhythmic, and tonal choices as good or as authentic sounding as theirs? Did you highlight words that had meaning and avoid emphasizing those that did not have meaning such as "the," "and," etc.? Did you look for the important words within each lyrical phrase and marry them to the important notes within your corresponding melodic phrase?

There is so much to be learned from this exercise; after all, you can't find a better collaborator than Bernie Taupin or Jackson Browne—or a better teacher than yourself.

A benefit from this activity is the original music you'll have created. If you like the music, but cannot hear it without the lyric (which is copyrighted and unavailable to you), then find a collaborator and ask that person to write an original lyric to your music. This, in fact, was a method that Oscar Hammerstein employed on a regular basis when he worked with Richard Rodgers; only Hammerstein reversed the process (something you can also try) and used music to help him write his superb lyrics. Hammerstein, whose grandfather was an opera house entrepreneur, was familiar with the great operatic arias and used the melodic phrases of arias as a method to assure that his lyric would work with music. Of course, he never told Richard Rodgers what aria he had used (I'm not sure if he ever told Rodgers he was, in fact, conspiring with the masters) and out of the genius of Rodgers would emerge such masterpieces as "You'll Never Walk Alone, "Some Enchanted Evening," and "Climb Every Mountain"!

Summary

Always keep in mind why you are writing a song, not a poem or an instrumental piece. You are writing a song because you want to enhance the meaning of your music with words and want to enhance the sound of your words with music. Words have a literal meaning, but are also sounds that can enhance not only the meaning of music but also the sound of your music. Although music is abstract, it has implications; the words you choose can make explicit what was once only implicit. Only through your sensitivity to the music you've written and its correspondence to words do these two disciplines meld into one that enhances both.

Activities

I. Begin a song with lyrics. Either create your own lyrics, or set the following ones that I've written.

1)   You never know,
You never know,
You never know just how it goes.
But it goes, it goes, it goes.

2)   Why, oh why did you ever leave me?
Why, oh why did you go away?

3)   Dance! Dance!
Let me see your body shake.
Move! Move!
Let me see what your body can say.

Procedure

I. Begin by setting lyrics to melodic rhythms

A. Read the lyrics through a number of times; be sure that you are reading them with feeling and are noticing what words are most important; those are the words that should fall on strong beats.

B. Compose melodic rhythms first; be sure that you compose to a groove (use a drum loop or a metronome, or tap your foot, clap your hands—whatever gets you involved physically.) Be sure to include some syncopation in your setting of the lyric.

C. Once you have created your melodic rhythms, add pitch to them.

D. Finally, add chords that enhance the music and the meaning of the lyric.

II. Begin with melodic rhythm

A. Begin a song with melodic rhythm, i.e., melody devoid of pitch. Use the example below as a rubric for this activity.

    a. Create at least two phrases. Use my example as a rubric.

In this example, the two matched phrases demand rhyme. The second phrase is a repeat of the first phrase with one slight alteration; the third beat in measure 3 changes from two eighths to a quarter note, making this is an inexactly matched phrase (Ex. 5.26) (▶ AUDIO 5.26).

Ex. 5.26

    b. Write lyrics to the rhythms you've composed (Ex. 5.27) (▶ AUDIO 5.27).

Ex. 5.27

Be sure your lyrics say something that you can get behind, that jump-starts your emotions. Without that happening, this will simply result in an academic exercise. With your emotions involved, you have a chance of writing a meaningful song.

    c.   Compose melodic pitches that heighten the feeling you want to generate (Ex. 5.28) (▶ AUDIO 5.28).

Ex. 5.28

I al-ways want-ed to lie by your side,   to tell the truth with no - thing to hide.

    d.   Add chords that enhance your melody and lyrics (Ex. 5.29) (▶ AUDIO 5.29).

Ex. 5.29

I al-ways want-ed to lie by your side,   to tell the truth with no - thing to hide.

The two methods I've outlined here have worked in songwriting classes I've taught and provide you with a way to begin to put words and music together.

6

Simple and Interesting

"Simple and interesting" is the magical formula for writing a successful popular song. Our songs are remembered because we provide our listeners with something they enjoy hearing and that they can respond to by participation in one form or another—either by simply listening, singing along, and/or dancing to them. In addition, our songs must have the ability to move people either physically or emotionally and, frequently, both physically and emotionally. This formula supposes that you have a feeling or a message you want to communicate to the masses and offers the most effective way to do that.

Our songs are remembered because we repeat certain patterns and phrases and use rhyme (another form of repetition). Repetition, however, is a two-edged sword and, more than any other element, can cause a song to become monotonous or annoying. The way to avoid monotony is to create interest—but attempts at creating interest may lead to complexities that go beyond what a mass audience can tolerate. The solution lies in how to combine these two attributes—but how is this done?

In order for a song to achieve this ideal, the songwriter must discover hidden complexities: musical and lyrical activities that affect listeners but are not necessarily perceived by them at the conscious level. These hidden techniques and exquisite choices made by talented songwriters cause their songs to be heard time and again without growing tiresome. Many of these techniques are contained within this book.

This chapter contains two examples of songs that are both simple and interesting, written by two great songwriters from two different eras: "Always" by Irving Berlin and "Imagine" by John Lennon.

"Always"

Irving Berlin was a masterful songwriter. He was not a formally trained musician, but was extremely talented both as a lyricist and composer who, during his heyday (which lasted about forty years!) had a pulse on the new nation and spoke to its people. Here is the chorus of one his most famous songs. It is a song of devotion and unconditional love. The chorus lyric is as concise and to the point as any lyric I've ever studied.

He begins the chorus with a rhymed couplet:

I'll be loving you	Always
With a love that's true	Always

He attaches the word "always" to each of his lines, carefully leaving some time after each of them so that we, the listeners, can feel the significance of the word.

Then the flow of the lyric changes, and we get three rhymed lines that lead to the title, which is then repeated.

When the things you've planned
Need a helping hand,

I will understand,
Always
Always

The chorus is at its midpoint and proceeds to repeat all the rhythm patterns that have previously appeared, but not all of its rhyme patterns. Instead of the three rhymes presented the first time around, Berlin chooses instead to use a device called *anaphora*, (Anaphora [a rhetorical device]: Beginning each new phrase with the same words.)

He repeats *Not for just* three times, and with each repetition, adds weight and meaning to the lyric by contrasting *an hour, a day, a year*, to the title, *Always*. This gesture also incorporates one of the most powerful lyric writing techniques: by using a polarity, *an hour* in this case, the polarity of *always*, the focus on the concept is heightened. What could be further from *always* than *an hour*? Yes, you could say *a second*, or *a minute*, but they might seem too extreme, and Berlin only had three musical phrases for his lyrics. Besides, *hour* is a better sounding word to sing on a long note because of its vowels. We feel an emotional crescendo as we move further away from time that can be measured to time that cannot—to the infinite.

The music of this song is rhythmically simple, but ingenious in its phrase order. The melodic rhythm of the first phrase is actually made up of two separate rhythmic *motives* (a *motive* is a musical seed, a short idea that can be developed) that initially are presented together and are then separated (Ex. 6.01).

Ex. 6.01

From these two motives, Berlin composes the entire song (Ex. 6.02).

Ex. 6.02

The order in which these motives are presented is:

a, b   I'll be loving you,   always

a, b   With a love that's true,   always.

a, a, a   When the things you've planned
            need a helping hand,
            I will understand

b, b   Always,   always.

The order by which these two rhythmic ideas are presented is one of the hidden complexities in the song. Each of these letters, a, and b, contains two measures of music, except for the two iterations of "always" at the end of the first half of the song, where each iteration lasts for one measure. This creates a section of sixteen measures, constituting the first half of the chorus. Notice how the change of the order of the phrases changes the flow of the song; also notice that each b-phrase contains the title. Berlin uses this exact rhythmic scheme to create the second half of the chorus.

The ascending contour of the melody also helps guide the listener to the title. The title word, "always," follows the natural contour of the spoken word and descends. Together the two phrases form an *arch contour* (Ex. 6.03).

Ex. 6.03 "Always" opening melodic motives, Irving Berlin

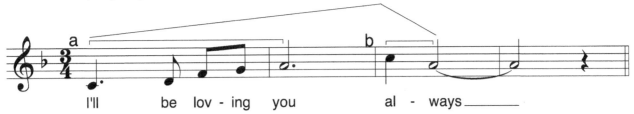

The return of the original motive occurs midway in the song and is immediately followed by the song's climax, one of the most beautiful phrases in song literature (Ex. 6.04).

Ex. 6.04 "Always" transformation of the opening motives

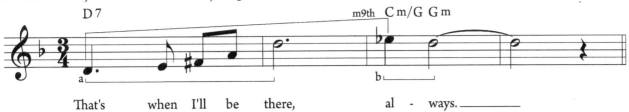

Notice the shape of the melody in the climax of the song. It again follows an *arch contour*, this time with a longer ascent and a shorter descent and highlights one of the sophisticated tonal choices made in the song. The climactic ascent, from the beginning of the phrase to its high note, is made up of the emotionally charged interval of a minor 9th and the chromatic note, E♭, that appears with the secondary dominant, D7 and poignant Cm/G harmony moving to G minor. Another point of interest (not shown) in this masterful song is a modulation to the key of A and a modulation back to the original key of F, created so elegantly that the listener is unaware of it except for the glow it leaves once it is heard. The simple rhythmic scheme that Berlin employs allows him to enrich the tonal areas of his song in order to deepen the effect of his lyric's expression of love and commitment.

To review: *simplicity* is achieved through the entirety of the song by two rhythmically based musical ideas and through the repetition of these ideas, as well as the repetition of the title. *Interest* is achieved through the order by which these two ideas are presented and the tonal choices consisting of melodic pitches and engaging harmonies as well as the modulatory activity within the song. The lyric, that is both simple and deep, encompasses a universal ideal: a declaration of a lifetime commitment of love.

"Imagine"

Masterful too was John Lennon. His song "Imagine" resonates into the 21st century and beyond because it addresses a universal: one of man's greatest hopes, that of a life without the dread of war. He asks us to imagine such a life and he achieves this in as simple and as direct a way as possible.

The entire song consists of two 2-measure phrases, an a-phrase followed by a b-phrase (Ex. 6.05). The a-phrase ends with a feminine ending: /-. The b-phrase ends with a masculine ending: -/.

Ex. 6.05 "Imagine" melodic rhythm, John Lennon

The **a** phrase	The **b** phrase
Imagine there's no heaven;	it's easy if you try

These two rhythmic phrases and the order presented continue throughout the entire song.

The simple form that Lennon uses in this song produces interest. The first verse consists of a balanced 4+4 measure structure—followed by another four measures. This creates an asymmetric structure of twelve measures, and we expect to hear the chorus; instead, the second verse enters and uses the same (4+4+4) structure. At this point, we are more than ready to hear the chorus, which is a simple 4+4 measure structure.

This effectively *simple* form and the use of a repetitious phrase grouping is only part of this music; the *interesting* pitches chosen for those rhythms transform them into a perfectly designed melodic plea (Ex. 6.06).

Ex. 6.06 "Imagine"

Ti, the seventh step, the leading tone in the major scale, is one of the most potent notes in tonal music. It pleads for resolution to the tonic and when the expected resolution does not occur—as in this song—when it moves instead to another unstable tone, in this case the sixth degree, *la*, it produces a feeling of great poignancy. The power of this song stems from this musical gesture being matched to a lyric that asks us to do something: to imagine.

What if the musical gesture did this instead (Ex. 6.07)?

Ex. 6.07

This musical gesture doesn't ask us a question; its melody is tonally closed and it doesn't work with Lennon's lyric. It does, however, provide us with a good example of poor prosody; instead of asking us to imagine, it stops us from imagining!

The harmonies that accompany John Lennon's simple melody add to its power.

As the leading tone arrives in measure 2 and thereafter, F, the subdominant harmony in C major, creates the tritonic relationship between B, the leading tone in the melody, and F, the 4th scale degree in the bass, producing a dissonance that asks for and receives immediate resolution, as the B moves to the A, the third of the F major triad. This simple gesture of a very dissonant note (*ti*) resolving to a less dissonant note (*la*) is very moving. (Remember that the melodic resolution is to the underlying harmony, but the note of resolution, *la*, is an unstable tone to the tonal center.) My analysis and words can only feebly describe this effect, but it can be fully appreciated simply by listening again to this song with this awareness.

Both songs presented in this chapter use the order in which the phrases appear and tone tendencies in powerful ways. In Irving Berlin's "Always" and in John Lennon's "Imagine" we see and hear that what we initially accepted as simple heartfelt expressions, actually contain astute choices and hidden techniques that produce interest.

Summary

The two great songs that I've used to demonstrate this basic principle for writing successful popular songs come from two different eras of songwriting. A "hidden" technique that appears in both songs is the use of repetition of two rhythmic phrases as a means to have the song sound simple and a change of the order of the phrases as a means to produce interest.

The elements that are used to produce interest are subject to stylistic change, but no matter what techniques are being used, the public embraces songs that outwardly appear to be simple but that contain intricate or complex hidden techniques. Whether these techniques occur because the writer is highly sensitive or because s/he has been trained in the craft of songwriting really doesn't matter; these techniques exist and this book attempts to expose and elucidate them.

Addendum

The two songs that I've used as models to exemplify the formula, simple and interesting, were chosen because they contain techniques exposed in the previous chapters 1–5. They are songs from two different eras of songwriting, eras that are far different from today's. You may be wondering if this formula is still valid in today's music. The answer is decidedly yes.

Styles change, societies change, but people remain the same. A major change in style often indicates that a style that has been around a long time has either become tired sounding and doesn't any longer reflect the mood of the society; the style has become too complex or too simple for the intended audience.

A stylistic change that has taken place in late 20th century and in the early 21st century has been the preponderance of songs that are loop-based and are steeped in technology. This combination has produced music that is simpler in its harmonic content but more complex in its other elements: unique synthesized sounds, more complex textures, more emphasis on rhythm, groove, and production. Hidden from the audience and many songwriters are some techniques that involve interesting uses of melodic rhythm, melodic phrase structure, and new approaches to harmony. These techniques are covered in the ensuing chapters in this book.

Since the two songs I chose to represent my "magical formula" were written by songwriters who had not been formally trained, you might be wondering to yourself "why don't I simply do what they did: use my intuition and forget about reading a book on the techniques of songwriting?" My answer to that pointed question is simply this: If you have the innate talent that John Lennon and Irving Berlin possessed, you probably don't need this book . . . although you might find it helpful. Most of us lesser mortals can use all the help we can get.

The next two chapters provide the basic vocabularies needed in order for you to fully grasp additional techniques that will be exposed throughout this text.

PART II

Tonal Environments

7

Traditional Major/Minor Environment

This and the next chapter will provide you with information that will help you grasp and control songwriting techniques that appear in the rest of the book. After studying these two chapters, you will understand how to establish a key and how the treatment of tonality affects style.

Precompositional decisions

Songwriters often make choices prior to actually writing a song. These *precompositional* decisions may include, e.g., whether to write a bluesy kind of song or to write an up-tempo dance tune. This conceptual way of dealing with your song has important consequences.

Tonal considerations are a part of the precompositional decisions you make as you attempt to get an overview of the type of song you want to write and what feelings you want to express. Various scales: major, minor, modal, blues, etc., and their derivative chords form what I term *tonal environments*. Each tonal environment has its own unique tonal hierarchies and assets. Many songs exist in just one tonal environment, but some mix environments to good effect. It is up to you to decide which tonal environment best suits the concept and type of song you are envisioning. We begin with the most familiar and still one of the most widely used of the tonal environments: traditional major/minor.

Traditional major—controlling your tonal materials

In order to control your tonal materials, the most basic thing you must be able to do is establish a tonal center. Once you are able to this, you can decide to either state the tonal center or simply imply it.

A tonal center can be established through purely melodic means, as demonstrated in Example 7.01. Unstable tones (marked with an asterisk *) moving to resolutions on stable tones produce a strong sense of key (▶ AUDIO 7.01).

Ex. 7.01 Establishing a tonal center through melodic means

Notice how *fa* beckons *mi*, how *la* beckons *sol*, and especially how *re* and *ti* beckon *do*. Also notice the length and metric placement of the tonic note.

Notes of a scale can be exposed linearly (horizontally) or with chords (vertically).

Diatonic chords are a result of piling up or verticalizing the notes of a given scale. If all the notes used in constructing a chord are stable (e.g., the I chord), then a stable chord results. If all the notes are unstable (e.g., the VIIdim chord), then an unstable chord results. If there are mixtures of stable and unstable tones in a chord (e.g., the IIIm chord), then a mixed result occurs, and like mixing chemicals, the result can be partially stable or partially unstable. Chords can be constructed using any interval, but because of the power of the harmonic series (the first overtones form a major triad), most chords are constructed in thirds (Ex. 7.02).

Ex. 7.02 Triads derived from the major scale

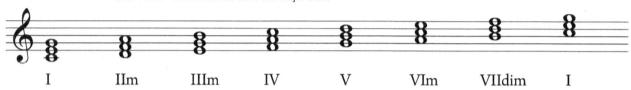

| I | IIm | IIIm | IV | V | VIm | VIIdim | I |

Triads that are derived from the scale form a hierarchal structure that can be measured from stability to instability (Ex. 7.03).

Ex. 7.03 Most stable to least stable triad

Stable--Unstable

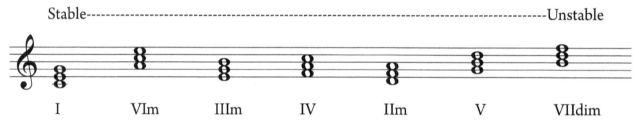

| I | VIm | IIIm | IV | IIm | V | VIIdim |

Especially important in establishing a tonal center is the order in which the chords appear and the metric placement of the chords. The I, IV, V, I progression, the movement of tonic (T) to subdominant (SD) to dominant (D) to tonic (T), exposes all the tones of the scale and serves as the template for the order in which chords often progress in this tonal environment. The chords progress from the most stable area (T) to a less stable area (SD) to the least stable area (D) to return to the most stable area (T). The tritone is important in establishing the tonal center in traditional major and minor because in those scales it consists of unstable tones. (This is not the case in most other modes.) When a dominant chord follows a subdominant chord, the tritone is exposed, and when it resolves to the stable tones found in the tonic chord, it establishes a key like no other device (Ex. 7.04).

Ex. 7.04 Establishing a tonal center with a chord progression

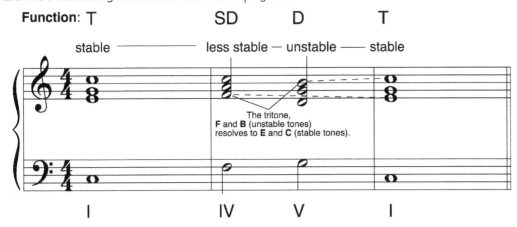

Traditional major/minor scales

You can easily establish a key using the major, melodic minor, harmonic minor, and natural minor scales in the manner demonstrated above. Each of these scales has unstable tones coinciding with the location of the tritone.

The tritone in the major scale is between *fa* and *ti*, the two most unstable tones in the scale (Ex. 7.05).

Ex. 7.05 Major scale (Ionian mode)

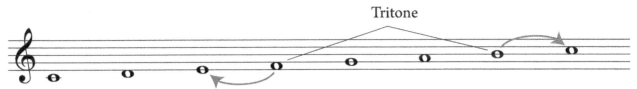

The tritone in the natural minor scale is between *re* and *le* (♭6), both unstable tones in the natural minor scale (Ex. 7.06).

Ex. 7.06 Natural minor (Aeolian mode)

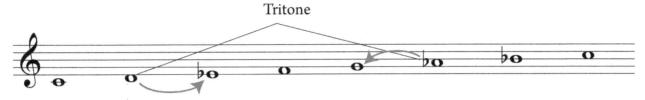

The tritone is between *fa* and *ti*, both unstable tones in the ascending melodic minor scale. An additional tritone exists in this scale, between *me*, ♭3, a stable tone that has no tendency to move, and *la*, an unstable tone that tends to resolve to *sol* (Ex. 7.07).

Ex. 7.07 Melodic minor ascending

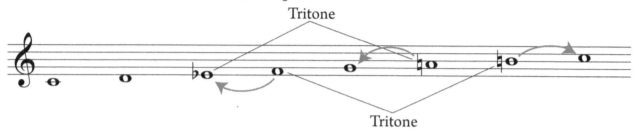

Two sets of tritones, all unstable tones, are found in the harmonic minor scale, *fa* and *ti* and *re* and *le*. These two tritones set up a tonal trap that makes this scale live up to its name—harmony being the main reason for this scale's existence (Ex. 7.08).

Ex. 7.08 Harmonic minor

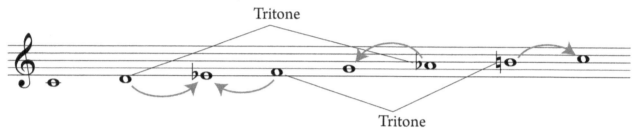

Functional harmony and chord progression in traditional major and minor

The need to establish a key and to easily modulate from one key to another was of tremendous stylistic importance to the development of music circa 1600–1900, during which time an elaborate tonal system called *functional harmony* was created and extensively employed. Functional harmony also drove the music of the *Great American Songbook* and is still a driving force in some of today's music.

Functional harmony is the grouping of like-sounding chords, chords that can function as substitutes for one another so that harmonic decision-making is made easier and more manageable. This technique, taught in traditional harmony courses, is very helpful to songwriters and will facilitate your ability to make harmonic choices in this tonal environment.

Triads that have two notes in common with the main function, either tonic, subdominant, or dominant, are placed in each of those families and are available as possible substitutes for one another (see Exs. 7.09–7.11, notes in common are in black). In a major key, *primary triads* are I, IV, and V; the other diatonic chords: IIm, IIIm, VIm, and VIIdim, are referred to as *secondary triads*. The function of each secondary triad is based on the function of its primary triad. The same harmonic functions exist in minor as they do in major, but because the minor key harmonic vocabulary is much larger, this study will first focus on major key harmony.

Major key harmony

The VIm and the IIIm chords each have two tones (shown in black notes, below) in common with the I chord (Ex. 7.09).

Ex. 7.09 Tonic function triads

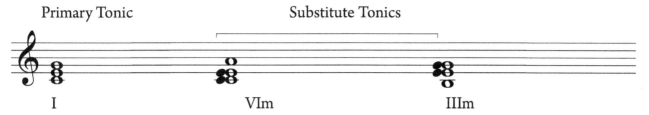

The IIm and the VIm chords each have two tones in common with the IV chord (Ex. 7.10).

Ex. 7.10 Subdominant function triads

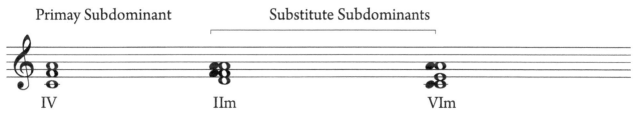

The VIIdim and the IIIm chords each have two tones in common with the V chord (Ex. 7.11).

Ex. 7.11 Dominant function triad

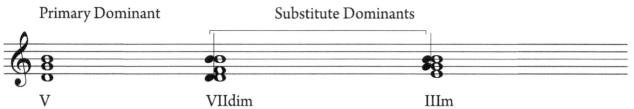

All triads are less stable than the I chord. The least stable diatonic triad is VIIdim, because it is made up of unstable tones and it contains the two most dissonant scale degrees, *fa* and *ti*. Two chords, IIIm and VIm, have dual functions because they contain both stable and unstable tones. The IIIm chord acts as either tonic or dominant, while the VIm chord acts as either a tonic or subdominant. These triads act in a chameleon-like way according to where they are located within a chord progression. Their functionality is built on the premise that chords move or progress from T to SD to D to T.

Once these stylistic expectations are established, a chord progression that moves from I to IIIm to IV sounds like a movement from primary tonic to a secondary tonic (the IIIm chord contains two stable tones, scale tones 3 and 5) to the subdominant. Since the IIIm chord also contains scale degree 7, the leading tone, and the one that helps define the dominant harmony, a progression that that moves I, IV, IIIm, I, sounds like a movement from tonic to subdominant to dominant to tonic. This means that the IIIm chord can act as either a substitute tonic or as a substitute dominant according to where it is located in the progression. Likewise, VIm has two notes in common with the primary tonic (scale degrees 1 and 3) as well as two notes in common with the primary subdominant (scale degrees 1 and 6). Therefore, it can act in either role. If VIm precedes V, it acts as a subdominant; if it follows a V chord, it functions as a substitute tonic (Ex. 7.12).

Ex. 7.12 Functionality in IIIm and VIm

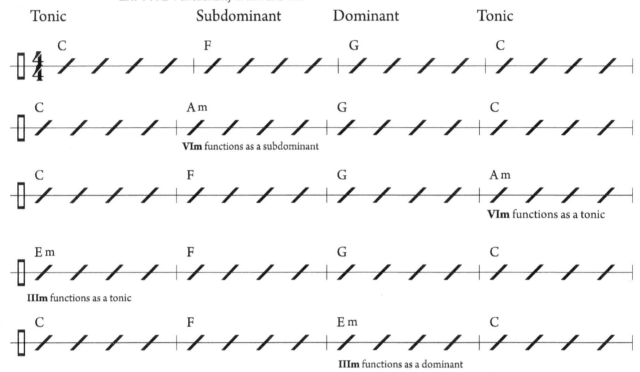

An understanding of functional harmony and the use of substitute chords increases the amount of harmonic options available to you by providing chord substitutions.

The most common and easy to recognize use of a chord substitution is found in the *deceptive cadence*. When a melody cadences on *do*, the "expected" chord is the I chord, but instead VIm, acting as a substitute tonic, appears in its place (Ex. 7.13).

Ex. 7.13 The deceptive cadence

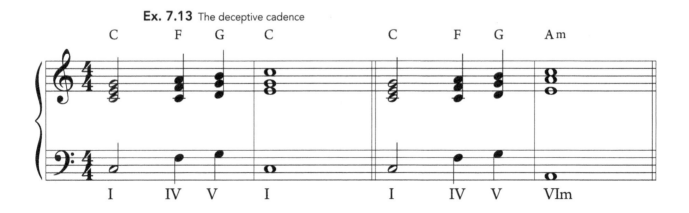

The first cadence in Sting's "Every Breath You Take" could have been to the I chord. The VIm chord, substituting for the I chord, provides a more open cadence, implying a continuance of both music and lyrics (Ex. 7.14).

Ex. 7.14 "Every Breath You Take" Sting

Note: When *do* appears as the final note of a melodic cadence, many chords are available and are used to substitute for the tonic chord in a deceptive cadence (e.g., IV, IVm, bVI, etc.), but VIm is the one most commonly used.

Strong root movements in traditional harmony

The progression from a stable area (T), to a less stable area (SD) to the least stable (D) forms a momentum that is the driving force that accounts for the establishment of strong root movements. Strong root movements that appear in the traditional major/minor scale environment are: P5↓, M2↑, M3rd or m3rd↓, ½ step ↑ or ↓, A4th or d5th ↑ or ↓.

These root movements appear frequently, because they reinforce the movement from tonic to subdominant to dominant to tonic that has permeated Western music for centuries, including the songs of the *Great American Songbook* as well as many well-known traditional folk and country songs (Ex. 7.15).

Ex. 7.15 Root movements that produce T, SD, D, T progressions

Down a perfect 5th or a diminished 5th

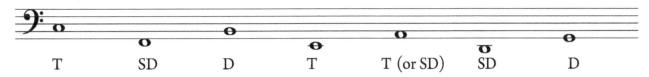

Up a major 2nd, up or down a minor 2nd

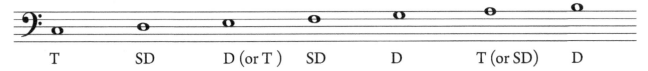

Down in diatonic thirds

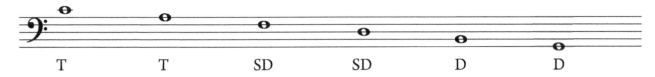

The chord progression in "Heart And Soul," a song from the *Great American Songbook*, was the favorite of doo-wop groups during the early years of R&B and rock and roll. The strong root movements in this song are either down in diatonic thirds or fifths (Ex. 7.16).

Ex. 7.16 "Heart And Soul" music by Hoagy Carmichael, lyrics by Frank Loesser

Adding diatonic sevenths to triads does not change how these chords function, nor does it change root movements; it simply adds dissonance, causing additional momentum and richness to the progression. The amount of dissonance is also an intrinsic part of style, so that in certain styles (e.g., jazz) we find many more seventh chords than we would in a simpler music such as folk or country music (Ex. 7.17).

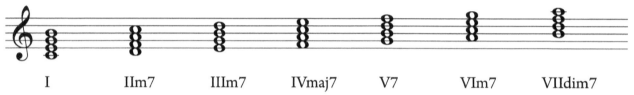

Ex. 7.17 Diatonic seventh chords

It is important to know what the strong root movements in traditional major and minor are, because they have been used so frequently and play a part in defining the style of song. Because of their overuse, many of these traditional harmonic moves, especially V to I and certain root movements, e.g., down a fifth, are now sometimes avoided. Although traditional major/minor is still in use, new styles and new harmonic vocabularies with different root movements have been installed into popular song. A historical study of the harmonic movement in popular songs from the *Great American Songbook* through rock and roll, R&B, and hip-hop demonstrates how important the blues, blues/rock, and modal vocabularies have been in altering how chords move and root movements occur. Chapter 8, "Blues and Modal Tonal Environments," will furnish you with these harmonic vocabularies and root movements and demonstrate through examples how these other tonal environments are used in well-known popular songs.

Chromaticism

Before we study other tonal environments, let's examine how traditional major/minor elaborated with chromaticism create a sumptuous harmonic vocabulary. The major scale is dynamic within itself, but when chromatic tones are introduced into it, it becomes not only a more dynamic and rich but also a less stable environment. Chromaticism (derived from *chromos*, the Greek word for "color") was the musical vocabulary used during the Romantic Era in classical music (1825–1900). It is found extensively in the music of Chopin, Brahms, Tchaikovsky, Wagner, Mahler, etc. The chromatic chord vocabulary that had developed in Europe permeated ragtime music and influenced the tonal vocabulary of the songs of the *Great American Songbook*.

When chromatic notes are used, the harmonic vocabulary expands considerably, creating more kinetic progressions due to the added dissonances. Chromatic notes also allow for richer harmonic colors, for short modulations (called *tonicizations*) that move away and then quickly return to the original key as well as more complete modulations that firmly establish new keys. The result of the extensive use of chromatic notes is a lush tonal environment suitable for both romantic melodies and lyrics.

Secondary dominants

Chromatically altering a secondary seventh chord, such as Dm7 in the key of C, by raising its third a half step, transforms it into a *dominant 7th type* chord (i.e., a major triad with a m7th). Any dominant 7th type chord other than the actual dominant 7th of the key is called a *secondary dominant*.

Ex. 7.18 Transformation of IIm7 into V7/V

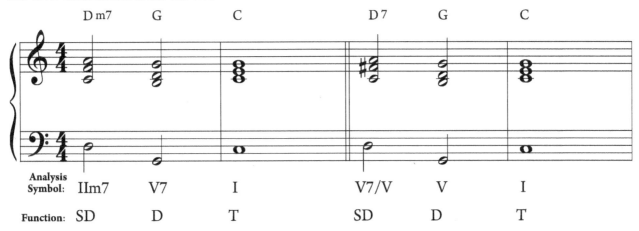

The IIm7 with a raised third, is called "five seven of five" and is symbolized by V7/ V (Ex. 7.18). Although this chord resembles the main dominant 7th of the key (i.e., it consists of a major triad and a minor 7th) it is only a *dominant seventh type* chord, not the actual dominant seventh of the key. Although the IIm7 has been altered into a dominant 7th type chord, its original function does not change: V7/V is based on IIm and is, therefore, a subdominant harmony.

The following diatonic progression: I, VIm7, IIm7, V7, VIm can be transformed into a more chromatic progression by simply raising the thirds of some of the secondary chords by a half step.

The chart (Ex. 7.19) demonstrates the evolution of a completely diatonic chord progression into one that includes chromatic chords that retain the same harmonic functions as their diatonic predecessors.

Ex. 7.19 Transformation of secondary seventh chords into secondary dominants

The result of this transformation is a chord progression found in the standard "Sweet Lorraine" that uses this exact progression within its eight-measure A section (Ex. 7.20).

Ex. 7.20 "Sweet Lorraine" music by Cliff Burwell, lyrics by Mitchell Parish

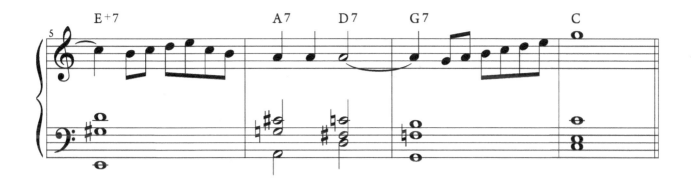

The melody of this great standard is nearly totally diatonic, while the harmonies are quite chromatic. The combination of a diatonic melody with chromatic harmony is common during this era of songwriting. This combination works so well because a diatonic melody is generally easier to sing than a chromatic one, while a chromatic harmony adds richness without otherwise making the music too complex.

In "Sweet Lorraine," the strong root movements highlight T, SD, D, T functions. Although these chords are chromatically altered, appearing as dominant 7th type chords, they are derived from and preserve their original function (Exs. 7.21–7.22).

Ex. 7.21 "Sweet Lorraine" root movements

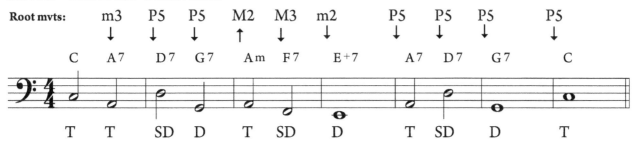

Ex. 7.22 Functional harmonic analysis of the chorus of "Sweet Lorraine"

Function in C:	T	T	SD	D	T

(**Function in A minor:** T   S.D

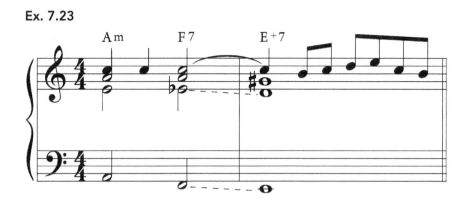

In measures 3–4 there is a temporary modulation (called a *tonicization*) to the key of A minor. The tonicization from C major to A minor is accomplished through a musical sleight of hand: F7, ♭VI7 in A minor, is a chromatic subdominant chord that easily slides down to its dominant, E+7. A complete modulation to A minor in measures 3–5 is withheld because the E+7 moves to A7, V7 of IIm in C (measure 5), instead of resolving to A minor (Ex. 7.23).

Ex. 7.23

This example exemplifies the type of chromaticism found in many songs of the *Great American Songbook*. Even though these types of chromatic chords are not extensively used in today's popular songs, it is important for you to know them because this vocabulary is part of our American musical heritage as well as a part of a professional musician's vocabulary.

In addition to dominant 7th type chords, many other chord types containing chromatic notes are used. George Gershwin used diminished triads and diminished 7th chords in an original and charming way.

Ex. 7.24 *"Someone To Watch Over Me" music by George Gershwin*

Every note in a chord has melodic power that helps determine where and how a chord moves. Since chromatic notes increase dissonance, they increase the kineticism of the progression. The results, apparent in Example 7.24, are the restless, lush harmonies found in the romantic music from this era of American popular song. Notice how Gershwin's choice of bass notes produces chord inversions. In the first two measures, the bass notes create a melodic bass line that contrasts beautifully with the vocal melody by moving in its opposite direction in the first two measures and in a similar direction to the vocal melody in the last two measures.

Note: The chromatic harmonic vocabulary consisting of secondary dominants, diminished chords, etc., resurfaces again in the sixties in a new context—in R&B and in R&B-influenced pop music (styles that will be covered in the next chapter).

Traditional minor scales and their diatonic triads

The minor mode has always presented problems to music theorists due to the startling fact that the minor third from the fundamental does not appear in the harmonic series! However, it is this very fact that causes minor to have its unique character. We are cultural beings as well as natural beings. We need the symbolism of the minor mode as the earth needs the moon as well as the sun. Minor is too often depicted as being "sad" and major as being "happy," but this reductionism works only for children. It is wiser to think of minor as being darker and more complex and holding more secrets, and to also think of minor in different tempi, not only as a tonal environment suited for a dirge. The minor mode can be very sensual and is often found in dance music (Exs. 7.25–7.27).

Ex. 7.25 *Natural minor*

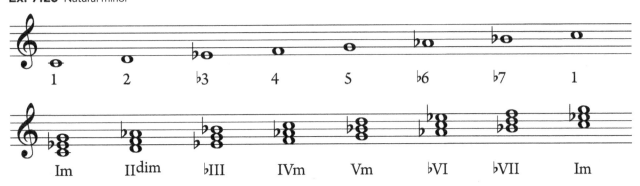

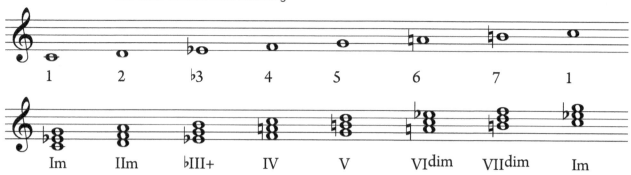

Ex. 7.26 Melodic minor ascending

1   2   ♭3   4   5   6   7   1

Im   IIm   ♭III+   IV   V   VIdim   VIIdim   Im

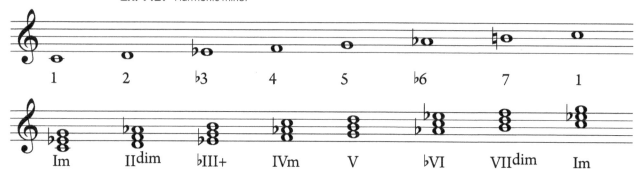

Ex. 7.27 Harmonic minor

1   2   ♭3   4   5   ♭6   7   1

Im   IIdim   ♭III+   IVm   V   ♭VI   VIIdim   Im

It is possible and not uncommon to find all three traditional minor scales used in one song, rendering a vast number of harmonic as well as melodic choices. Scale degrees ♭6, 6, ♭7, 7, are all found in traditional minor, rendering a vast group of triads (Ex. 7.28).

Ex. 7.28 Triads in the key of C minor (derived from all the traditional minor scales)

Cm   D dim   Dm   E♭   E♭+   Fm   F

Im   IIdim   IIm   ♭III   ♭III+   IVm   IV

Gm   G   A♭   A dim   B♭   B dim

Vm   V   ♭VI   VIdim   ♭VII   VIIdim

"Hotel California" (1971), a hit song by the Eagles that depicts the underbelly of the LA scene, uses richly diverse harmonies. As chromatic as this harmonic progression sounds, all the notes are derived from the various B minor scales (Ex. 7.29).

118

Ex. 7.29 "Hotel California" verse chord progression, Don Felder, Glenn Frey, Don Henley

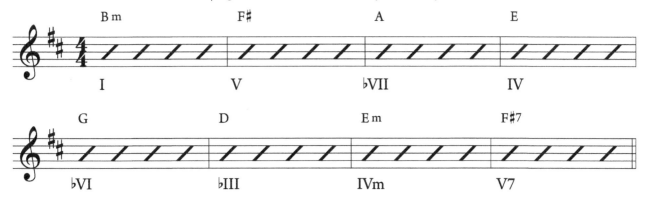

The harmonic vocabulary in minor is especially rich in choices of subdominant chords. In C minor, the subdominant chords you have available are: Fm, F, Ddim, Dm, A♭, and Adim. The second chord in all the examples below are subdominants.

Ex. 7.30 Subdominants in C minor

Modal interchange

In the songs by the greatest songwriters: Schubert, Berlin, Gershwin, Porter, John Lennon and Paul McCartney, Joni Mitchell, Paul Simon, Carole King, and Stevie Wonder, there is an abundant mixture of minor within major and major within minor. We live in a world that is neither major nor minor all the time; from moment to moment our feelings can and often do change. Through the mixtures of major and minor we come much closer to finding symbols in a tonal environment that matches or reflects what we experience in life.

When a chord found in a minor key occurs in a parallel major key—or vice versa—that chord is considered borrowed and the term "modal interchange" is used to describe this activity.

One of the most common borrowings from minor that occurs in major is the scale tone ♭6. It occurs in the IVm and the IIm7(♭5) chords and, with an additional borrowing of ♭3, it also occurs in the ♭VI chord.

Of all the composers from the golden age of popular song, the one most attracted to modal interchange was Cole Porter (Ex. 7.31).

Ex. 7.31 "All Of You" Cole Porter

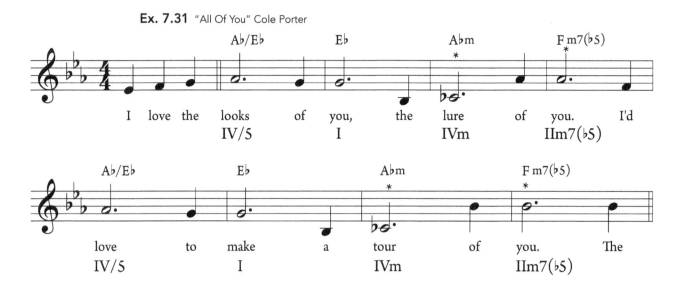

"All Of You," in E♭ major, borrows from its parallel minor, E♭ minor. (C♭, the ♭6 scale degree, appears in the both the melody and in the harmony, giving the song its unique, piquant flavor (* indicates modal interchange occurrences).

Modal interchange is one of the defining sounds of the Beatles. Again, ♭6 provides the tonal color that captures the flavor of the minor mode in a song based in major. The song is in the key of G major, so when the E♭ appears in Cm6, it is poignantly unexpected, as is A♯ found in the D augmented chord, since it also implies G minor (A♯ = B♭, the third of G minor). Because of these implications, the major third, B♮, the last note of the chorus (on the word "glad") automatically puts smiles on our faces (Ex. 7.32).

Ex. 7.32 "She Loves You" John Lennon, Paul McCartney

Summary

Gaining control over your tonal materials will help you become a better musician and a better songwriter. If you know how to establish a key and understand harmonic functions, you will be able to substitute one harmony for another and control the tonal movements within your song. Traditional major and minor form the backbone of the *Great American Songbook*, so knowing this vocabulary will allow you to enter into a deeper understanding of some of the greatest popular songs ever written. Traditional major/minor however is only one of a number of possible tonal environments. The next chapter deals with some others.

Activities

Knowing how to navigate in all of the diatonic major and minor keys is a tremendous help in becoming a professional a musician and songwriter. Be able to do the following:

- Name, play and sing all the diatonic notes in all the major keys and in the three forms of minor keys. That is a big order, but daily practice consisting of naming various scale degrees quickly (Example: Name scale degree 6 in the key of E, in the key of B♭, in the key of F#) will get you there. It may take six months or a year, but by that time you will have learned to navigate in any given key.
- In songs you've already written, look for possible substitute harmonies: secondary chords that might work better than the primary chords you may have in place; try substituting a chromatic chord or a modal interchange chord for a diatonic one.
- Analyze the melodies and chords of two of your favorite songs in traditional major or traditional minor. Play and sing the songs, analyze the chord progression, and, once you have memorized them, transpose the chords of the songs in at least two other keys.

8

The Blues, Rock, R&B, and Modal Environments

Blues

The blues is the most influential American roots music, affecting the sound of popular music from W.C. Handy's "St. Louis Blues" through the inception of rock and R&B, straight through to today's popular music. One of the main sources of the blues is the minor pentatonic scale (Ex. 8.01).

Ex. 8.01 Minor pentatonic scale

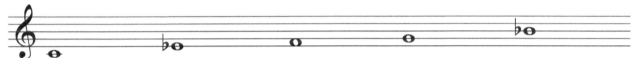

When the minor pentatonic scale combines with the basic I, IV, V chords found in functional harmony, a new chemistry is created, one that immediately produces a uniquely poignant sound that easily evokes an emotional reaction. The blues is the only music that fully embraces the comingling of major and minor, i.e., both the major and minor third are diatonic in the blues. Rather than using the term "modal interchange" for the blues I use the term "modal integration." Dissonances that occur between melody and harmony, that would otherwise have had to be resolved in other tonal environments, are accepted and are, in fact, one of the defining factors and main attractions of the blues.

The chart below contains the primary chords in C major with the C minor pentatonic scale (Ex. 8.02).

Ex. 8.02 Dissonant melody/harmony relationships found in blues

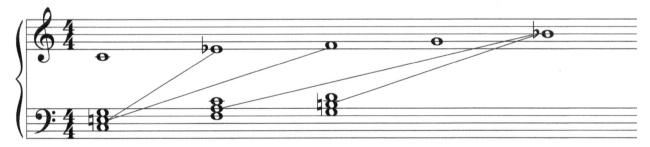

In a traditional harmonic setting, an F or E♭ in a melody sounding over a C major chord would be expected to resolve to a E, and a B♭ in the melody over a G major chord

would be expected to resolve to a B. In blues songs and performances, these dissonances may or may not resolve to the underlying harmony. These modal contradictions (major and minor occurring simultaneously) are not only accepted, but are the lifeblood of the blues! The dissonances, used authentically, resonate deeply within our souls and are a reflection of the pathos that is so much a part of the history of American music and of America itself. The power of the blues has moved it well beyond this land. The poignancy that this music evokes resonates with all humans who have felt pain, suffering, injustice, the pleasures of sex, the contradictions in life—the life force itself.

The authentic sound of the blues is best represented by the voice and the guitar, where vocal inflections, bent notes, notes that exist between the major third and the minor third live. Both the voice and the guitar can bend and inflect notes in a similar fashion. The piano cannot. Because of this, when blues music—notated and arranged for piano and voice—first appeared in published form, the dissonant clashes between the minor pentatonic scale and the major chords in the harmonic underpinning were some-what ameliorated. To make notated piano music compensate for the piano's inability to bend notes and also to have the music look like it made sense, the ♭3, a characteristic note in the blues, often appeared in major keys as ♯2.

These are some attributes of early blues songs:

• Sections of songs that sometimes appear in major and parallel minor.
• The I chord often incorporates the ♭7 found in the minor pentatonic scale and produces a I7 harmony.
• The ♭3, found in the minor pentatonic scale, produces the IV7 harmony.
• The thirds of all major chords are subject to modal contradictions by the appearance of their minor thirds in the melody.

All of these attributes are found in W.C. Handy's "St Louis Blues," published in 1914. The blues had existed long before it appeared on record and in sheet music. W.C. Handy's contribution to the blues and to American popular music was his ability to create songs that incorporated the blues vocabulary and publish them in written form. Wisely, W.C. Handy self-published his "St. Louis Blues" in 1914 after having had his song turned down by many publishers on Tin Pan Alley, resulting in a prosperous career and many honors bestowed on him.

Ex. 8.03 "St. Louis Blues" W.C. Handy

The four-measure introduction of the original piano/vocal arrangement written by W.C. Handy is in G minor. The music of the verse that follows (Ex. 8.03) is in G major! This immediate modal contradiction sets the stage for the first theme, which continues in this bimodal environment. In measure 1, the G major chord contains a ♭3 grace note that is written as a ♯2 (A♯ = B♭). The next measure has a ♯5 (the D♯ = E♭) leading to 6, but more importantly, this D♯ is the disguised minor third of the C major chord. Most major chords are treated in this bimodal (major and minor) way. Every third of a major chord can be "worried," a term itinerant blues players used in referencing a frequency some-where between major and minor that is at the heart of the blues. The minor third of the tonality (B♭ in G major) appears in the melody on beat 3 of measure 2, a further indication that this is the environment in which these wild flowers grow.

The form of this very original song is ABC, three different sections that use the blues tonal vocabulary and retain the same tonal center. Handy writes the A section in the traditional twelve-bar form and treats the lyric form in the traditional struc-ture: an opening line that repeats, followed by a line that rhymes with lines one and two. In this most famous of blues songs, B, the middle section beginning with "St. Louis Woman / with her diamond rings" is a sixteen-measure section in G minor, the parallel minor to G major, reinforcing the bimodal environment of the entire song. This section sounds like a chorus and is followed by a return to the twelve-bar form. The C section marked by Handy as "Chorus" is again, a twelve-bar blues, with a mel-ody that is more urgent sounding than the one in the A section. Its lyric does not fol-low the traditional structure; it contains three different lines that all rhyme. Unlike most blues sung by iterant blues performers, with verses that change lyric direction frequently, this blues has a concept and theme with both the introduction and the B section set in a tango rhythm (the tango was all the rage in 1914) because Handy was intent on making this not just another twelve-bar blues, but a commercial blues song.

The malleability of the blues, its ability to function not simply in the traditional twelve-bar form but in any song form, allowed it to influence and become an integral part of the sound of American popular song. George Gershwin, Harold Arlen, and Duke Ellington are among composers from that era who understood and used the power of the blues in their songs.

Gershwin's use of the blues is often very subtle. Songs that seemingly have no associ-ation with the blues, such as "A Foggy Day," "The Man I Love," and "Somebody Loves Me" (Ex. 8.04), have blues elements so beautifully integrated that we don't even notice them and we simply assume that these songs just sound kind of "jazzy." The incorporation of blues attributes is, in fact, one of the reasons those songs are heard as jazz songs.

Ex. 8.04 *"Somebody Loves Me" music by George Gershwin, lyrics by Ira Gershwin*

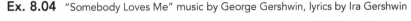
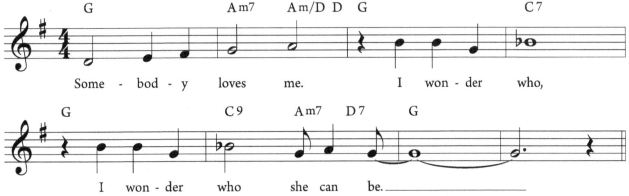

The minor third of G appears twice within the first eight measures of the melody and harmony in "Somebody Loves Me" (measures 4 and 6) although the song is clearly in G major. This blues note gives the song it's poignancy and probably inspired its lyric.

Blues in early rock and roll

Early rock and roll songs were nearly all blues, often appearing in the most common form: the twelve-bar blues. But unlike blues performed by traditional blues players—with their somewhat random-sounding lyrics appearing in each verse—early rock song forms included verse/chorus, verse/refrain, and AABA structures. Songwriters such as Chuck Berry, Willie Dixon, and Leiber and Stoller demonstrated how malleable the form of the blues can be by writing songs in myriad forms. Innovative songwriters at Motown Records, such as "Smoky" Robinson, Holland, Dozier and Holland, Marvin Gaye, and Mickey Stevenson also used blues elements in their songs that further demonstrated how the blues can flavor songs that otherwise would not be so tasty.

The English groups, especially the Rolling Stones, The Kinks, The Who, The Yardbirds, The Beatles, The Spencer Davis Group, and Cream, along with Jimi Hendrix and some American groups, such as Creedence Clearwater Revival and Aerosmith, created a new harmonic vocabulary derived from the blues, and transformed the sound of rock and roll while retaining its roots. In doing so, they established a harmonic vocabulary that marked the first significant harmonic change in popular song in over fifty years.

The transformation of the blues: rock and R&B

The power of the blues in contemporary song is often underestimated and is too often ignored by present-day songwriters, who can benefit from its many attributes. The blues/rock harmonic vocabulary developed in the 1960s and is still heard today.

Blues/rock harmonies developed from combining the minor pentatonic scale with major triads. This amalgamation generates a group of new harmonies and harmonic movements. When major triads are used to harmonize the minor pentatonic scale, the overall sound retains the modal contradictions that form the main characteristic of the blues (Ex. 8.05).

Ex. 8.05 Harmonization of the minor pentatonic scale with major triads

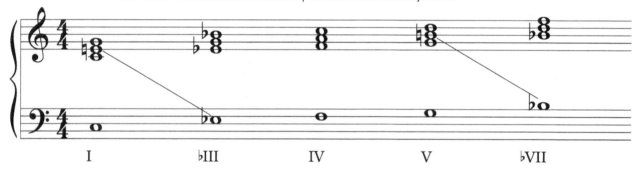

I   ♭III   IV   V   ♭VII

The modal contradictions that define the sound of the blues is retained when the minor pentatonic scale is harmonized with major triads. The third of the I chord is major, but the root of the next triad, ♭III, contradicts it, producing what in traditional harmony pedagogy is called a "cross" or "false" relationship, a dissonance that students in traditional harmony classes are warned to avoid. But this dissonance is exactly the sound that defines the blues! It is the sound of major and minor coexisting in the same environment.

Other chords added to this harmonic vocabulary that reinforce the sound of the blues include the II, ♭VI, and the VI chords (Ex. 8.06).

Ex. 8.06

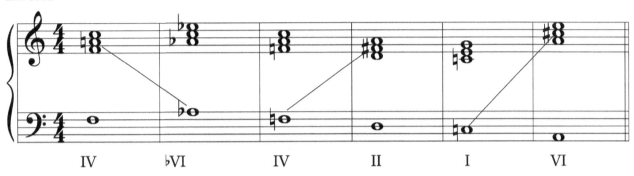

Harmonic movements used in rock and R&B songs are not based solely based functional harmony and often contradict the usual root movements found in traditional functional harmony (Ex. 8.07). Instead of chords moving down in fifths, rock chords often move down in fourths; instead of moving up a whole step, rock progressions often move down a whole step; instead of only moving down in thirds diatonically, rock progressions contain major triads that move up or down by minor thirds. Not only did the rhythm of rock music change the sound of popular music, but the entire tonal environment changed as well.

Root movements in blues/rock

Ex. 8.07 Common root movements found in the blues/rock tonal environment

John Fogerty, leader and main songwriter of the group Creedence Clearwater Revival, used this blues-conceived introduction in his iconic song, "Proud Mary." The song, in the key of D, begins with the startling sound of a ♭VII chord. Notice the modal contradictions that exist between the C chord to the A chord and the F chord to the D chord (Ex. 8.08).

Ex. 8.08 "Proud Mary" John Fogerty

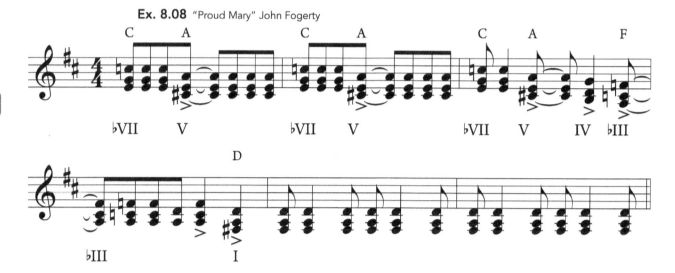

The Beatles came under the spell of early rockers such as Chuck Berry and Little Richard and helped develop and popularize the blues/rock vocabulary (Ex. 8.09).

Ex. 8.09 "Back In the U.S.S.R" John Lennon, Paul McCartney

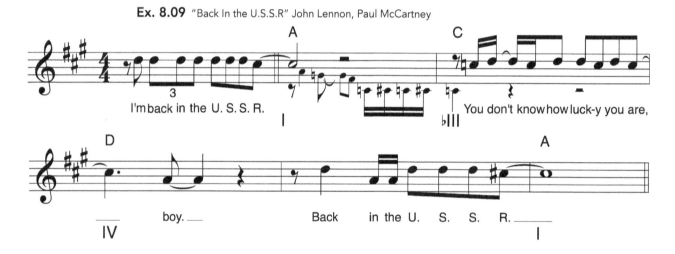

Notice all the delightfully contradictory thirds in the melody in this song's chorus: major 3rd, minor 3rd, major 3rd, and how the chords reflect the blues, with the roots moving up a minor third from A to C and down a fourth from D to A.

The chord pattern in "Hey Joe," Jimi Hendrix's first hit, remains the same throughout the song. All roots move down in P4ths. The chords and melody are located either in the E Aeolian, E Dorian, or E Mixolydian scales. (The key signature is somewhat of an anomaly here, as it is in many blues songs; it indicates E major, but D# is nowhere to be found in either the melody or the harmony.) What binds these chords together is the same tonal center (E) and the common tones that exist between the various scales. The total integration of the major and minor modes found in this song renders the unmistakable sound of the blues (Ex. 8.10).

Ex. 8.10 "Hey Joe" chords with common tones

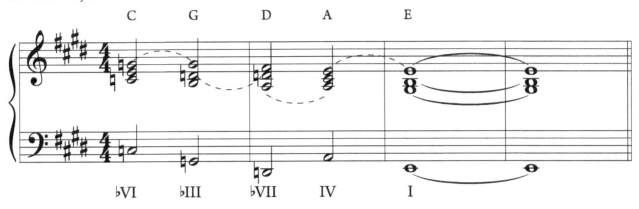

The scale that results from these chords provides the melodic materials that include the major 3rd, the minor 3rd, the flat 6th, and the natural 6th (Ex. 8.11).

Ex. 8.11 "Hey Joe" scale

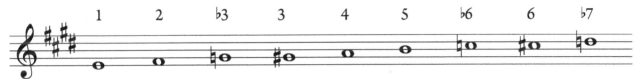

Within the context of the entire song, Jimi Hendrix sings the minor third, the major third, and the blues note that lies in between them. In addition, both ♭6 and ♮6 appear in the melody (Ex. 8.12).

Ex. 8.12 "Hey Joe" Billy Roberts

Hey ⸺ Joe,   where you go-in' ⸺ with that   gun in your hand?

"Gimme Some Lovin'," a hit back in 1966 by the Spencer Davis Group, has a blues-based chord progression that moves up in minor 3rds between I and ♭III and IV and ♭VI. Notice the common tones between those chords that help bind these disparate chords together (Exs. 8.13–8.14).

Ex. 8.13 "Gimme Some Lovin'" chord progression, common tones

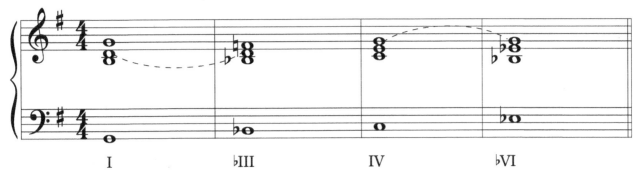

129

Ex. 8.14 "Gimme Some Lovin'" Spencer Davis, Stevie Winwood, Muff Winwood

So glad we made___ it   So glad we made___ it   You got to

Gim-me some lov-in'   Gim-mie, Gim-mie, some lov-in'

The only notes sung throughout the entire melody of "Gimme Some Lovin'" by Stevie Winwood are 1, ♭3, 3, 4, 5, and 6, a blues-based hexatonic scale (Ex. 8.15).

Ex. 8.15

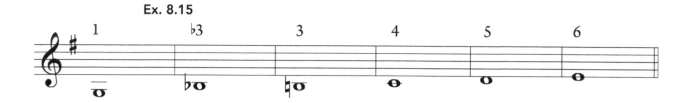

Adele had a gigantic hit with "Rollin' In the Deep" in 2012, a song that has its roots in the blues and in the Black Christian church (Ex. 8.16).

Ex. 8.16 "Rollin' In the Deep" Adele Atkins, Paul Epworth

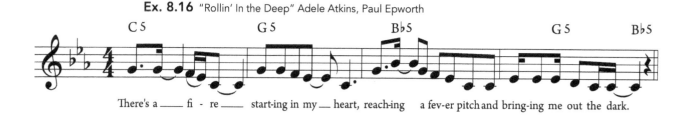

There's a ___ fi - re ___ start-ing in my ___ heart, reach-ing a fev-er pitch and bring-ing me out the dark.

The dyads C5, G5, B♭5, consisting only of the root and the fifth of each triad, played on the recording initially by an acoustic guitar, allow for a greater choice of notes in the melody and also provide an interesting texture to the production. The root movements, G to B♭ back to G, up and down in minor 3rds, are indicative of the blues influence.

Adele sings a minor hexatonic scale throughout (Ex. 8.17).

Ex. 8.17

Mixing blues harmonies with traditional major/minor harmonies

Blues-derived harmonies are sometimes used in conjunction with more traditional functional harmonies and root movements. More than any other group, The Beatles integrated both traditional major/minor and the blues into one environment.

"Hey Jude" is written completely in traditional F major until the coda, when the following blues derived progression occurs (Ex. 8.18):

Ex. 8.18 "Hey Jude" John Lennon, Paul McCartney

Na, na, na, na-na-na na.   Na-na-na-na. Hey,   Jude.

Neil Young's "Old Man" in the key of D, begins on a ♭IIImaj7, incorporating a major 7th chord into an otherwise blues/rock harmonic environment (Ex. 8.19).

Ex. 8.19 "Old Man" Neil Young

Old man,   look at my   life;   I'm   a-lot like   you   were.

"Black Velvet" is one of the finest rock songs ever written. The vocal on the original recording by Alannah Myles is extraordinary, but the music that inspired it is equally so. In a mainly blues environment, root progressions from traditional major/minor appear, yet everything is of a piece. The verse of the song is in E minor; the chorus implies G major and is best analyzed in that key until its final cadence (Ex. 8.20).

Ex. 8.20 "Black Velvet" chorus, David Tyson, Christopher War

The chord movement in the chorus of "Black Velvet" begins with a traditional harmonic root movement down a fifth. The harmonic implication of the progression, Am7 to D, is to move to G. Instead, the Am chord appears again and moves to F, ♭VII in G, contradicting the F♯ that appeared in the D chord in measure 2. The root movement, F to C, down a fourth, is one of several blues-derived root movements that includes V moving to IV7. IV7 in G is the common chord or *pivot chord* that transmutes to ♭VI7 in E minor leading to V7ˢᵘˢ that finally beckons the goal, E minor. The melody is completely diatonic in both G major and E natural minor.

The blues/rock harmonic vocabulary was presented on albums of songs right besides songs that stem from a European folk tradition and that seemingly have no relationship to the blues. However, many of the same root movements that are found in blues are also found in traditional folk music that uses modes such as the Mixolydian, the Dorian, and the Aeolian. Because of this kinship, it is no wonder that modal music coexisted in the1960s "British Invasion," right along with the blues in bands such as The Beatles, Led Zeppelin, Jethro Tull, and Fleetwood Mac.

"Rhiannon" by Stevie Nicks has a verse in the key of A Aeolian, alternating the Am and F chords, two measures each for eight measures (not shown here). The chorus of this very original, haunting song, however, hints at C blues (Ex. 8.21).

Ex. 8.21 "Rhiannon" chorus, Stevie Nicks

Styles within the R&B tonal environment

Rhythm & blues songs are written in many different substyles. There are songs that incorporate the blues and sound like they come right out of the Black Baptist or Pentecostal churches; there are funky, highly rhythmic songs that practically eschew harmony and mainly use the minor pentatonic scale, and there are romantic, sensual songs that combine blues notes with jazz harmonies.

All R&B music, however, demands healthy rhythmic grooves that permeate the songs bottom up through to the melody. Often the bass riff is as important as the vocal melody. *Call and response* is a typical type of activity that involves the soloist answered by group members, backup singers, or instruments. Often the melody is embellished with melismas (two or more notes sung to one syllable), most notably popularized in the vocal stylings of, e.g., Aretha Franklin, Mariah Carey, and Christina Aguilera.

Traditional, church-influenced R&B

Traditional R&B, whose roots are in the blues and in Black Gospel music exemplified by artists such as Ray Charles, Aretha Franklin, Wilson Pickett, and Otis Redding, is characterized by these factors:

- The minor pentatonic scale is often the basic raw material for the melody.
- Blues notes in the melody sound simultaneously with both diatonic chords and chromatic chords such as secondary dominant chords or a diminished 7th chords in the harmony.
- Extensive use of melisma.
- Background vocals, responding to the lead vocalist, or vice versa, produce *call and response*, a characteristic of African music.
- Harmony is mainly triadic with prominent use of the IV chord, the most prevalent progression being I to IV or IV to I (the *plagal* or "amen" cadence).
- Secondary dominants, diminished chords (remnants of ragtime music), and blues-derived chords are all part of the harmonic palette.
- Diatonic chords, often with their diatonic 7ths included, often move either up or down by diatonic steps.
- Root movements from both traditional major/minor and blues/rock vocabularies are used, often appearing next to one another.
- The physicality of the music, the syncopated rhythms, and grooves are essential.
- Compound meters (6/8, 9/8, or 12/8) are often used in ballads.

Otis Redding's great "I've Been Loving You For Too Long" has many characteristics of church influenced traditional R&B (Ex. 8.22).

Ex. 8.22 "I've Been Loving You Too Long" Otis Redding, Jerry Butler

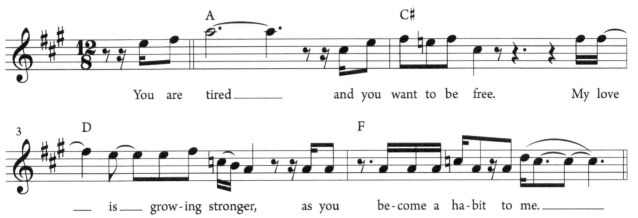

133

The E♮ in the melody that appears against the chromatic E♯ in the C♯ chord in measure 2, the blues note, ♭3, C♮, in the melody in measure 3 and 4, the 12/8 time, the blues-generated chord progression of D moving to F in measures 3 and 4, and Otis's use of melisma, all point to the church tradition—the roots from which this song grew.

Romantic R&B

Romantic R&B has roots in both the Black church, in the music of the *Great American Songbook*, and in jazz-based songs. It is exemplified in many songs from the mid-1960s through the 1990s sung by artists such as Al Green, Barry White, Marvin Gaye, Patti Austin, Al Jarreau, Stevie Wonder, Jerry Butler, Lou Rawls, and George Benson. To the above list of traditional R&B characteristics, these new ones may be added:

• The melody often contains *tensions* (the upper extensions of chords built in thirds: 7ths, 9ths, 11ths, 13ths).
• A richer harmonic palette than is found in traditional church-based R&B. These include jazz chords, tonicizations, and modulations.

Al Green's gigantic hit "Let's Stay Together" is typical of romantic R&B songs. It contains minor 7th and minor 9th chords with roots that often move up or down a step diatonically and with a melody often based around a 9th or 7th of the harmony (Ex. 8.23).

Ex. 8.23 "Let's Stay Together" Al Green, Willie Mitchell, Al Jackson Jr.

Mariah Carey's first hit, "Vision Of Love," is a beautifully conceived romantic R&B song with influences from both the Black church (note the 12/8 time signature and the secondary dominant chords) and jazz (Ex. 8.24).

Ex. 8.24 "Vision Of Love" Mariah Carey, Ben Margulies

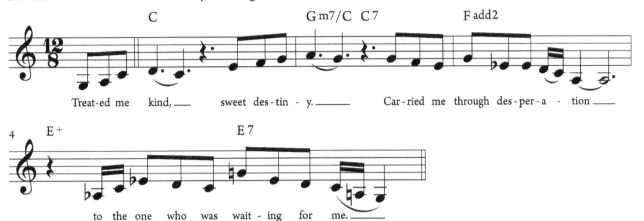

Jazz chords, blues notes, and melismas appear throughout the song. There is a tonicization of the IV chord that takes place almost immediately in measures 2–3 (Gm7/C, C7, F). Notice the 9ths that appear in the melody (the major 9th in measure 3 and the ♯9 in measure 4) as well as the choice dissonances produced by the juxtaposition of the C minor pentatonic scale containing an E♭ sung over the chromatic E+7 and E7 chords in measure 4.

Funk

The main exponents of funk are James Brown, Sly Stone, and George Clinton. This style contains the following traits:

- Riff-based songs with very few chords (see chapter 15, "Riff-Based Songwriting").
- The prominence in the melody of the minor pentatonic scale.
- The bass line is often very important in creating the groove and establishing a riff.
- Emphasis is on rhythm with an intricate web of rhythms full of syncopations, performed perfectly in sync with one another, forming a matrix of nearly nonstop propulsion.

Sly Stone's "Sing A Simple Song" makes it clear from its inception that this is a blues-inspired funk-based piece (Ex. 8.25).

Ex. 8.25 "Sing a Simple Song" Sly Stone

The riff in the introduction, which runs throughout the verse section of the song, is a good example of the kinds of bass or guitar riffs that define funk. The E7 in measure 2, played by the organ and guitar, pits the major third, G#, against the minor third, G♮, sung by the lead female vocalist. Sly Stone often combined pop elements into his songs. "Sing A Simple Song" has a section in the chorus (not shown here) that changes tonal environments rather radically, when bass player/vocalist Larry Graham sings an ascending E major scale, replete with solfege syllables, *do, re, mi,* etc., that uses the unbluesy *ti* found in traditional major as an example of how to sing a simple song. This impish ironic gesture slyly acknowledges its intended integrated audience.

Traits of varied R&B styles can, of course, be found in the same song. This is the case in "I Heard It Through The Grapevine," a song that combines elements of funk with church influences (Ex. 8.26).

Ex. 8.26 "I Heard It Through The Grapevine" Norman Whitfield, Barrett Strong

The chorus melody of "I Heard It Through The Grapevine," notated here in E♭ major, is made up of the minor pentatonic scale. The syncopated chords move back and forth from I major to IV7, a typical harmonic pattern in Black church music. The minor third is sung in the lead vocal while the background vocals sing the major third of an E♭ major triad! The funky bass line/riff, the backup vocals that include call and response, the soulful nuances of Marvin Gaye's voice, and the groove produced by the Funk Brothers, the Motown rhythm section, help to further stylistically define this masterful song.

Many songs that came out of Berry Gordy's Motown records and later, Philadelphia International, the record company owned by the excellent writing/producing team of Kenny Gamble and Leon Huff, combined elements of pop music with more traditional R&B elements to appeal to the widest possible audience (Ex. 8.27).

Ex. 8.27 "Love Train" Kenny Gamble, Leon Huff

This anthemic song (it was the theme of the popular TV dance show "Soultrain") has a blues-influenced sound that emanates from the harmony. The II9 chord followed by the IV chord does the trick, with the F# of the D9 contradicting the F♮ of the F chord. The melody in C major is totally diatonic. The call and response (in this case, the lead singer responds to the group vocals) and the relentless rhythm section all add to the R&B traits.

Twenty-first-century R&B and hip-hop

Twenty-first century R&B and pop music often resemble one another; the two music charts' titles often overlap. Secondary dominant chords are rare, probably because they hint at an older church-related R&B style. Even the traditional sound of the blues, the "B" in R&B, is sometimes missing in contemporary R&B and hip-hop songs. Although the minor pentatonic scale is still very much a part of today's music, the Aeolian mode is equally important. The sounds and overall production in hit R&B and hip-hop songs is slick and enticing. Sometimes only two chords appear in an entire song, as in the highly syncopated 2008 hit by Ne-Yo, "Closer" (Ex. 8.28).

Ex. 8.28 "Closer" Magnus Beite, Mikkei Eriksen, Tor Hermansen, Bernt Stray, Shaffer Smith

The "R" of this style, rhythm, has dominated the sound of both pop and hip-hop for some time now, with rap a major influence, especially on rhythm and rhyme. Harmony is simple but sometimes very intriguing, as demonstrated in "Crazy In Love" (Ex. 8.29).

Ex. 8.29 "Crazy In Love" Beyonce Knowles, Rich Harrison, Shawn Caeter, Eugene Record

Got me look-ing so cra - zy right now. Your love's ___ got me look-ing so cra - zy right now.

Got me look-ing so cra - zy right now. Your touch's ___ got me look-ing so cra - zy right now.

"Crazy In Love" in D minor, contains blues/rock chords that move hypnotically between B♭, the ♭VI chord, and G, the IV chord, with the B♭ and the B♮ contradicting each other throughout the chorus, giving it a blues flavor while accentuating the frenetic subject of the lyric

Modes

Modes is another name for scales. There are six common modes, three that are major: Ionian, Mixolydian, and Lydian, and three that are minor: Aeolian, Dorian, and Phrygian. Two of the commonly used modes have been touched on in the last chapter: the Ionian (the major scale) and the Aeolian (the natural minor scale). The use of modes can often lead to interesting and unique songs. Each individual mode has two characteristic notes that define it. The first characteristic note is its third because it defines the mode as either major or minor. The second characteristic note, represented by the darkened notes in the charts below, help to further define the mode within its major or minor grouping.

The tritone within each mode is also indicated because its placement determines how stable or unstable a mode is. An arrow emanating from a member of the tritone indicates that it is an unstable note within the tonality and seeks resolution to the note indicated by the arrowhead. The word "stable" placed over one of the notes of the tritone indicates that it is not dissonant to the tonality and, therefore, has no need to resolve.

Only in the Ionian and Aeolian modes are both members of the tritone composed of unstable tones. This gives these two modes the most potential to easily establish a key (accounting for the popularity of the use of these two modes). In all the other modes, only one member of the tritone is an unstable tone. Because of the placement of the tritone in both the Mixolydian and Dorian modes, ♭7, an unstable note, resolves a whole step up to *do*. This accounts for their weaker ability to establish a key (Ex. 8.30–8.31).

Ex. 8.30 Major modes

Ionian

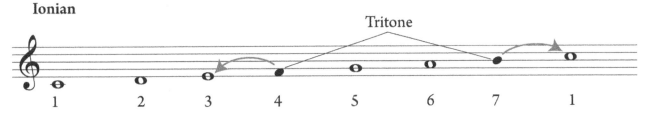

Mixolydian

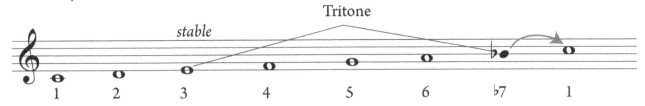

Lydian

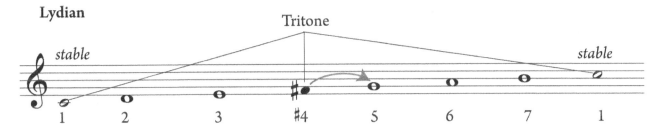

Ex. 8.31 Minor modes

Aeolian

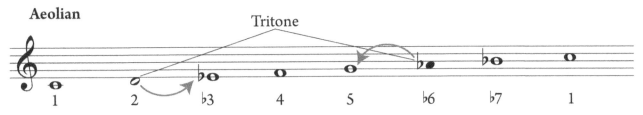

Dorian

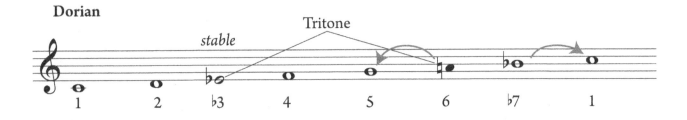

Phrigyian

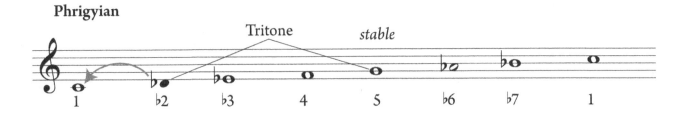

The diatonic triads in the modes

In (Exs. 8.32–8.45), each triad that contains the characteristic note of the mode appears with darkened notes. The I chord of the relative Ionian mode is contained in a rectangle. The relationship of other modes to the Ionian is emphasized in these charts because of the incredibly strong pull of the tritone to resolve to the stable tones in the Ionian mode, the mode that most easily establishes a key. If you allow this to happen, you would leave the mode you are in and modulate to the relative Ionian. A modulation to the relative Ionian should not always be avoided; it can be a very strategic move, as demonstrated in chapter 16, "Tonal and Rhythmic Strategizing," but it should not happen by accident.

The modes most likely to establish a strong tonal center or key are listed starting from the strongest to the weakest:

Ionian-------------------most stable
Aeolian
Mixolydian
Dorian
Phrygian
Lydian-----------------least stable

The modes most often used in popular song are the Ionian, Aeolian, Mixolydian, and Dorian.

Aeolian

Ex. 8.32 Diatonic triads in the Aeolian mode

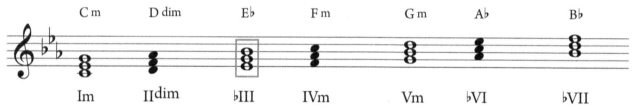

The pure minor or Aeolian mode is a great tonal environment to use in dance music and pop music. Its tritone, scale degrees 2 and ♭6, consists of two unstable tones that present possibilities for strong harmonic cadences, but do not close as strongly as the cadences found in traditional major or minor environments. By simply choosing to be in a minor mode, you avoid the "too good to be true" effect that traditional major sometimes has, and by choosing the Aeolian mode you avoid the too obvious leading tone. The ♭7, found in the Aeolian mode, is a less dynamic scale tone than the leading tone and, therefore, the cadences it produces are less pronounced occasions. This is a very positive attribute because if there are obvious cadences in a dance song the music has the effect of stopping and starting—and stopping and starting is hardly a desirable result in a dance-oriented song. Think of the many dance hits by Madonna, such as "Dress You Up" (Ex. 8.33), "Holiday," and "Papa Don't Preach"—all in the Aeolian mode. Obviously, tempo is also an important factor in the effect music has. Minor is more colorful than major; it seems to hold more secrets and, when combined with a medium or up-tempo groove, the effect it has on us is often very sensual.

Ex. 8.33 "Dress You Up" Andrea LaRusso, Peggy Stanziale

The Aeolian mode isn't confined to dance music. "Ain't No Sunshine" by Bill Withers and "Fallin'" (Ex. 8.34) by Alicia Keys employ the bare-bones sound of the minor dominant (Vm) to create songs with a very powerful expression of longing.

Ex. 8.34 "Fallin'" Alicia Keys

Mixolydian

Ex. 8.35 Diatonic triads in the Mixolydian mode

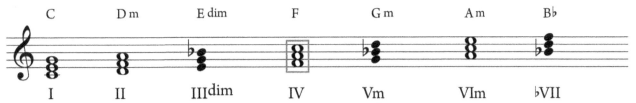

Due to the differences in each mode's tone tendencies, each separate mode beckons certain root movements. The Mixolydian mode often contains root movements down in P4ths, as demonstrated in Example 8.36, "Automatic." In modes, such as this one, that do not have strong harmonic cadencing attributes, the melody often is crucial in defining the tonal center.

Notice how the stable tones in F Mixolydian are highlighted in the melody of "Automatic" with the inclusion of a melodic dominant to tonic axis and how *re* resolves to *do* in both melodic phrases. The country star Miranda Lambert has had several of hits in the Mixolydian mode, a tonal environment that helps define this artist's identity or "sound."

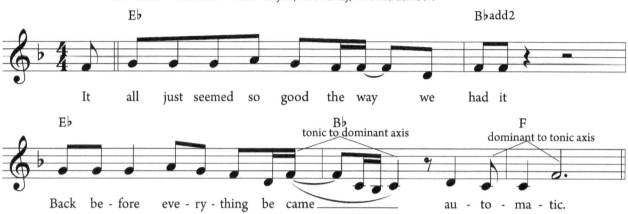

Ex. 8.36 "Automatic" Nicole Galyon, Nat Henby, Miranda Lambert

It all just seemed so good the way we had it

Back be - fore eve - ry - thing be came_____ au - to - ma - tic.

In order to demonstrate the power of the melody to define the key in modal writing, I've used the same chords as the original and have rewritten the melody of "Automatic." To highlight B♭, the relative Ionian mode of F Mixolydian, I created a melodic dominant to tonic axis in the key of B♭ and highlighted the stable tones in Bb.

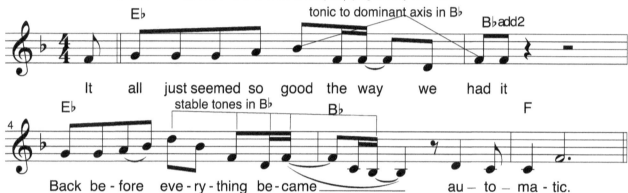

Ex. 8.37 "Automatic" rewrite of the melody implying the key of B<flat>

It all just seemed so good the way we had it

Back be - fore eve - ry - thing be - came_____ au — to — ma - tic.

Now the song sounds as though it were composed in B♭, not F. The F chord that ends the excerpt now sounds like the dominant of B♭ Ionian, not the tonic of F Mixolydian. Conclusion: the importance of melodic choices when using modes cannot be denied.

Dorian

Ex. 8.38 Diatonic triads in the Dorian mode

C m	D m	E♭	F	G m	A dim	B♭
Im	IIm	♭III	IV	Vm	VI^{dim}	♭VII

There are fewer popular songs written completely in the Dorian mode than in the Aeolian mode. This is because it is harder to establish the tonal center in the Dorian mode due to the location of the tritone that occurs between the stable ♭3, and the unstable 6th scale degree. The 6th scale degree in the Dorian mode, being a whole step away from the 5th scale degree, doesn't generate the same amount of tension/release that occurs in the Aeolian mode, where ♭6 is a half step from 5 and moves easily to it. Many songs written in the Dorian mode do not use the fairly difficult to hear and sing 6th scale degree in the melody and, instead, hide it in the harmony.

Ex. 8.39 "It's Too Late" Carole King, Toni Stern

Carole King's "It's Too Late" uses the flavor of the Dorian mode without ever having the F♯, the 6th degree of the A Dorian mode, appear in the melody. Instead, the F♯ is embedded in the D6 chord. The IV and IIm chords in Dorian, because they contain the characteristic 6th scale degree, are used extensively in order to define the sound of this mode.

The melody in the verse of The Beatles' "Eleanor Rigby" begins in the Dorian mode. The 6th scale degree makes a pungent appearance in the melody, but soon reverts to the ♭6, C♮, to cadence in the more stable Aeolian mode.

Ex. 8.40 "Eleanor Rigby" John Lennon, Paul McCartney

The Dorian mode often moves to the parallel Aeolian mode because the Aeolian is a more stable mode than the Dorian and offers easier access to a tonal cadence.

Van Morrison's "Moondance," for instance, moves from a Dorian verse to an Aeolian chorus, with both sections using the same tonal center.

The Phrygian and the Lydian modes are interesting but are rarely employed throughout an entire song. This is probably due to the difficulty in cadencing in these two modes.

Phrygian

Ex. 8.41 Diatonic triads in the Phrygian mode

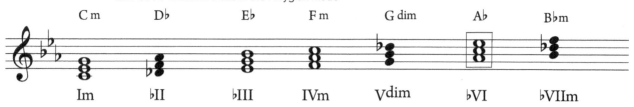

The Phrygian mode can conjure up a typical Spanish sound because of its characteristic ♭2 scale degree that also generates the ♭II major chord. Gloria Estefan, who grew up with the sound of Latin music, gravitated toward this intriguing mode in her 1987 #1 song, "Cant Stay Away From You." The song begins in G Phrygian but as it moves to its chorus it strategically modulates to the relative Ionian key of E♭.

Ex. 8.42 "Can't Stay Away From You" Gloria Estefan

Lydian

Ex. 8.43 Diatonic triads in the Lydian mode

The Lydian mode, along with the Lydian ♭7 mode, (this latter mode, made up of the Lydian mode with ♭7 substituting for ♮7 is used extensively in jazz), is found throughout most of Leonard Bernstein's masterpiece "West Side Story." Bernstein begins "Maria" in the Lydian mode, an extremely unstable mode due to the location of the tritone (one member of the tritone is the tonic!). When he wants to cadence, he wisely reverts to the parallel Ionian mode.

Ex. 8.44 "Maria" music by Leonard Bernstein, lyrics by Stephen Sondheim

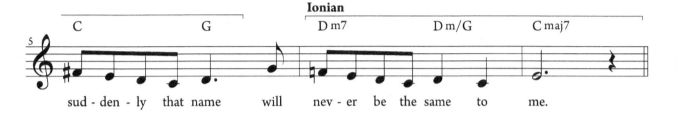

The last two song examples, one in the Phrygian mode and the other in the Lydian mode, begin in those modes, but because of their tonal instability eventually move to either the *relative* Ionian mode (in a relative mode, the two modes share the same notes but the tonics are different [Ex. 8.42]) or the *parallel* Ionian mode (in a parallel mode, the tonic of the two modes is the same but some of the notes of the two modes are different [Ex. 8.44]).

Other examples of how modes are used within songs appear in chapter 16, "Tonal and Rhythmic Strategizing."

Pentatonic scales

Ex. 8.45 Major and minor pentatonic scales

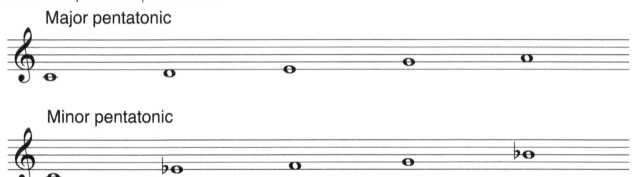

Pentatonic scales that contain no half steps were probably among the first scales used by man; they are found in all cultures. The reason for this is their close relationship to

the overtone series—both the major and minor pentatonic scales lack half steps and the interval of the tritone. They are scales from a simpler time. Why then do they permeate the sophisticated technology-driven pop music of the 21st century? The answer, my friend, is that they provide that essential ingredient, simplicity, a main ingredient in popular songwriting but, more importantly, they are tribal. They connect with everyone—they invite you to participate—to sing along!

Ed Sheeran has connected with a worldwide audience through his talents as a performer/songwriter and through his seductively physical grooves, his rap influenced melodies, and his abundant use of the pentatonic scales—a potent combination that appeals to all cultures (Ex. 8.46).

Ex. 8.46 "Shape Of You" Ed Sheeran, Steve Mac, Johnny McDaid, Kandi Burruss, Tameka Cottle, Kevin Briggs

When used in a postchorus as a chant, the pentatonic scale becomes practically tribal.

Contemporary treatment of tonality—avoiding the obvious

What if you did not want to establish the tonal center at all in the entire song but, instead, only imply it? This is what many contemporary songwriters choose to do. By choosing to imply rather than state the tonic throughout, the music becomes more alight, buoyant, intriguing, and, possibly, more inviting. Although the traditional progression of T, SD, D, T has not been completely abandoned, the avoidance of this progression, especially the avoidance of V moving to I—is apparent in many contemporary songs. Very different perceptions of the tonal center are generated in #2 and #3 in Example 8.45 by rearranging the order of the three primary chords in C major, thereby metrically emphasizing functions other than the tonic.

In Example 8.47, the three primary triads in traditional major placed in different order.

- # **1.** is the traditional, straight-ahead statement of the tonality in the usual order, T, SD, D, T, leaving no doubt as to what the tonal center is.
- # **2.** can be heard as C Ionian but sounds more authentic as G Mixolydian.
- # **3.** can be heard in C Ionian, but could also easily be heard in F Lydian.

Ex. 8.47 Primary chords in major placed in different order

1. **Ionian**

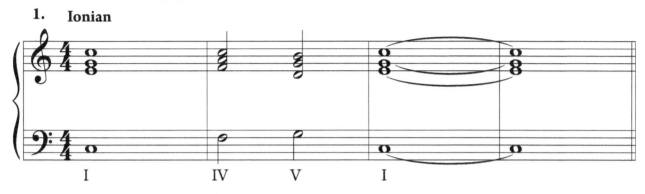

	I	IV	V	I

2. **Mixolydian**

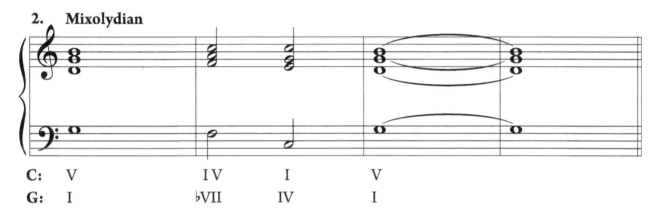

C:	V	IV	I	V
G:	I	♭VII	IV	I

3. **Lydian**

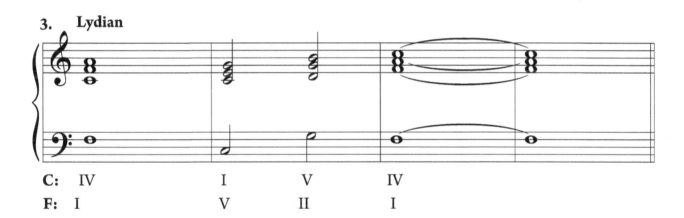

C:	IV	I	V	IV
F:	I	V	II	I

In popular song today, any chord in the diatonic environment can move to any other diatonic chord. As a songwriter, you must be sensitive to how harmonic movements and the quality of the chords (whether they are major or minor, etc.) affect the melody, lyric, and emotional milieu that you are attempting to create.

Although the concept of functionality is hardly passé, this new approach to the use of diatonic chords presents fresh possibilities in chord movement. I use the term "movement" here because I hesitate to use the term chord "progression," simply because "progression" implies movement toward a goal area—a type of harmonic movement that you may—or may not—want to achieve.

In present-day pop songwriting, there is not much interest in having a large harmonic vocabulary that includes chromatic chords or tensions that can be added to basic triads. Nor is there much interest in modulating within the song. Instead, we often find chord patterns that repeat and create a somewhat ambiguous diatonic tonal environment that often implies more than one tonal center. Typically, a harmonic carpet is laid out in a four-measure repeated pattern usually consisting of four chords. Emphasis is placed on the melody, on melodic hooks and melodic phrases that create interest and contrast through (1) effective use of nonchord tones, (2) placement of the melodic phrases in relationship to the harmonies, and (3) changes in the melodic rhythms in different sections. These methods along with changing the tessitura are important ways to create interest and contrast from section to section in a song. Other means used to create contrast include arranging and production techniques such as the use of novel sounds and radical textural changes such as dropping out the drums for an entire section of the song.

Songs written in recent times demonstrate that, when using less traditional root movements, the major scale is still a viable and vibrant environment in which to create songs. The two song examples that follow (Ex. 8.48, Ex. 8.49) contain root movements that do not use typical T, SD, D, T progressions and avoid moving from the dominant chord to the tonic chord.

Ex. 8.48 "Payphone" Adam Levine, Ammar Malik, Benny Blanco, Robopop, Shellback, Wiz Khalifa

Notice that the looped chord movement in "Payphone" (Ex. 8.48) never cadences on the I chord. In fact, when the I chord does appear in the metrically weak second measure, it is a suspended chord, making it an even less obvious tonal resting place. Nearly every melodic phrase ends on an unstable tone, and every harmonic phrase ends on a suspended chord or on the dominant, which is found at the cadence, creating a sense of instability. The prosody in this song is excellent; the music heightens the emotion expressed in the lyric as it reflects the singer's unsettled state of mind.

Ex. 8.49 "Call Me Maybe" Carly Rae Jepsen, Josh Ramsey, Tavish Crowe, René Dif

"Call Me Maybe" (Ex. 8.49) was the breakout hit of the summer of 2012. The chorus's arpeggiated melody captures the sense of adolescent-like playfulness, reinforcing the lyrical concept. Notice that the melody is nearly completely made up of stable tones in the key of G. However, the chord progression that mainly moves down in P4ths, never cadencing on G. The melody's relationship to the harmony creates delightful dissonances that transform what could have been dull into something delightful. The placement of the chords is also unique, adding to the rhythmic call-and-response activity occurring between the strings and the vocal; when the string figure stops, the vocal takes over. Hence, no clashes occur between the melodic line and the chords.

Both "Payphone and "Call Me Maybe" use loop-based chord patterns throughout the song. The chord movement in "Payphone" is: IV, I^{sus}, VIm, V. The chord movement in "Call Me Maybe" is: IV, I, V, VIm, IV, I, V.

Summary

The amount of space given in this chapter to the blues is an indication of its importance in popular songwriting. The use of blues and modes as well as new approaches to traditional scales can enliven your harmonic and melodic vocabulary and help spark your creativity.

As demonstrated throughout this chapter, the root movements of chords created by blues and modes are radically different from the way they move in functional harmony. These blues-generated root movements have influenced root movements in songs that are mainly set in more traditional tonal environments. This expansion of harmonic movements provides a greater freedom for expression, giving you options otherwise not available.

The tonal environments presented in this and the previous chapter are just a part of the available choices you have. Try experimenting with scales that you create as well as all the scales and tonal environments I've listed.

Activities

- If you are attempting to expand your own stylistic vocabulary, allow for the necessary time to listen to the styles you are not yet familiar with. Sing and play along with those songs that have intrigued you. Once you learn a song, attempt to play and sing it in at least two other keys. By doing this, you will reinforce your kinesthetic memory in various keys as you learn the rhythms and textures as well the tonal environments of the songs.
- To absorb the blues vocabulary, practice Ex. 8.50. Sing the minor pentatonic scale as you play the I, ♭III, IV, V, ♭VII chords. Enjoy the modal contradictions, the poignant dissonances that are the lifeblood of the blues. Do this in several different keys.

Ex. 8.50 Blues exercise

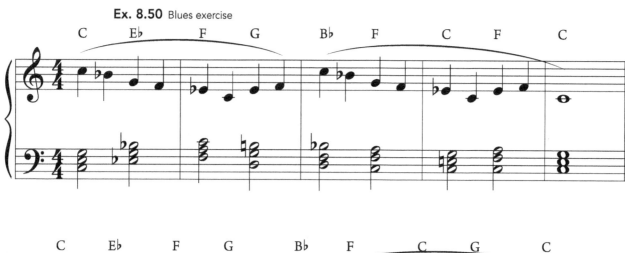

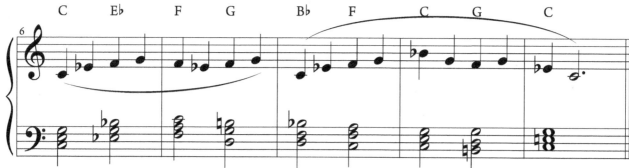

- Write a song that uses the blues/rock harmonic vocabulary.
- Sing and play all the modes, paying close attention to the characteristic notes and the location of the tritone. Practice in all keys. This activity and the following one will take extensive time, but will be worth it.
- Play the diatonic triads in each of the modes, noting the quality of the chord (major, minor, diminished) on each scale degree. Notice what the characteristic note of each mode is and in what chords it appears. Practice in all keys.
- Create a chord pattern in a major key that avoids a V to I cadence and is somewhat tonally ambiguous. Write a section of a song or an entire song using your chord pattern.

PART III

Large Considerations

9

Developmental Techniques

A song idea is often a fragment—either a lyric phrase, a title, or a musical fragment—that asks us to develop it. It is a seed waiting to blossom into something extraordinary; and it is our challenge to allow this seed its life. To develop an idea, some of that idea must be repeated. In a sense, the art of writing a popular song is learning how to repeat ideas, both musical and lyrical, that nonetheless manage to keep the listener involved. Developing and transforming a musical idea has been defined as the ability to create contrast within similarity and similarity within contrast.

Many songs created in this century do not contain a great deal of development; instead, they rely on pure repetition and use of interesting sounds, great grooves, and production devices to enliven the recording. Nonetheless, there are some contemporary songs that do present us with great examples of how to take an idea and with simple developmental techniques such as sequence, extension, truncation, rhythmic displacement, etc., create a song that is both unified and interesting. These techniques do not usually occur in a pristine manner. Rather, they are combined, sometimes with new material, making any formal methodology of teaching this important aspect of composition difficult to fully categorize or communicate. Difficult—but not impossible. If you are open to thinking creatively, you will see and hear in the following examples ways of perceiving musical ideas and their consequences that will open doors that may have previously been closed to you.

The musical idea, the motive

A musical idea for a song often occurs as a rhythmic idea bound to an interval or shape, a musical gesture that has enough interest or potential to induce the composer to continue it and develop it. It is called a *motive*. The motive in (Ex. 9.01) is used in the subsequent examples to demonstrate how developmental techniques can be employed.

Ex. 9.01 Original motive

Repeat the rhythm/change the pitch (rrcp)

Possibly the simplest and most effective thing you can do with a *motive*, beyond simply repeating it verbatim, is to strip the pitch from it, leaving only its rhythm—and when the motive is repeated, change the pitch content. I call this technique *repeat the rhythm, change the pitch*, henceforth referred to as simply: *rrcp*. Let's look the at the moyive stripped of its pitch (Ex. 9.02; ⊙ AUDIO 9.02).

Ex. 9.02 Motive, melodic rhythm

You may choose to change some of the pitches or all the pitches. In (Ex. 9.03A), the last two pitches have been changed from the original motive, while in (Ex. 9.03B), the first three pitches have been changed (⊙ AUDIO 9.03A and B).

Ex. 9.03 Rrcp (retain the pitch, change the rhythm)

In (Ex. 9.04; ⊙ AUDIO 9.04), the original motive is stated and then repeated with every note except the last one changed. I have changed the direction for the first two notes as well as last two notes. Notice how beautifully the two phrases work together. One reason for this natural flow is that the last two notes of the original motive furnish the first two notes of the second phrase. This could easily be the beginning of a song.

Ex. 9.04 Interesting transformation

Original Motive   Transformation

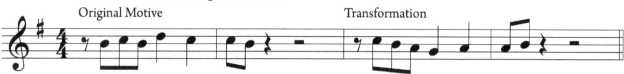

You may want to retain the contour of the melody and repeat the idea, retaining the size and the direction of the intervals but place it at another pitch level. This technique is a more specific use of *rrcp* and produces a *sequence*.

Ex. 9.05 Sequence

original motive   sequence

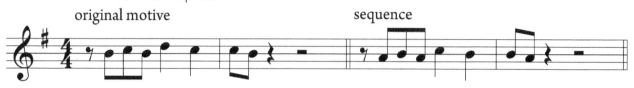

I simply take the original motive in (Ex. 9.05; ▶ AUDIO 9.05) and move every pitch down a *diatonic* second. If I had used the exact quality of the interval (e.g., the first interval in the original motive is a half step, not a whole step), the piece would have modulated to another key.

Here is a motive from a hit song (Ex. 9.06). Do you recognize it?

Ex. 9.06 Motive from hit song

The two measures in (Ex. 9.07) are made up of two phrases, the first referred to as the *antecedent phrase* and the second referred to as the *consequent phrase*. Sometimes this type of two-phrase occurrence is called a *question and answer*. I prefer to use the terms "antecedent" and "consequent," because the actual music in the phrases might indeed imply two questions, or an answer followed by a question.

Ex. 9.07 Antecedent/consequent relationship

The addition of harmony makes this music richer and more interesting (Ex. 9.08).

Ex. 9.08 The melodic motive complete with harmony

Conjunction

Possibly, in an attempt to repeat a motive, it may occur to you to connect phrases to each other. This is usually accomplished with one or more notes. This is a useful device, a developmental technique I've named *conjunction*. It is the musical parallel to the grammatical term (e.g., "and," "but," "then," and idiomatic phrases such as "as well as").

Eric Bazillian, the writer of "One Of Us," brilliantly used a conjunction to make the opening of his song ear-catchingly unique. Here is what Eric wrote (Ex. 9.09):

Ex. 9.09 Conjunction

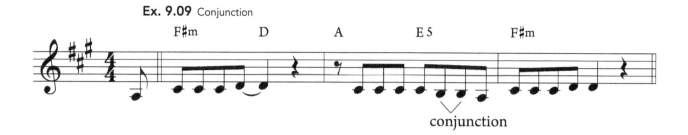

conjunction

Note that the third measure, except for a lack of a tie, is the same as the first measure. What began as a one-measure phrase answered by a one-measure phrase now is a one-measure phrase answered by a two-measure phrase. Bazillian simply added the two-note *conjunction* to the end of his consequent phrase and extended it with the repetition of his original motive.

The opening motive is now also found at the end of the second phrase! This interesting development allows for a lyric with more continuity to emerge. Notice that the lyrical conjunction "and" occurs with the musical conjunction just described (Ex. 9.10).

Ex. 9.10 "One Of Us" Eric Bazillian

If God had a name, what would it be? And would you call it to His face

Extension

Extension is one of the most natural and effective developmental techniques available; simply repeat the motive and add one or more notes to it. In (Ex. 9.11; ▶ AUDIO 9.11), the initial phrase is made into a more complete statement.

Ex. 9.11 Original motive with extension

extension

The use of *extension* also lends itself to the use of parallels in the lyrics. Beginning the second phrase with the same motive often leads naturally to the use of anaphora (Ex. 9.12; ▶ AUDIO 9.12).

Ex. 9.12

If I could find the an-swer, If I could on-ly give you one good rea - son.

Stevie Wonder's lyrics in "Isn't She Lovely" mirror the music; the first two notes of the two phrases receive the same two words (Ex. 9.13).

Ex. 9.13 "Isn't She Lovely" Stevie Wonder

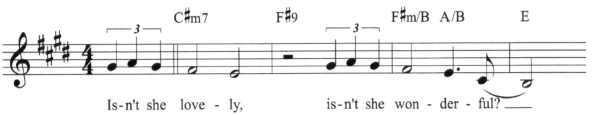

Is-n't she love - ly, is-n't she won - der - ful? _____

In "Overjoyed," Wonder states his musical idea and then restates it. He accelerates it by not leaving as much time between iterations and extends the phrase by repeating the motive two more times, changing the pitches on the last iteration. This allows him to create a musical narrative for his lyric. Here we see how repetition and *extension* combine to produce an extraordinary whole (Ex. 9.14).

Ex. 9.14 "Overjoyed" Stevie Wonder

O - ver time _____ I've been build - ing my cas - tles of love _____

Bruno Mars, a great vocalist, is also a substantial songwriter. "Just The Way You Are," a title potent enough to produce two different #1 songs (this one and Billy Joel's), abundantly displays the use of *melodic extension*. The initial motive in the chorus leads to an extension of that motive (Ex. 9.15).

Ex. 9.15 "Just The Way You Are" initial motive Bruno Mars, Philip Lawrence, Ari Levine, Khalil Walton, Kari Cain

The second phrase is derived from the first. It appears with one of the repeated first notes missing and with an additional *extension* of four notes, transforming the entire melody into a musical narrative (Ex. 9.16).

Ex. 9.16 *"Just The Way You Are" phrases 1 and 2*

When I see your face, ___   There's not a   thing ___ that I ___ would change,

As this music grows, each musical gesture is born from the previous one. A unified, completely organic sounding chorus emerges like a butterfly emerging from a chrysalis (Ex. 9.17).

Ex. 9.17 *"Just The Way You Are" extension*

thing ___ that   I ___ would   change, ___

The music for the title (Ex. 9.18) is derived from the extension (Ex. 9.17) by simply changing the pitch of the first two notes!

Ex. 9.18 *"Just The Way You Are" title phrase*

Just ___   the   way ___ you   are. ___

There is prosody at play here, as the same motive is retained while the lyrics state, "There's not a thing that I would change 'cause you're amazing just the way you are." Was this perfect occurrence of music and words coincidence, serendipity, or rational choice? Possibly a bit of all three!

Truncation

Truncation shortens the motive or phrase. Example 9.19 (▶ AUDIO 9.19) states the original motive, truncates it, and immediately sequences the truncation. This is an example of how developmental techniques are often combined to create interesting music.

Ex. 9.19 Truncation combined with sequence

You may try many variations of truncation and extension until you find something you can use. Here is another variation. Notice that the three phrases form a natural sounding musical whole (Ex. 9.20; ▶ AUDIO 9.20).

Ex. 9.20 Motive followed by two examples of truncation

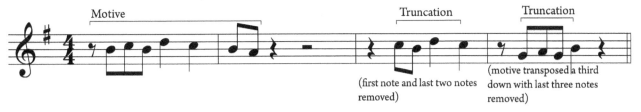

(first note and last two notes removed)

(motive transposed a third down with last three notes removed)

"Umbrella," one of Rihanna's biggest hits, benefits from the use of truncation. Notice that the lyric "under my umbrella" is also truncated along with the music. If only a small portion or segment of the phrase is used, the term *segmentation* can be applied (Ex. 9.21).

Ex. 9.21 "Umbrella" Christopher Stewart, Terius Nash, Thaddis Harrel, Shawn Carter

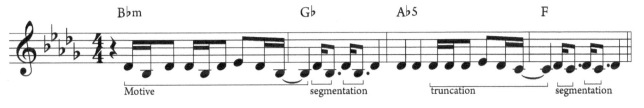

You can stand un-der my um-brel-la ____ el-la, el-la, eh, eh, eh. Un-der my um-brel-la ____ el-la, el-la, eh,

Rhythmic displacement

Another very useful developmental technique is *rhythmic displacement*, where a rhythm that appears in one metric area is displaced to another metric area. This technique is most powerful if the repeating figure is placed in a contrasting metrical setting, e.g., if a rhythmic figure begins on an upbeat, it is effective to begin the next phase using the same figure on a downbeat, or if a figure begins on a strong beat (e.g., the first beat of a measure), it is effective if the same figure begins on a weak beat of a measure (e.g., the fourth beat) (Ex. 9.22; ▶ AUDIO 9.22).

Ex. 9.22 Rhythmic displacement

159

Possibly the most famous use of this device is by George Gershwin. His brother, Ira, could not help but use the unique rhythmic effect that George had created as the genesis for the title of the song (Ex. 9.23).

Ex. 9.23 "Fascinating Rhythm" music by George Gershwin, lyrics by Ira Gershwin

Fas-cin-a-ting rhy-thm, you've got me on the go! Fas-cin - a-ting rhy-thm, I'm all a quiv-er

The first phrase, beginning on the downbeat of measure 1, contains seven eighth notes including the eighth-note rest. This same phrase then begins on the upbeat of beat 4, rhythmically displacing the phrase by an eighth note. This activity of alternating downbeat and upbeat positions continues with the last iteration of the motive rhythmically changed in order to get back to a more regular sense of meter.

Taylor Swift uses both *rhythmic displacement* and *segmentation* in the setting of title "Shake It Off" (Ex. 9.24). Swift grabs just a segment of her motive that appears in measure 1 on beats 2 and 3 and has it reappear in measure 3 on beat 1 on a strong beat, and then on beat 4, a weak beat. The resulting syncopation creates an infectious hook.

Ex. 9.24 "Shake It Off" Taylor Swift

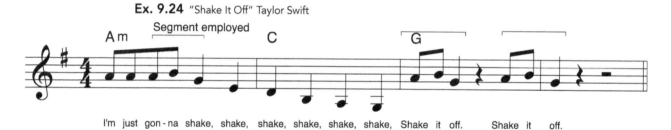

I'm just gon-na shake, shake, shake, shake, shake, shake, Shake it off. Shake it off.

Rhythmic displacement is a great commercial writing device. The hook phrase repeats here with little danger that it will be monotonous, since it appears in different parts of the measure each time (weak beat 2, strong beat 1, weak beat 4)—it's a hook with two barbs!

Lady Gaga and Rob Fusari use all three developmental techniques: rrcp, extension, and rhythmic displacement in their hit song "Paparazzi." The rhythm, the melodic contour, the interval of a descending P5th, all help define the almost Beethovenian idea (Ex. 9.25).

Ex. 9.25 "Paparazzi" motive

A repeat of the motive follows, but now with an added pickup note acting almost as a conjunction to help connect the idea to itself. When the idea is repeated for a third time, two pickup eighth notes are used (Ex. 9.26).

Ex. 9.26 *"Paparazzi" Stephanie Germanotta and Rob Fusari*

After three repetitions, usually something must change in order to avoid monotony. (You might want to consider this a compositional rule of thumb). This is a composer's moment of truth; at this juncture, the entire idea may either be abandoned or it may be developed into something unique and wonderful. Lady Gaga and Rob Fusari prove in this moment, in this choice, that they are talented and savvy songwriters (Ex. 9.27).

Ex. 9.27 *"Paparazzi" verse development*

This choice took courage—the courage to create new material. But be aware that even the new material is derived from a rhythm we already know. Four different specific developmental techniques occur in this example. First, the rhythmic motive is transformed by changing the pitch (rrcp) (Ex. 9.28).

Ex. 9.28 Transformation of the original motive using *rrcp*

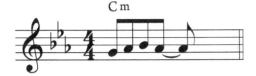

The transformed motive is then extended (Ex. 9.29).

Ex. 9.29 Extension of the motivic transformation

Extension

In the next phrase of the song something even more extraordinary occurs; it is a slight variation on *rhythmic displacement* (Ex. 9.30). The writers take the extension of the fourth phrase—the last five notes of the phrase—and begin the next phrase with them on the downbeat of the new measure. Two notes (D and C) are added in the middle of the phrase, on beats 3 and 4 in the first measure to make the phrase feel more rhythmically comfortable. This is a use of *extension*.

Ex. 9.30 Rhythmic transformation

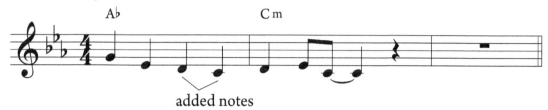

added notes

What was once the middle and end of a melodic phrase has become the beginning of the new melodic phrase. Both phrases melodically end the same way. This last time, however, the melody is harmonized by the I chord instead of the ♭VI chord.

There is something almost magical in creating an idea and then transforming it until a unified whole is achieved. But it is not magic that makes it work; it is the knowledge of how to transform and develop your idea that creates the illusion of magic. I believe it helps you to know that these transformations are possible. Now that you know, isn't it exciting!

One question that students invariably ask me in songwriting classes is: "Do you think that the writer actually thought about all these techniques while writing this song?" My answer is, "No, . . . the writer may not even know the name of a technique that s/he is using, but because of years of attempting to compose and, in the process, gradually accumulating knowledge of what seems to work and what doesn't, s/he has absorbed all sorts of techniques." Thinking about techniques while writing will usually slow down the process, but knowing these techniques and the possible options they offer as well as you know your name allows you to write the song. You should work on these techniques until they become second nature to you. This may take some time, but it is a process that produces lasting results.

Circling back process

An important practice in writing a song is to circle back on what you've already written. Circling back and playing with these ideas, removing or adding a note or a part of the phrase, extending it, or rhythmically displacing all or part of the original phrase may be just what is needed to inspire a fresh idea. Only you will know that this "new" idea is in part borrowed from or generated from something you've already created. Once you have successfully completed the section of the song using this circling back technique, you will have created a section that has an organic connection to the previous section, yet is different enough to sound new.

Basic developmental techniques can be isolated from one another, but as already viewed in "Paparazzi," they are most often combined with one another. This is another indication that compositional choices do not emanate entirely from the rational mind but from a feeling for a desired effect—something that is usually more subtle and elusive. However, if the rational mind is primed to participate in the creative process, it can provide options and possibilities as well as necessary information so that the creative flow is not interrupted or stopped.

Retrograde

This is a technique that usually begins as an intellectual exercise, but can lead to interesting, even extraordinary, results. What if you start your motive from its last note and write it backward? This is a developmental technique called *retrograde*. Here is the motive I've been using as an example throughout this chapter, followed by its exact retrograde (Ex. 9.31; ▶ AUDIO 9.31).

Ex. 9.31 Retrograde of original motive

The resulting music is very usable; this could easily be the beginning of a song.

Inversion

Ex. 9.32 Original motive and inversion

The term "inversion" refers to inverting the direction of the intervals used (Ex. 9.32; ▶ AUDIO 9.32). If a melody moves up a diatonic second, then its inversion moves down a diatonic second. (It is best to think diatonically, so that the quality of the interval, e.g., whether it is a major 2nd or a minor 2nd, is not a factor.) If you invert your motive only to discover that the results are not satisfying, try to combine it with another technique, e.g., try transposing the inversion up or down to see if that can produce a better result (Ex. 9.33; ▶ AUDIO 9.33).

Ex. 9.33

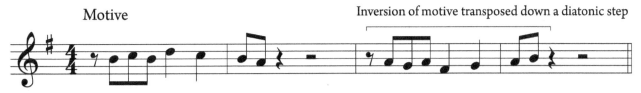

By transposing the inversion down one diatonic step, I achieved a more satisfying result.

Retrograde and *inversion* seldom appear in their pristine form in popular song. These techniques more often appear in a general, gestural way, as they do in the "Up On The Roof," Carole King and Gerry Goffin's gem from 1962.

Carole King has a glorious gift for melody and the developmental know-how to unify a song. The DNA of the melody of "Up On The Roof" is found in its opening ascending P4th interval and in measure 2, where the interval of a descending P4th shows up in the melodic outline. King develops it further in measure 3, where the melody, having arrived at the tonic, skips down yet another P4th (Ex. 9.34).

Ex. 9.34 "Up On The Roof" music by Carole King, lyrics by Gerry Goffin

Within this melody are several developmental techniques that defy exacting labels. Part of the verse incorporates something close to *inversion* in a couple of areas. The opening two notes of the first phase of the song, the ascending P4th, have repercussions throughout this song. The end of the first phrase on the lyric "getting me down" contains a P4th on beats 1 and 2 with an eighth note that appears in between them (Ex. 9.35).

Ex. 9.35 The main motive of the song

Carole King masterfully uses melodic extension. She takes the second half of the first phrase and begins the second phrase with a slightly altered version of it (She adds an eighth-note C on the first beat, followed by the B and G on the second beat and third beats respectfully) and then extends that phrase (Ex. 9.36).

Ex. 9.36 Beginning of A section

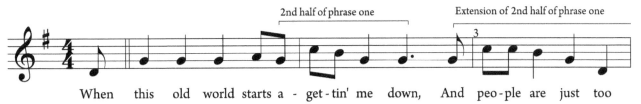

When this old world starts a-get-tin' me down, And peo-ple are just too

much for me to face,

Although this melody contains the developmental devices and techniques demonstrated, nothing is totally prescribed or academic. Rather, the techniques employed hint at and demonstrate ways of approaching music that allow for fluidity and exploration of the materials that allows you to create something original, memorable, and organic.

The A section itself is worthy of making this song stand out from the pack, but what completely takes this song to another level is the B section or bridge. The three-note motive derived from measure 2 of the A section begins the B section, this time stated in quarter-note values that are *rhythmically displaced* twice, and those magical measures are then *sequenced* up a third and then extended. (The sequence does not appear in Ex. 9.37, but if you know the song, you can't help but hear it).

Ex. 9.37 "Up On The Roof" bridge

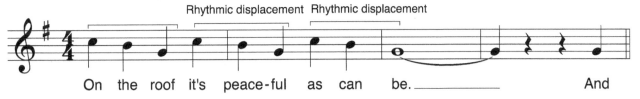

On the roof it's peace-ful as can be. And

The last phrase of this song continues the transformation of the original motive (Ex. 9.38). The motive has been transformed using the same shape—but is inverted. The 2nd goes up, as does the 3rd and the P4th, this time rising up on the roof . . . up to pop music heaven!

Ex. 9.38 "Up On The Roof" comparison of beginning and ending

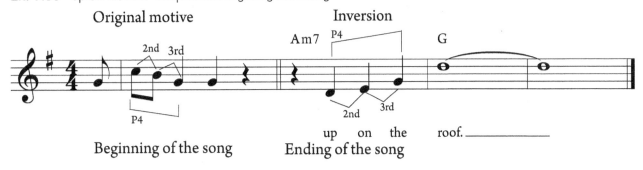

The topography of the phrases

No doubt, you will find more developmental techniques in the *Great American Songbook* than in today's popular songs. Alan Menken, one of today's most talented songwriters, continues that tradition in his writing for the theater and for the movies. "Beauty And The Beast" is a song in which Menken takes one motive and stays with it until he develops it into a completely satisfying song. He first composes a five-note motive, then retains the rhythm while varying both the pitch and the melodic contour (Ex. 9.39).

Ex. 9.39 "Beauty And The Beast" lyrics by Howard Ashman, music by Alan Menken

Most striking in this example is the way the phrases are spaced, what I refer to as the *topography of the phrases*, the layout of the musical landscape. There are six beats between the last articulated note of the first phrase and the beginning of the second phrase, and six beats between the last articulated note of the second phrase and the beginning of the third phrase; but there are only two beats that separate the last note of the third phrase from the beginning of the fourth phrase and two beats the separate the last note of the fourth phrase from the beginning of the fifth phrase. This is an example of *phrasal acceleration*, a technique that provides another way to capture our interest. It also allows the last two musical phrases to support one lyrical phrase.

Notice the change in melodic contour that occurs in measures 5–7, an example of retrograde of the pitch content but one that retains the rhythm of the original phrase. Howard Ashman, a highly sensitive and talented lyricist, reacted perfectly to this music. As the contour of the phrases change direction, moving from ascending phrases to descending ones, the lyric references this change: "then somebody bends unexpectedly."

Paul Simon has managed to combine his poetic sensibility with a grasp of what has mass appeal. Though difficult to pin down, his writing is well worth studying. One transcendent song, that became a #1 Adult Contemporary hit in 1975, is "My Little Town." The topography of the phrases in this song is natural and interesting—the phrases change meter and contain organic melodies that spin on and on following their own logic. They are laid out in a completely natural conversation-like way, ignoring the usual demands found in most popular songwriting.

The song captures the feeling shared by those of us who have long ago left our own little towns for the big city or for the world at large. This song is an example of Simon's ability to take a melodic idea and transform it.

Ex. 9.40 "My Little Town" Paul Simon

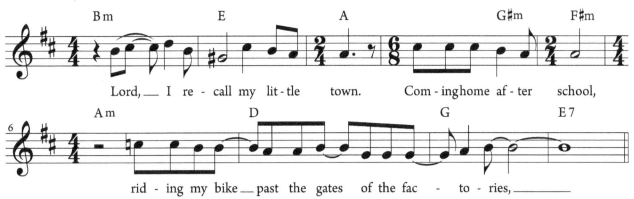

The music in measure 4, the 6/8 measure, obviously derives its melodic pitches from the end of the previous phrase and rhythmically transforms them. The phrase that follows, in measure 6, begins to restate the melody, originally in A major, in the parallel minor key, A minor—but, instead, extends and modulates it to the key of G. The long four-measure phrase beginning in measure 6 in (Ex. 9.40) possibly inspired Simon to write that he went "past the gates," just as the phrase itself had gone past the anticipated metric stopping point. Whether that was a conscious decision, that kind of event happens when a writer's muse is in the room.

All the music in (Ex. 9.40) is derived from the first vocal phrase of the song (Ex. 9.41).

Ex. 9.41 "My Little Town" opening phrase

Observe how the last three notes in (Ex. 9.40) are derived from the first three notes of the opening motive of the song. Everything connects to everything else, yet nothing is literally repeated.

Summary

You can perceive from the Paul Simon and the Carole King examples that while developmental techniques can be isolated and demonstrated in an academic way, the actual process of composition often involves combining possibilities, developments, and permutations of a motive that may not be so obvious. Nonetheless, I strongly advise you to learn each of these individual developmental tools in a pristine way. Once your mind has absorbed the information, it will automatically develop ideas in ways that you may not be able to name, but that have a logical and poetic connection to one another.

Once you create a motive, you should first study it carefully. Be cognizant of its rhythm, its shape, the intervals in it, how it sounds with different harmonies, etc. Play and sing it many times so that it really becomes a part of you, and then act freely with your original materials, and always strive to surprise and delight yourself. If you succeed, it will practically assure that your song will surprise and delight others.

Activities

- Create a motive
- Repeat the motive, retain the same rhythm, and change the pitch
- Extend the motive or connect the motive using a musical conjunction.
- Be aware of the contour of each phrase as well as the contour of the larger sections of the song; try to ensure that all the phrase contours are not the same.
- Develop just the extension.
- Sequence all or part of it.
- Be aware of the topography of the phrases; change the amount of time that occurs between phrases.
- Experiment: try to work with the inversion and the retrograde of the motive.
- Try transposing an inversion or retrograde. Try to find a way to make one or both logically follow something you've already created.
- Does the motive lend itself to rhythmic displacement? If so, attempt to rhythmically displace it.
- As you compose, keep circling back to use something that has already occurred. This will help you achieve unity in the song.
- Play with the clay.

10

The Melodic Outline and the Melodic Step Progression

The melodic outline

The *melodic outline* defines the basic architecture of a melody. Once you start to see it and use it, you will be able to design and control your melodies over a greater span of time. Locating or defining the melodic outline initially may seem to be a daunting task, but is fairly easy once you know what to be aware of. A melodic outline is made up of:

• Notes that fall on the strong beats of the measure.
• The highest notes and the lowest notes in the phrase or group of phrases.
• Longer value notes and repeated notes.
• Notes that begin and end phrases.

The melodic outline is also useful as an analytical tool to help give you a bird's-eye view of your song. It is one of the strongest means to control directionality and progression in your melody.

Melodic step progression

The scale is the foundation of most music and it provides you with one of the most powerful of melodic tools: the *melodic step progression*. In order to strategically use melodic step progressions, you must look to the melodic outline that provides the architecture of the melody.

Here is a scale: its descent from E♭3 down to E♭2 initially may not call to mind any song that you know; yet the scale itself provides the melodic outline and foundation for the iconic "Over The Rainbow" (Exs. 10.01–10.02).

Ex. 10.01

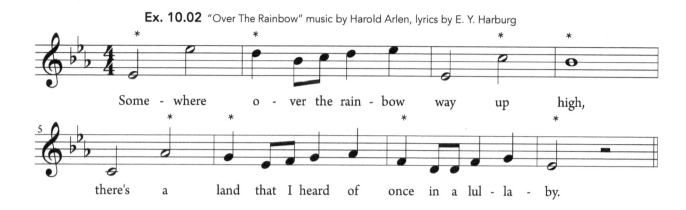

Ex. 10.02 "Over The Rainbow" music by Harold Arlen, lyrics by E. Y. Harburg

Some - where   o - ver the rain - bow   way   up   high,

there's   a   land that I heard   of   once in a lul - la - by.

Notice in Example 10.02 that the melodic step progression (marked with asterisks) is formed on beats 1 and 3, the strong beats in 4/4 time.

You've no doubt heard remarks such as "The melody didn't seem to go anywhere" made in an attempt to critique a melody that either you or someone in a songwriters' group had written. You might have wondered, as I have, what was meant by that remark. How could you make a melody "go somewhere"? Since a scale is the easiest type of melody to sing and to follow, one possible answer is: use a melodic step progression, because a melody that is built on a melodic step progression is automatically provided with directionality.

The Rolling Stone's "Angie" contains a memorable melody. What makes it memorable are a number of factors, including its rhythm and its lyric. But what gives it cohesion and direction, as well as memorability, is the melodic step progression it contains (Ex. 10.03).

Ex. 10.03 "Angie" Keith Richards, Mick Jagger

An - gie,   An - gie,   when will those clouds dis - ap-pear? _____

A melodic step progression can propel a melody over a long distance. In the standard "For Once In My Life," simply shown here with its melodic outline, the progression of *mi* to *fa* to *sol* takes sixteen measures (Ex. 10.04). Within those measures is another melodic step progression from *la* to *ti* (marked with **).

Ex. 10.04 *"For Once In My Life" lyrics by Ronald Miller, music by Orlando Murden*

For once in my life I have some one who needs me; Someone I've needed so long.   For

once unafrid,   I will go where life leads me,   And somehow I know I'll be strong.

The main function of a melodic step progression is to cause the melody to progress in a logical, memorable manner. However, there should be nothing that sounds academic or overly prescribed in the resulting melody. Of course, this is true in most aspects of music making, whether you are performing on an instrument or composing. You must be vigilant in keeping your creative light burning, understanding that the best techniques go unnoticed.

Here is a descending E Mixolydian scale that descends from its fifth. I will use it as an outline or guide for a melody (Ex. 10.05).

Ex. 10.05 *Descending E Mixolydian scale*

Here is an elaboration of it (Ex. 10.06):

Ex. 10.06

This result is okay, but a bit too academic sounding; it moves too logically and predictably.

Here is a more creative rendering (Ex. 10.07):

Ex. 10.07 *"Norwegian Wood" John Lennon and Paul McCartney*

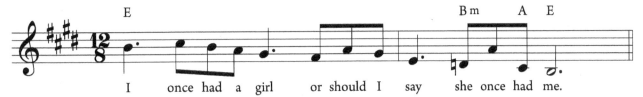

I   once had a girl   or should I   say   she once had   me.

Most likely the genesis for the melody to John Lennon's and Paul McCartney's little masterpiece is the descending Mixolydian scale. Although this melody moves logically, it is not governed by any strict adherence to following each scale degree by using the same pattern. Nonetheless, it is the scale that gives the melody its direction and unity.

"Lonely Tonight," a 2015 country hit sung by Blake Shelton, uses melodic step progressions throughout its verse section (Ex. 10.08). Its prechorus section also contains a melodic step progression that could have easily have become too predictable and less interesting if the final note had been the expected stable C instead of the delightfully unexpected unstable B♭. *The melodic step progression in this example and in others that follow are marked with asterisks*.*

Ex. 10.08 "Lonely Tonight" Brent Anderson, Ryan Hurd

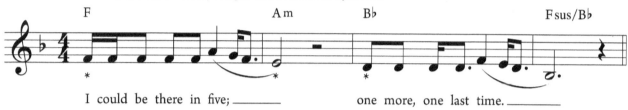

One of the greatest exponents in the use of melodic step progressions was Richard Rodgers, who for over fifty years wrote masterpieces of popular song with an amazing breadth, from the insouciant "Lady Is A Tramp" to the sentimental "The Sound Of Music."

One of the ways that Rodgers highlighted the directionality of the melodic step progression was to create a melodic pedal point of one or two notes, either at the top of the melody or at its bottom, and by doing so, craft a point of reference so that the melodic movement could more easily be measured and, more importantly, felt by the listener.

Here is a song that Rodgers wrote with his first major collaborator, Lorenz Hart, for the iconic Broadway musical, "Pal Joey" (Ex. 10.09):

Ex. 10.09 "Bewitched" music by Richard Rodgers, lyrics by Lorenz Hart

Another of Rodger's songs, this one written with his second major collaborator, Oscar Hammerstein, uses the same technique but reverses the placement of the melodic pedal, this time making it a low note in the melody (Ex. 10.10).

Ex. 10.10 "The Surrey With The Fringe On Top" music by Richard Rodgers, lyrics by Oscar Hammerstein

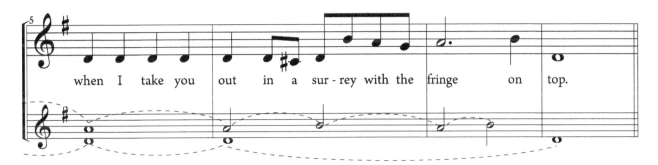

Rodgers showed the world how to use *solfege* (i.e., to sing using musical symbols) and, in the process, fortuitously showed composers how to use a melodic step progression (Ex. 10.11).

Ex. 10.11 "Do-Re-Mi" music by Richard Rodgers, lyrics by Oscar Hammerstein

One of the most popular songs of the last century (it was recorded by over 1,500 artists), "Stardust," initially seemed to me to be a strange candidate for such popularity because of its melodic angularity and almost continual change in melodic direction (Ex. 10.12). This anomaly prompted me to examine its melodic outline—and there it was: an almost perfectly outlined scale!

Ex. 10.12 "Stardust" music by Hoagy Carmichael, lyrics by Mitchell Parrish

Some - times I won - der why I spend the lone - ly night

dream - ing of a song; ___ the mel - o - dy haunts my rev - erie, ___

Many songs from the Golden Age of American Popular Song (circa 1915–1950) use this technique. So, too, do today's songs. However, today's melodic step progressions may appear in more subtle ways.

Ariana Grande had a #1 hit in 2014 with "Problem," a song that showed off her extraordinary range with the help of a melodic step progression. Notice how the end of the first phrase moves to the high F♯ that drops down to the D♯, while the end of the second phrase moves to the F♯ and continues on by step to high G♯ (Ex. 10.13).

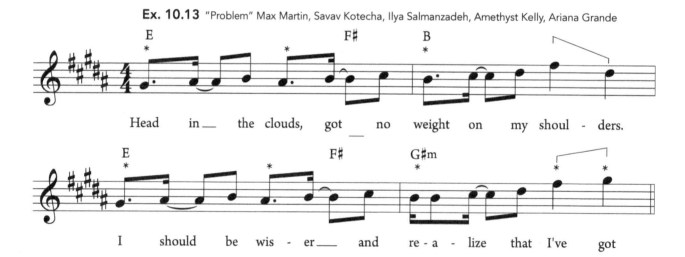

Ex. 10.13 "Problem" Max Martin, Savav Kotecha, Ilya Salmanzadeh, Amethyst Kelly, Ariana Grande

Head in ___ the clouds, got no weight on my shoul - ders.

I should be wis - er ___ and re - a - lize that I've got

You may wonder: must your melody keep the same direction—up or down the scale—in order to employ this technique? Absolutely not! Sometimes a melodic step progression will gradually move between only two or three scale notes, but if those notes are strategically placed, the listener will experience a real sense of progression.

The next example, "The Climb," demonstrates this, and in doing so, also exposes the power of prosody. The melody attempts to climb, to reach the peak by moving from *do* to *re* to *mi*. Moving from *do* to *re* is no problem, but since the primary tone tendency of *re* is to move down to *do*, the melody initially capitulates to that tendency. Only after a Sisyphus-like effort is made does *re* progress to *mi*. This striving for and failing, and finally succeeding, occurs in the music, which perfectly reflects the lyrics (Ex. 10.14).

Ex. 10.14 "The Climb" Jesse Alexander, Jon Mabe

This example also demonstrates how a melodic outline containing a melodic step progression can keep a listener focused over a great many measures.

The chorus of Lady Gaga's "Paparazzi" contains the same movement of *do* to *re* to *mi*, but this time without the struggle; instead, it is an expression of pure joy (Ex. 10.15).

Ex. 10.15 "Paparazzi" Stephanie Germanotta, Rob Fusari

Quite often, two melodic step progressions occur within a melody, one made up of the highest notes and one made up of the lowest notes; this is what occurs in "Paparazzi."

The melodic outline in relationship to the actual melody

Not all melodies contain a melodic step progression within their melodic outline. The melodic outline might contain leaps that demand connections that the actual melody usually provides by stepwise motion in the form of either scales or embellishing patterns.

Richard Marx, a talented songwriter with a special gift for writing memorable melodies, wrote and performed "Right Here Waiting," a number 1 pop hit in 1989 (Ex. 10.16).

Ex. 10.16 "Right Here Waiting" Richard Marx

Where-ev-er you go, ____ what-ev-er you do, ____ I will ___ be right ___ here wait - ing for you. ___

If you play or sing just the melodic outline of Marx's song, the beauty of the complete melody is hardly discernible. The details, the notes in between the melodic outline, obviously make a big difference. Nonetheless, the melodic outline, like the walls and ceiling of a handsome room, defines its structure. Let's take a closer look at the furniture and paintings that occupy and decorate this room (Ex. 10.17).

Ex. 10.17 The notes in between the notes of the melodic outline

Where-ev-er you go, ____ what-ev-er you do, ___ I will   be right ___here wait - ing for you. ___

The melodic outline contains a number of disjunct intervals, skips of P4ths and M3rds. Notice that in the complete melody all but one of these intervals are filled in with conjunct intervals. In fact, all the notes that connect the notes of the melodic outline are either scalar patterns or ornamental or embellishing patterns.

In demonstrating this aspect of melody writing, I am not suggesting that you begin your melody with the melodic outline. Rather, I believe that as you create your melody, you should simply be aware of the outline of your melody as you progress in your writing.

Process

The following is a demonstration of my process in composing a melody. Although the melodic outline is only one of many aspects of the melody that I take into consideration, it is one of the most important, because it helps me grasp the architecture and progression of the melody over a large span of time.

Once I compose a phrase, I spend a short time examining it, musing if I should write a new phrase or repeat it. I try to hear where the phrase might lead. In Example 10.18, I am aware of the F, G, C, E melodic outline as well as the melodic step progression of E, F, G, F, E. I am also aware of an arch contour made up of the highest notes of the melody (⊙ AUDIO 10.18).

Ex. 10.18 Phrase #1

I decide to repeat the first phrase with a slight alteration; I omit the first F and remove the tie, slightly changing the rhythm (Ex. 10.19; ⊙ AUDIO 10.19).

Ex. 10.19 Phrase #2

I start the next phrase on the downbeat in order to contrast it with the previous phrases and choose to make the next phrases grow in intensity by using a melodic step progression starting on the note A (following the highest note of the last phrase, G). I increase the intensity with a B and then allow the melody to retreat back down to G and to the gravitational pull of C, the tonic. I then start the next measure after the downbeat and enliven it with two sixteenth notes and truncate it by leaving off the last note (Ex. 10.20; ⊙ AUDIO 10.20).

Ex. 10.20 Phrases #3 and #4

The fifth phrase can work as a sequence, so I begin the sequence on F, the next logical note derived from the downward movement of A to G. The movement from F to E now seems to be asking for the last phrase to move to D, which it does (Ex. 10.21; ⊙ AUDIO 10.21).

Ex. 10.21 Phrases #5 and #6

As I listen to the entire eight measures, the too-predictable phrase structure bothers me; there are too many one-measure phrases. I decide to combine measures 7–8 into one complete two-measure phrase. This is more musically satisfying.

I also use this as an opportunity to highlight the melodic step progression of F, E, D by placing the D on the downbeat of measure 8 (Ex. 10.22; ⊙ AUDIO 10.22).

Ex. 10.22 Rewrite of phrase #5 and #6 into phrase #5

Here are the completed eight measures (Ex. 10.23; ⊙ AUDIO 10.23):

Ex. 10.23

The following analysis indicates the most important notes in the melody. Certain notes within the melody carry more weight because of their metric placement or because of their length, and form the melodic outline, designated by straight lines. The melodic outline also helps delineate the melodic step progression, designated with asterisks (Ex. 10.24; ⊙ AUDIO 10.24).

Ex. 10.24 The melodic outline and the melodic step progression

Harmony almost always adds an enhancement to the melody. Keep in mind that this melody was written first and chords were then added to it (Ex. 10.25; ⊙ AUDIO 10.25).

Ex. 10.25 Melody with harmony

Melodic contour

A melody's outline also reveals the contour of the melody, affording us a better view of the song's architecture. There are a number of ways of seeing and hearing the contour of a melody. You may look at each individual phrase and perceive its contour. If too many phrases have the same contour, it might indicate monotony is developing and that a change of direction in some of the phrases might be needed. This observation is important within a section, but is especially important from section to section because a change in melodic contour is a powerful contrasting device used between sections.

There are only five basic melodic shapes or contours: an *ascending* contour, a *descending* contour, a combination of the two that form either an *arch* or an *inverted arch*, and a *stationary* melody that doesn't move much at all (Ex. 10.26).

Ex. 10.26 Melodic contours

Ascending

Descending

Arch

Inverted Arch

Stationary

Although the contour of your melody is usually not your first consideration when writing a song, it is wise to listen and observe what direction your phrases have taken, whether all the phrases have the same shape (which might produce monotony), whether the entire section is moving in one direction—upward or downward—or whether your melody has progressed at all.

Ex. 10.27 "Can You Feel The Love" music by Elton John, lyrics by Tim Rice

The first four measures of this beautifully written song have an overall directionality that is very satisfying (Ex. 10.27). The first phrase is an arch contour, the second is also an arch contour with a shorter descent, and the third (measures 3–4) is a longer arch. When we trace the overall contour from measure 1 to measure 5 we see that the entire melody gradually ascends with a slight descent at its very end. We also perceive a melodic step progression (marked with asterisks) in measure 3 and 4 that moves from B♭ to C to D to E♭ back down to D and C.

Summary

The process of writing a song is one that involves zooming in on important details and zooming out so that the overall direction of the melody and the architecture of the entire song are healthily maintained. Being aware of the melodic outline is an important part of the zooming out process.

Once you are conscious of the melodic outline, the importance of directionality, and how to incorporate melodic step progressions into your writing, your melodies will become stronger, have more direction, and be increasingly memorable.

Activities

- Study the melodies of songs that attract you. Look for melodic step progressions, especially those that occur in the melodic outline.
- Revisit songs you have written. Are melodic step progressions present? If not, consider rewriting some or part of your melodies if you feel they can be enhanced by the inclusion of a melodic step progression.
- Study the melodic structures of sections of songs that have attracted you and examine the melodic contour of each section. For example, in a verse/chorus song, is there a noticeable difference in the melodic contour of the verse section from the chorus section?
- Perform the same study in songs you have written.

11

Form and Function

Song forms

The *outer form* of a song, i.e., the entire form of the song, is important because it is the vessel that holds the cargo, the bottle that holds the wine. But like a wine bottle, whose shape is practical and houses wines that may range from $1.98 to those that sell for $998.00 or more, song form does not alter the value of the song; as in wine, it is the content of a song that determines its worth.

It is important for you to choose the most effective outer form for your song so that it can provide the proper vehicle for your message. However, do not get the notion that you simply choose a form and fill it in, like painting by numbers. The choices you make within every section, the *inner form*, i.e., the phrase structures that occur within each section, whether it is balanced or unbalanced, the order of the phrases, the amount of space between phrases, etc., along with the content of the entire song are more important determinants of how a listener tunes in to your song. The actual function of your song, your ideas and how you present them, ultimately determines its form.

Popular songs are compact, usually lasting two-and-a-half to four-and-a-half minutes. If a song is to become popular, repetition is obligatory; therefore, all popular song forms repeat or contain repeated sections.

Verse, verse, verse

Songs using a *strophic form*, in which all verses or stanzas of the text are sung to the same music, have provided a simple and effective way to record the aural history of a people or a tribe from time immemorial. Verses that follow one upon another serve well to tell stories and to relate chronological or historical events.

"1913 Massacre" by Woody Guthrie is a song written in strophic form that chronicles and comments on the unfortunate incident that resulted in seventy-three children being trampled to death because of a panic in a dance hall after somebody jokingly yelled "Fire!" Guthrie begins it this way:

> Take a trip with me in 1913,
> To Calumet, Michigan, in the copper country.
> I will take you to a place called Italian Hall,
> Where the miners are having their big Christmas ball.

Here is a summation of the ten verses that Guthrie wrote:

"1913 Massacre" by Woody Guthrie

Verse 1
Guthrie invites you the listener to copper country, Calamut, Michigan, where a Christmas party is being held in the Italian Hall.

Verse 2
He verbally paints the scene of the party that is taking place up a high staircase in the dancehall, where adults are dancing and children are gathered around the Christmas tree.

Verse 3
Guthrie furnishes more verbal painting of friendly people singing and dancing as you join in.

Verse 4
You ask about pay and discover that even though they risk their lives daily, they make only a dollar a day in the copper mines.

Verse 5
You listen to a girl play the piano and the author reminds you that the bosses and thugs are milling outside.

Verse 6
One of the thugs yells, "There's a fire!" But that is denied immediately by a woman, who asks that everyone continue to party.

Verse 7
Some people, however, try to get out, but the thugs hold the door closed.

Verse 8
Panic sets in, and people rush down the steep staircase to the door and are trampled on while the bosses and thugs outside laugh.

Verse 9
The terribly sad result is then described: seventy-three dead children are carried to the Christmas tree.

Verse 10
The piano plays a funeral tune as the bosses are met by the moans and wailing of the bereaved "See what your greed for money has done."

It is obvious that the focal point in this song is the reporting of the events, the content of the lyrics—not the music. The song form is functional, a vehicle that repeats and repeats and, in doing so, becomes transparent after a short time and allows the listener to fully focus on the story being told.

Any number of subjects works well in this form, especially if there is some sort of list involved. Gordon Lightfoot's masterful, "The Wreck Of The Edmond Fitzgerald," which contains a heartfelt narrative of the events that led to the sinking of an ore carrier, the *Edmund Fitzgerald*, in Lake Superior in 1975, when twenty-nine members of the crew perished. It is also a great form for social protest, where a listing of statements can build in intensity, e.g., "Masters Of War," Dylan's devastating indictment of the perpetuators of the Vietnam debacle. This form can also serve as a kind of travelogue, e.g., Jimmy Webb's 1967 hit "By The Time I Get To Phoenix," a song sung by a man who has just left his wife and who tells us what he pictures her doing as he drives away from her, listing the places he plans on reaching as he progresses on his trip—Phoenix, then Albuquerque, and finally Oklahoma.

The verse/refrain form

A verse/refrain song differs from a simple verse, verse, verse form, in that it contains a culmination point, a point of arrival that houses the central statement. The line or two that appears at the end of *every* verse is called the *refrain*. The refrain may be and often is the title. The difference between a verse/refrain song and a verse/chorus song is that a refrain is an intrinsic part of the verse and ends the verse section; the chorus of a verse/chorus song is an entirely different section.

There are various ways to highlight the refrain line. The easiest and most natural way is to simply place it at the end of a balanced section of music. This gesture alone is satisfying to the listener, but simply doing it and nothing else runs the risk of having the refrain line taken for granted. Therefore, a very important musical consideration when writing a refrain is what occurs musically at the final cadence, where the refrain line resides.

Since there are only a certain number of ways to cadence, and since many melodies that coincide with a harmonic cadence have been overused, both your harmonic choices and, particularly, your melodic choices must be carefully considered to avoid composing something too generic or clichéd. Here the notion of a "hook" serves us well. We need something to "hook" our audience. This can be provided by using an unexpected but effective interval or rhythm in your melody. Other effective means for highlighting a refrain include leaving some space before the refrain line or repeating it, possibly with different chords or repeating it in a different rhythmic setting.

Dylan's setting of the refrain line in his "Blowin' In The Wind" is a gem (Ex. 11.01). He accelerates the phrase structure with the help of an inner rhyme, "friend/wind," then removes "friend" when he repeats the line, shortening it and strengthening its impact with a 3-stressed line instead of duplicating the previous 4- stressed line. "The **answer**, my **friend**, is **blowin'** in the **wind**, the **answer** is **blowin'** in the **wind**").

Ex. 11.01 "Blowin' In The Wind" Bob Dylan

Bruce Springsteen chose to use the simplest harmonic cadence available to set his title/refrain line at the end of his verses. Nevertheless, he created a memorable refrain by using an emotional sound, "Oh," set in three half notes to lead to it (Ex. 11.02).

Ex. 11.02 *"I'm On Fire"* Bruce Springsteen

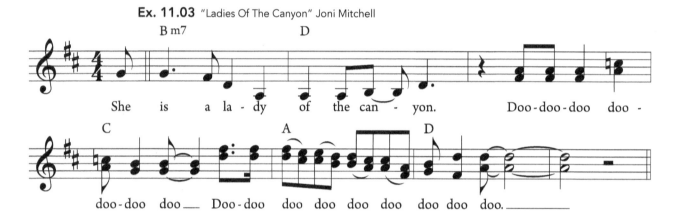

Joni Mitchell's setting of her refrain line in "Ladies Of The Canyon" is memorable because of the intervals and shape of its unique melody and because of its equally unique and memorable vocal aftermath (Ex. 11.03).

Ex. 11.03 *"Ladies Of The Canyon"* Joni Mitchell

Stevie Wonder used a rich harmonic palette and a beautifully poetic line to lead to a segment of a maxim, "All is fair in love and war," to create his title/refrain line (Ex. 11.04).

Ex. 11.04 *"All In Love Is Fair"* Stevie Wonder

Title at the beginning of the verse

There are also many songs that place the title at the beginning of the verse instead of placing it at the end of the verse. Beginning with the central idea demands that the first lyric line and the first musical phrase be strong enough to propel the entire song;

the rest of the song is then based on these initial motives and relies on your ability to lyrically and musically develop them. This form works especially well if the song is a reminiscence.

I am an admirer of Alan Jackson's writing. He succeeds in creating popular songs using materials that are simple, interesting, and emotionally honest.

Alan Jackson's #1 country song "Remember When" begins and ends each verse with the title. This song, a first-person narrative, is a reflection on the major events in his married life. It is written in strophic form, the perfect vehicle for it. This is another excellent example of the use of a list and anaphora.

Here are the first lines from each of the six verses:

Verse 1
Remember when I was young and so were you

Verse 2
Remember when we vowed the vows and walked the walk

Verse 3
Remember when old ones died and new were born

Verse 4
Remember when the sound of little feet was the music we danced to

Verse 5
Remember when thirty seemed so old

Verse 6
Remember when we said, "When we turned gray . . ."

Ex. 11.05 "Remember When" Alan Jackson

"It Was A Very Good Year" is a well-known strophic song that begins in verse 1 with "When I was seventeen," in verse 2 with "When I was twenty-one," and in verse 3 with "When I was thirty-five." Anaphora is very effectively used here, with each iteration of "When I was . . . [the singer's age] . . . it was a very good year." Erwin Drake conceived the song for the folk group the Kingston Trio; hence, he wrote modally, using the Phrygian mode and referencing the parallel major. In doing so, he created a unique song that eventually received a stunning arrangement by Gordon Jenkins and a great vocal performance by Sinatra. Here is the beginning of the song (Ex. 11.06):

Ex. 11.06 "It Was a Very Good Year" Erwin Drake

The B section or bridge of an AABA song

The multiple verse song or the verse/refrain song are both great for composing a chronology or list, but their downside is that the repetition of one verse followed by another, followed by another, can lead to monotony. The writers in the late 1950s and early 1960s, who had gravitated to this form because of the influence of folk music, were now compelled to create a contrasting section: a bridge.

The verse/refrain section became an A section that, once repeated, was followed by a contrasting B section, the bridge. The bridge was followed by a return to the A section. This model, AABA, had been the main form used within choruses of songs from the *Great American Songbook*, reinforcing the truism "The more things change, the more they remain the same."

The songs that were written in the rock era that used this form, however, took a slightly different turn than the AABA choruses of the earlier era. This occurred because of function. The new songs written in this form were not choruses, but were verse/refrain songs with a bridge, and had more of a storyline or narrative driving them. There are many examples: Billy Joel's "Just The Way You Are," Paul Simon's "Still Crazy After All These Years," Bruce Springsteen's "I'm On Fire," etc.

The term "bridge" is one of the best descriptive terms in the musical lexicon. It hints at the main function of a bridge, which is to contrast to the previous sections. The function of an actual bridge is to transport you from one familiar area, like a highway, over an unfamiliar area, e.g., over a river that would be impassable by other means, back to familiar territory, e.g., the highway. As you enter the bridge, you are transported to a contrasting area, and as you leave it, it gently lowers you to familiar territory.

B–Bridge

A–Highway / A–Highway   A–Highway

Techniques to create contrast in writing a bridge

The most important characteristic needed in a bridge is contrast. Here is a list of devices that work in creating contrast in the bridge:

• Change the tessitura of the section.
• Change the melodic rhythm.
• Change the harmonic rhythm.
• Change the phrase lengths.
• Begin melodic phrases in a different area than those of the verse.
• Begin the bridge on a different chord than the chord that began the verse.
• If necessary, modulate to another key.
• Change the rhyme scheme.
• Provide a new slant on the lyrical content.

The last item on the list of contrasting elements, "Provide a new slant on the lyrical content," is one of the most important functions of the bridge. An example of the bridge lyric fostering a new angle on the central idea is found in Billy Joel's "Just The Way You Are." In the verses we are told many of the reasons why he wants his lover to not change, elaborations of the opening phrase, "Don't go changing to try to please me"—all except for one. That reason is withheld until the bridge and is found in this line: "What will it take 'til you believe in me the way that I believe in you." Until that line appears, the listener is under the impression that the singer is simply expressing his pure unconditional love. But in that one line, we realize that the singer has an ulterior motive: he is very insecure and the reason he keeps asking his lover not to keep changing is his fear that she doesn't believe he loves her enough and, therefore, changes her appearance to have him pay more attention to her. He finds these changes very threatening to him. This information provides us with a deeper understanding as we simultaneously enjoy the musical contrast that Billy Joel has created for this section, which includes changes of phrase lengths and a modulation to a new key midway through the bridge followed by a modulation back to the original key as it returns to the A section.

Unifying the bridge to the previous sections

You should be aware of the amount of musical contrast provided by your bridge section. If the bridge starts sounding like it is from another song, obviously, you've gone too far in your use of contrasting devices. A well-written bridge usually contains more than one of the contrasting devices listed above while it retains some elements found in the A section to create unity in the piece. Sometimes simply treating these elements in a different way, e.g., changing the phrase length and the harmony, is enough to provide the necessary contrast.

Here is the opening of the verse section of Billy Joel's "My Life" (Ex. 11.07):

Ex. 11.07 "My Life" Billy Joel

Got a call — from an old —— friend, we used to be real —— close.

The bridge contrasts nicely with the A section, while providing similar materials. It starts on the VIm chord implying a modulation to the relative minor, while the melodic rhythms and repeated notes and melodic contour are similar to those found in the A section (Ex. 11.08).

Ex. 11.08 "My Life" bridge

I nev-er said you had to of-fer me a sec-ond chance.

Lennon and McCartney's "Yesterday" provides us with an example of a successful bridge that contains the perfect amounts of contrast and similarity. This song is written in an AABA form with the title at the beginning of the verse section and is yet another reminiscence (Exs. 11.09–11.10).

Ex. 11.09 "Yesterday" the A section, John Lennon, Paul McCartney

Ex. 11.10 "Yesterday" bridge

The *contrasting elements* in the bridge of "Yesterday" include:

- Slower rhythms, especially the opening half notes.
- Longer phrases; there are only two 4-measure phrases in this section, as opposed to the verse's one- and two-measure phrase lengths.
- The verse section is an unstable fourteen measures long (a seven-measure section that repeats) while the bridge is a balanced eight-measure section (four measures plus four measures).
- The verse begins in the key of F and moves to D minor. The bridge begins the key of D minor and moves to F.
- The harmonic rhythm in the bridge is somewhat faster; this is especially due to the pronounced quarter-note stepwise bass motion in measures 2 and 6.
- The verse uses only end rhymes, while the bridge uses inner rhymes as well.

The use of inner rhymes plus the change in harmonic rhythm, both accelerating devices, cause the bridge to have a sense of urgency not present in the verse section, which is more ruminative in nature.

- The bridge is the only place in which the singer attempts to explain what happened in his lost love affair, although he can't (or won't) divulge the reason for the breakup except that he said "something wrong."

The *similar elements* in the bridge of "Yesterday" that help unify the two sections include:

- The keys employed in both sections (F major and D minor) are intimately related and are used in both sections.

- The second measure of the verse contains the same chord progression as the first measure of the bridge.
- The last note of the verse is the same note that begins the bridge and the last melodic figure of the bridge leads the listener in quarter notes right to the note, G, that begins the verse, connecting the two sections in a natural and expected way.

Too many songs contain bridges that are simply filler. This is a mistake; the bridge can be the high point of a song and can sometimes be so prominent that it sounds like it could be the chorus, an occurrence I've noticed especially in country songs. Good examples can be found in Richard Leigh's masterful "Cold Day In July," sung by the Dixie Chicks, or in James Otto's 2008 #1 country song, "I Just Got Started Loving You." The bridge of Billy Joel's "She's Always A Woman" also resembles a chorus and is a high point in that song.

To modulate or not

You may wonder how far you should go tonally to create contrast, e.g., or whether your bridge should modulate to another key. The answer really depends on style and how harmonically elaborate your A section is. If in your verse all the diatonic notes have been used and a few chromatic notes have been introduced already, then a change of key in your bridge is probably necessary. But if the A section is mainly diatonic, simply choosing one of the harmonic functions that hasn't been highlighted in the A section may provide enough contrast. Or you may simply install one new harmonic color, even a common chromatic chord, e.g., a flat seven (<flat>VII) chord or a secondary dominant may provide just enough harmonic contrast to satisfy.

You will know if your bridge is musically successful once you hear the return of your A section. If the return gives you a sense of "Ah, it's so nice to hear the A section again, although I thoroughly enjoyed that last section," then you've achieved your goal.

The length and importance of the bridge depends on the length of the previous sections. A rule of thumb in an AABA form is to have your bridge be about the length of one A section. If the bridge occurs after a verse/chorus, verse/chorus, its importance is somewhat diminished. If it comes after a verse/prechorus/chorus; verse/prechorus/chorus, its length and importance are further diminished; in this latter form, a bridge is often shortened and used simply to modulate to the chorus in a higher key.

The chorus

The function of a chorus is to state the central idea, repeat it and/or elaborate on it. The one thing the chorus should not contain is verse material, i.e., the narrative or the background information that leads to the chorus. Ideally, it should provide balance to the song and be approximately the same length as the verse or the verse and prechorus combined. The inner structure of every chorus is different, but one of the traits of well-written choruses is that they contain memorable phrases that are repeated within the chorus itself. Most of the time, both the music and lyrics in choruses remain the same. Indeed, the origin of the chorus section in popular song points to the importance of repetition and the sing-along quality of this section. The verse/chorus form became popular during minstrelsy. The chorus section is the section of a verse/chorus song that was originally sung by the entire minstrel troupe following the verse section sung by a soloist. The actual chorus sang the chorus! Every performer and professional songwriter knows that one way to involve your listeners is to invite them to sing along. The "sing-along" quality is still an important part of nearly every chorus, and it is, therefore, wise to include some background harmony in arranging your chorus, even if only one person sings a harmony part.

We can easily trace a continuum from the verse/refrain song to the verse/chorus song. If a refrain line is continually repeated, the refrain line starts to sound like it is a chorus. Examples of songs that use one or two lines that sound as though they could have been the refrain lines of verses but, instead, act as choruses include Bruce Springsteen's "Born In the USA" (in fact, Bruce Springsteen has recorded this song as a verse/refrain song in a less commercial setting than his hit recording.), and John Mayer's "All We Ever Do Is Say Goodbye."

Songs that use repetitious phrases that almost act like mantras are found in the choruses of Dave Mason's "Feelin' Alright," "Holding Back The Years" ("I'll keep holding on") recorded by Simply Red, "Na, Na, Hey, Hey (Kiss Him Goodbye") recorded by Steam, and "Gimme Some Lovin'" recorded by the Spencer Davis Group.

Choruses with repeated music and lyrics; the midpoint of the chorus

The simplest choruses are balanced and often split in two parts, the second part being a musical—and sometimes lyrical—repetition of the first part.

Here is the lyric to the anthemic chorus of a #1 song in 2015, "We Are Young," recorded by the group Fun. The writers could have chosen to write additional lyrics when the music repeated, but instead chose wisely to simply repeat them.

"We Are Young" chorus,   Nate Ruess, Andrew Dost, Jack Antonoff, Jeffrey Bhasker

Tonight
We are young,
So let's set the world on fire.
We can burn brighter
Than the sun.
Entire 5 lines repeat

Another example of a song that simply repeats both the lyric and music within the chorus is "Human Nature," recorded by Michael Jackson.

"Human Nature"   lyrics by John Bettis, music by Steve Porcaro

If they say "why, why?"
Tell 'em that it's human nature
"Why, why does he do me that way?"
Entire 3 lines repeat

One of the questions to ask yourself after writing a section of music, especially a chorus section is, "How many elements contain exact repetition?" Do the melody, the harmony, and the lyrics all repeat? If the repetition of all the elements works, then fine— leave the section alone. If they, instead, prove to be monotonous, try changing one or two of the elements. Try changing the harmony or slightly altering the melody or, especially, changing the lyric to provide some additional interest to a section.

The melodic and lyrical changes in the third line, the midpoint of the chorus of Sam Smith's hit "Stay With Me" add to the emotional heft of this simple but highly effective song. While the lyrics change, the melody only does a slight variation and the harmony remains the same the same. Another obvious commercial move found in this song is having the title appear in both the first and last lines.

> Oh, won't you stay with me
> 'Cause you're all I need
> [midpoint]
> This ain't love, it's clear to see.
> Won't you stay with me.

The midpoint of a chorus is often a crucial area, as can be seen and heard in the three preceding examples. When the second half of the chorus musically repeats the first half, it causes a rhythmic closure (the term used to designate rhythmic closure is "fragmentation"). Although there is nothing wrong with fragmenting the chorus, i.e., dividing the chorus into two symmetric parts, there are subtler and more interesting ways to treat the division of the chorus.

In Example 11.11 "(I've Had) The Time Of My Life," the harmonic phrase structure defines the midpoint (measure 5) but the melody and lyrics, which began in the first half of the chorus, reach over into the second half and create an asymmetric structure that, nonetheless, feels totally comfortable. The result is an interesting chorus structure with enough repetition to make it memorable. Instead of a simple 4-measure plus 4-measure structure, the chorus is nine measures long, with a melody that is laid out: 2½ + 2 + 2 + 2½ measures (Ex. 11.11).

Ex. 11.11 "(I've Had) The Time Of My Life" music by John DeNicola, David Markowitz, lyrics by Franke Previte

Other chorus structures

All the examples of choruses presented so far have repeated sections. What other kinds of successful choruses exist?

Carole King and Toni Stern's "It's Too Late" is eight measures long with a four-measure turnaround (The lyric "oh, no," which occurs in the turnaround section, acts as both part of the emotional aftermath of the chorus and as a means to get back to the verse). Nothing literally repeats, although there are considerable connections between the individual phrases. The harmonic phrase structure of the chorus can be divided evenly into two 4-measure phrases. The melody in the first half consists of thee phrases: "And it's too late, baby / Now it's too late / 'Though we really did try to make it." The second half consists of one long phrase: "Somethin' inside has died and I can't hide and I just can't fake it." The listener hears the satisfying connection of rhythm and rhyme of "inside, "died," "hide" and "make it" and "fake it" and feels the balance of the 4 + 4 measure structure that connects the first half of the chorus to the second half.

Even though there is no repeated section in the chorus, there are other repetitions that compensate for this: the title repeats in the first two phrases with different emphasis: "It's **too late**" and "**It's** too late. Adding to the lyric pleasures is the natural development and seeming inevitability of the melody.

The coda of the song is also an area where the title is highlighted by three repetitions (Ex. 11.12).

Ex. 11.12 "It's Too Late" coda, Carole King, Toni Stern

This is a good commercial move, but is also an honest, emotionally driven one—a statement that needs repeating so that the singee fully realizes that it's really over. This is commercially viable music that is also artistic and honest. The truth found in a well-written song is one of its most important and most powerful elements—one that helps connect the song to all of us.

Choruses with an added phrase

One of the best strategies for making a chorus more interesting and memorable is to first create a balanced chorus and then add a phrase. I refer to this added phrase as the cherry on top of an ice cream sundae—not a necessity, but a definite plus. In the Corrine Bailey Rae hit "Put Your Records On," the chorus is in two symmetrically constructed four-measure halves.

Girl, put on your records on,
Tell me your favorite song,

You go ahead and let your hair down (measures 1–4)
These 4 measures are balanced by:
Sapphire and faded jeans,
I hope you get your dreams
Just go ahead and let your hair down (measures 5–8)
The added line then appears:
You're gonna find yourself somewhere, somehow. (measures 9–12)

Although the title doesn't appear in the added line, a very important lyric containing the central idea does, and makes this chorus stand out (Ex. 11.13).

Ex. 11.13 "Put Your Records On" added line in chorus, Corinne Bailey Rae, John Beck, Steve Chrisanthou

The verse/chorus song

We have looked at verses in relationship to refrain lines and we have looked at choruses alone. Now let's examine the way verses relate to their choruses. The verse/chorus form has been and still is the most prevalent of all song forms. The most important function of a verse in a verse/chorus song is to lead the listener to the chorus section.

Here are some general characteristics of the verse section in relationship to the chorus section:

• A verse contains lyrical ideas that lead to the chorus.
• A verse contains more conversational-type rhythms rather than declarative-type rhythms.
• A verse contains more details in the lyrics than does the chorus.
• The tessitura of the verse section is usually different than and usually lower than that found in the chorus.
• The harmonies that immediately precede the chorus are usually less stable than those found in the chorus.
• The movement from verse to chorus is often a movement from unstable to stable. How you create that movement can be achieved through some or all your resources: harmony, melody, rhythm, and lyrics.
• The two most important lines of your verse lyric are the first line and the line that leads into your chorus.

Here are some general characteristics of choruses:

• The most important function of the chorus is to state the central idea of the song.
• Placement of the central idea.

• A more stable, usually balanced, rhythmic structure than that of the verse or verse/pre-chorus that precedes it.
• A more stable tonal structure.
• The length of the chorus usually balances the section (verse) or combined sections (verse/prechorus) that precede it.

The following analyses of two great verse/chorus songs should convince you that each song is its own entity with the demands of the lyric concept and inner structure determining the actual shape of each section, demonstrating how flexible the verse/chorus structure is in housing songs of very different sensibilities.

"Fire And Rain"

James Taylor's "Fire And Rain" is a great reminder to us that each well-written song is unique. We learn in the verse that the singer has lost someone close to him, someone he loved so much that he felt compelled to write her a song. The choice that James Taylor made in using direct address—singing to the dead girl, Suzanne—makes this song unusually poignant. You might surmise that a lyric that is so highly emotional would produce an unstable or imbalanced structure. But this is not so. The melodic phrase structure of the verse is symmetric: a (two measures), b (two measures), a (two measures), b (two measures). Each melodic phrase in this verse ends on a stable tone, including the last phrase of the verse, which ends on *do*. This, however, is not enough to stop the forward motion created in the verse.

The verse music of "Fire And Rain" achieves its forward motion toward the chorus through the sensitive use of unstable tones, nonchord tones, and interesting rhythms in the melody, and especially the tonal environment consisting of the Mixolydian mode and one chord, G7, borrowed from the parallel Ionian mode (Ex. 11.14).

Ex. 11.14 "Fire and Rain" first lines in verse 1, James Taylor

The first lines of the lyric are unforgettable; you are obliged to listen intently after hearing them. As the lyric continues, "I walked out this morning and I wrote down this song; I just can't remember who to send it to," the first two musical phrases repeat, creating a symmetric section. Nonetheless, after hearing them, we are left unfulfilled, feeling empty. This is caused by both the second and fourth phrases ending on <flat>VII, a very unstable chord, its instability highlighted by the chord preceding it, the V chord borrowed from the parallel Ionian mode, that promises—but does not deliver— tonal fulfillment. Everything in this set of matched phrases that rhyme (a, b, a, b), indicates that all is right in the world—except for that last harmony (B<flat>maj7) and the last two melody notes, E and C, nonchord tones that do not resolve to the underlying harmony. The effect of this is like watching and listening to a person who is standing upright and seems perfectly all right, but then suddenly realizing that everything inside him is crumbling. This example demonstrates the enormous power of harmony and the melody/harmony relationship to create great prosody, interest. and forward motion when used strategically. But the effectiveness of both the tonal environment and the harmonic progression of this verse are not fully realized or appreciated until the chorus appears (Ex. 11.15).

Ex. 11.15 "Fire and Rain" first four measures of the chorus

When the chorus begins in the more stable parallel Ionian mode, the listener feels a satisfactory sense of arrival. The functionally strong harmonic progression, SD, D, T, occurs three times and cadences each of those times on the tonic chord, C, with either the stable *sol* or *mi* in the melody. The stability of the music works with a statement concerning the deep life experiences the singer has experienced. Only in the fourth phrase, in the last line, "But I always thought I'd see you again"—a painful declaration that reestablishes the sense of loss this song is centered on—does Taylor once again return to the Mixolydian tonal environment, a weaker and less stable tonal environment. This results in bringing his sense of loss directly to the listener. But again, in the chorus, this emotion is housed in a symmetric structure—four matched phrases that rhyme and, by doing so, James Taylor presents these deeply felt emotions in a contained, dignified way.

"Fire And Rain" contains three verses, each one furnishing the listener with more information and insight into what the singer is feeling and how he is coping. The first verse informs us of the sad news and the reason the song is being sung. The second verse is a plea for help to Jesus to give the singer the strength to continue, and the third verse is a look to the future when some sense of normalcy can be restored to his life. The chorus is an statement of the rewards and punishments life has already dealt him, a statement of his own internal strength gained through life's experiences, how much he has already withstood, and finally, an admission that he never expected this event to occur.

The mournful feeling coupled with dignity that this powerful song generates emanates from a man almost numbed by the devastating news that has recently been relayed to him. James Taylor's method of expressing this is practically stoic—both music and words are devoid of even a hint of romanticism or sentimentality, defining not only an event in his life but also how he is dealing with it. Through this great song, we realize the importance of choosing the perfect tonal environment and form for capturing and presenting the essence of what and how emotions are felt and communicated.

"Friends In Low Places"

"Friends In Low Places," Garth Brook's gigantic hit, was the first single from his *No Fences* album and received both the Academy of Country Music and the Country Music Association awards in 1990 for Single of the Year. It's an amazingly well written song. It invites you to sing along to it as its lyric surreptitiously encourages you to drink along to it as well.

The first line is one of the two most important lines in any song, and this one is a winner: "Blame it all on my roots / I showed up in boots / and ruined your black-tie affair." We immediately know that this unwanted guest has made an unruly appearance in a place where he doesn't belong. We soon realize, because he is using direct address, that he is singing to a former girlfriend.

As the song progresses, we learn more and more about the relationship of the singer to the singee. This detailed information shows up in the long verse section, which is in two parts. The length of this verse is needed to communicate the important storyline to the listener.

In verse 1 we learn the protagonist is an unwanted guest and we get that he is there to do damage. We learn that he was not invited to this swanky party and, judging from his outrageous actions—he grabs a glass of champagne from the table of her new boyfriend or fiancé—he's had quite a few. That's enough information to lead to the chorus, which centers on the fact that he's got friends in low places, places where he can drink and behave outrageously and still be accepted.

A second verse must add more interesting information and again lead seamlessly to the chorus. But before that happens, the writers give us, the listeners, a break. After a lot of lyric information, it is a good idea to insert a long turnaround or, as they do here, provide an instrumental that uses eight measures of the chords of the chorus as its foundation. The second verse provides us with both a sloppy apology, right in character for someone who is drunk, "Hey, I didn't mean to cause a big scene," and an insult, "Just give me an hour and then, well, I'll be as high as that ivory tower that you're livin' in." We are now ready to hear the chorus again and again, and again . . . Have another drink, sing along!

Now, let's find out how all that lyric information in the verses gets passed on to us in such a succinct, seductive, and memorable way and how the music of the chorus corrals us into singing along with it. Repetitive patterns are great for helping the listener remember a song, and wisely chosen matched phrases that rhyme are the basis for the verses of "Friends In Low Places." The pattern is a (one measure), a (one measure), b (two measures), a simple pattern that repeats four times, yielding the entire sixteen-measure verse (Ex. 11.16).

Ex. 11.16 "Friends In Low Places" verse rhythm, Dewayne Blackwell, Earl Bud Lee

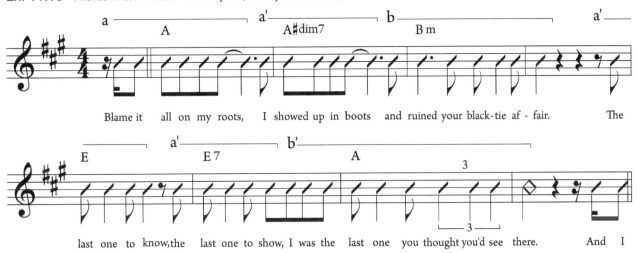

The order of the melodic phrases: a, a, b, a, a, b, is simple and effective. The possible monotony caused by repeating this pattern throughout the verse is completely avoided here through the use of inexactly matched phrases, wonderfully inventive tonal choices in both melody and harmony, and a very natural, conversational type lyric.

Although rhyme, especially perfect rhyme, can be a problem by sounding too contrived, Dwayne Blackwell and Bud Lee have to be admired for pulling off great lyrics that are full of perfect rhymes that never get in the way but, instead, enhance the story they tell.

The chorus contrasts with the verse in many ways:

• It contains the central idea and its elaboration.
• It makes declarative statements using longer rhythmic values.
• The melody's range is larger (both lower and higher) than that of the verse.
• It is tonally more stable than the verse, both beginning and ending on the tonic chord.
• The topography of the phrases changes drastically from those found in the verse. Melodic phrases are longer (the first phrase in the chorus is a two-measure phrase elided with a three-measure phrase, making it five measures long). The chorus has long phrases needing lots of breath control in order to sing them, followed by shorter phrases with lots of space surrounding them, whereas the phrases in the verse are much more regular.
• The harmonic rhythm changes. Chords in the verse are held for one or two measures, whereas chords in the chorus are held longer; the I chord is held for entire four measures at the beginning and midway through the chorus.

The chorus's sixteen-measure length perfectly balances the verse section. The title of the song appears at the top of the chorus and also at its ending, a commercial move that can sometimes sound forced, but not in this song. The sing-along quality of this chorus is firmly established at its midpoint, where repetition of the rhythm of the chorus's first melodic phrase appears.

There are some wonderful changes that take place between the first part of the chorus and the second part. Compare Example 11.17, the first part of the chorus, to Example 11.18, the midpoint of the chorus. The first melodic setting of the title phrase plunges down to the low A on the word "low," but at the midpoint, instead of diving down, the melody rises to a high note, F<sharp>, on the "O" of "Oasis. By doing this, the writers not only offer up a more interesting chorus, capture the sense of the singer's out-of-control-drunkenness, and captivate us but also show off Garth Brook's enormous range and emotional heft.

Ex. 11.17 "Friends In Low Places" first part of the chorus

'Cause I got friends in low pla - ces where the whis-key drowns and the

Ex. 11.18 "Friends In Low Places" midway through the chorus

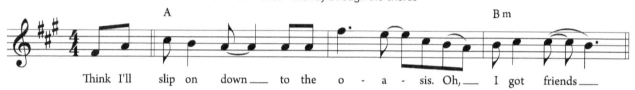

Think I'll slip on down __ to the o - a - sis. Oh, __ I got friends __

The chorus of "I've Got Friends In Low Places" is what is called a "sing-along," a feel-good song meant to involve as many people joining in as possible. As befits a feel-good song, it is a major key throughout. The verse/chorus form provides the perfect vehicle for a sing-along: Its opening two verses give the intended audience the necessary background information, made more cogent because the singer directs it to his ex-girlfriend (while having the intended audience identify with him) that leads to the sing-along chorus, followed by two more verses, followed by chorus/chorus/chorus, etc.

The prechorus

The function of a *prechorus* is to create tension and interest to lead to the chorus. The prechorus is an actual section of a song, not simply one added phrase tacked on to a verse. It can be thought of as a second part of a verse, but with certain conditions. This section is usually needed because the verse sounds and feels tonally and rhythmically static because not enough interest and momentum have built up to call forth the chorus. Repeating the verse structure would not solve the problem; it might even exacerbate it. The problem often occurs if the music in the first part of the verse (usually four measures) repeats, causing the eight-measure section to *fragment*.

When fragmentation occurs, the song needs some energy and direction, and that is what this new section, the prechorus, should provide.

The music for the verses in Carole King's and Gerry Goffin's "(You Make Me Feel Like) A Natural Woman" is sixteen measures in length and fragments midway through at the end of measure 8 (measures 1–8 are repeated in measures 9–16). The lyrics of lines 2 and 4 further help to close the section with perfect rhymes coupled with matched phrases.

"(You Make Me Feel Like) A Natural Woman," line endings in verse 1
Verse 1
Line 1: morning rain   a
Line 2: so uninspired   b
Line 3: another day   a
Line 4: so tired   b

The need for another section is, therefore, demanded to maintain the listener's attention and create tension and more forward motion to the chorus.

The prechorus serves to destabilize or imbalance the entire first section of the song; by "first section," I mean the combination of the verse and prechorus, the two combined sections whose function is to lead to the chorus. Another way to think about a prechorus is that it is a second part of the verse—but on steroids! Its job is to make the listener ache for the chorus (Ex. 11.19).

Ex. 11.19 "(You Make Me Feel Like) A Natural Woman" prechorus, music by Carole King, lyrics by Gerry Goffin

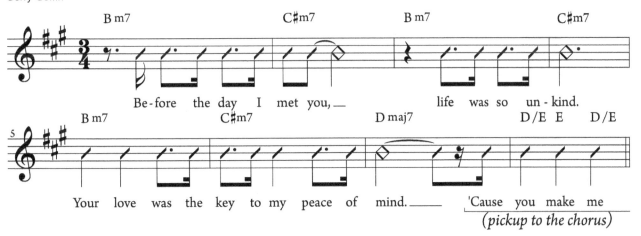

The prechorus in "A Natural Woman" is half the length of the verse and, therefore, unbalances the entire front part of the song. (I define the front part of the song as the combined length of the verse and prechorus [verse: sixteen measures; prechorus: eight measures]). Notice how the prechorus's unstable harmonies build tension as the IIm7 to IIIm7 chords repeat three times leading finally to the subdominant and dominant harmonies. Adding to the structural instability are its unbalanced three phrases. The prechorus contains accelerated rhythms and allows for the important back-heavy lead-in to the chorus, a phrase that is actually the melodic beginning of the chorus that enters at the end of the prechorus's last harmonic phrase. (See chapter 14, "The Melodic Phrase/

The Harmonic Phrase.") All these attributes contribute to the prechorus's function of beckoning the chorus.

Although prechoruses are generally one half the length of the verse, there are some that are the same length as their verses. If that is the case, it usually uses harmony as the main device to create the necessary tension. Creating harmonic tension doesn't mean that you must seek out highly dissonant chords—the harmonies can be as simple as, e.g., using only the V and IV chords throughout the prechorus and avoiding the I chord, especially in a cadencing position. The two strategies, rhythmic and tonal, are often combined. The prechorus section frequently ends open tonally, rhythmically and, possibly, lyrically (rhyme is not always needed), with all the elements combined to create the necessary tension.

"California Gurls" is another verse/prechorus/chorus song that exemplifies why and how this form works.

The rhythms of the verse melody are playful, as is the groove that features syncopated chords set against a steady beat. The verse consists of the same basic four-measure melody and harmony repeated four times. This amount of repetition, perfect for a teenage audience, can only work if the melodic rhythm and groove are infectious (they are) and if the lyric is fun (it is). This section, nonetheless, is symmetric and demands a section that unbalances it and creates harmonic tension—in other words, a prechorus is called for.

The prechorus to "California Gurls" fulfills all the stated requirements for this song section: it is eight measures long, one-half the length of the verse, and is harmonically unstable. This section creates a need in the listener to hear a balanced section and the tonic chord again (Ex. 11.20).

Ex. 11.20 "California Gurls" first four measures of the prechorus, Katy Perry, Bonnie McKee, Lukasz Gottwald, Benjamin Levin, Max Martin, Calvin Broadus

The sixteen-measure chorus restores the verse's chord pattern, groove, and strong tonal stability (notice how much of the melody in the chorus resides on *do*). It contains a melodic rhythm that is even more infectious than the verses and has a more assertive rhythmic profile. The melody is a bit unusual, because it has a lower tessitura than that of the prechorus but is, nonetheless, the most powerful musical statement of the three sections (Ex. 11.21).

Ex. 11.21 "California Gurls" first four measures of the verse

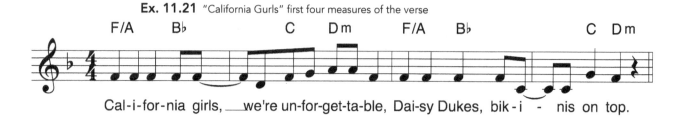

These three sections represent only part of the total form of this song. As in many songs using loop-based harmonic and rhythmic patterns, form in this song has been expanded. After the return to the verse section, this time pared down to eight measures, the prechorus and chorus occur followed by a rap section (twenty measures), followed by the chorus and a postchorus section, all taking place over the same chord pattern that appeared in the verse and chorus sections.

The prerefrain

A prerefrain functions the same way that a prechorus does, except that its destination is the refrain rather than the chorus. When a verse/refrain song contains a prerefrain, the refrain may be highlighted so drastically that is causes the prerefrain coupled with the refrain to almost sound like a chorus. Paul Simon's "Bridge Over Troubled Water" and Smokey Robinson's "Tears Of A Clown" contain refrain lines that feel almost chorus-like because of this. You can easily argue that "Tears Of A Clown" actually has a chorus rather than a refrain, but debating it would only illustrate how mutable and ambiguous some of these forms are. This should also inform you that in composing a song you are not dealing with inactive forms into which you place your phrases, but rather, a creative activity that produces varied results due to your choices.

The hooky prechorus (the luxury airliner)

In recent years, the prechorus has started taking on another function, especially in commercially oriented songwriting. The prechorus is no longer being asked to simply lead to the chorus; it is also being asked to provide additional listener satisfaction by housing yet another hook. Upon hearing this added approach to a prechorus, the listener may actually feel that the chorus has arrived, but is then redirected by something in the song that indicates there is more to come. In this new addition to the prechorus, the function of the prechorus is to not only lead to the chorus but also to provide a memorable arrival point—but one that is not the final destination. This experience might be likened to going on a trip, getting on board a luxury airliner, being served caviar and champagne, and enjoying it so much that you momentarily forget that you are still traveling to your main destination—until you actually arrive there. The name I've fabricated for this is *the luxury airliner*.

Does the following section of a song (Ex. 11.22) sound like a transition or an arrival or both?

Ex. 11.22 "Locked Out Of Heaven", pre-chorus, Bruno Mars, Ari Levine, Philip Laurence

When I first heard this section I heard it as an arrival point. The song is in D minor, and the verse has been signaling D minor or F major as a point of resolution and tonal stability, so the return to D minor harmony with a hooky melody and a lyric, "Cause your sex takes me to paradise" easily could be mistaken as the title of the song. When I heard the same phrase repeat, I assumed that it was the chorus because repetition of the title phrase is one the main characteristic of a chorus, but there was an extension added to it, one that was leading somewhere, a characteristic of prechoruses: "and it shows." The phrase that completes the entire statement, "'Cause you make me feel like / I've been locked out of heaven" reveals itself in the new section, the actual chorus! It is here that we find more chorus-like characteristics and more tonal stability, the relative major, F. The section is a balanced sixteen measures (8+8) with the title repeated midway through, leaving no doubt that it is the chorus. No complaints from this traveler, we've had a good time!

Multiple hooks

If you are attempting to write commercially, you should be aware that finding additional hooks, like the ones already shown in Example 11.22 can help you achieve popular success. Concentrating on writing hooks can be a bit tricky, because it may lead to overkill and possibly detract from the natural flow of a song. "Heart Attack," by an army of six writers, manages to install a number of hooks without losing its integrity as a well-written song. It has two major hooks in the chorus, the first (Ex. 11.23), a memorable legato melody, the second (Ex. 11.24), a more rhythmic one.

Ex. 11.23 "Heart Attack", Demi Lovato, Mitch Allen, Jason Evigan, Sean Douglas, Nikki Williams, Aaron Phillips

Ex. 11.24

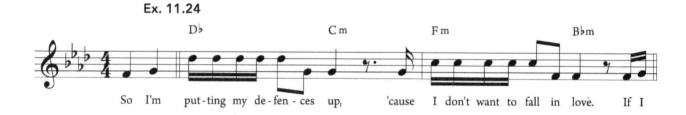

The song as a chorus

We are now taking a step back in time to examine the choruses of much older songs. Doing so functions as both a tribute to those songs and as information you may find very helpful. Since most of the songs in the *Great American Songbook* are called complex choruses because they contain four sections, they provide us with many great examples of how to elaborate both musically and lyrically on a theme. All the lyrics of the choruses of, e.g.,

"'S Wonderful" or "Embraceable You" by Ira Gershwin are, as befitting of the chorus form, elaborations on the title. You well may wonder what happened to the verses of those songs.

When the verses of these songs were originally written, they were an intrinsic part of a Broadway musical. It is always difficult to move from dialogue to singing in a live show because the audience must participate in a suspension of disbelief. The main function of verses in Broadway shows is to provide a transition from the spoken word to the chorus of the song much the same way a recitative leads to an aria in an opera. Some of the verses from these songs from Broadway shows go well beyond this pedestrian function and are gorgeous. Some of them that work beautifully out of the context of the shows for which they were originally written are still sung in cabarets or in more formal settings like pop-concerts. But most verses for these now ancient songs function less well when removed from the Broadway context for which they were written. Many of these Broadway-generated songs dropped their verses the way Darwin theorized that living forms as they evolved, species dropped appendages. In fact, during the late 1950s through the 1970s, some songs, e.g., Sammy Cahn and Jimmy Van Heusen's songs, written specifically for Frank Sinatra, such as "All the Way," "Come Fly With Me" and "Only the Lonely," were written as choruses without verses.

The two forms of choruses found in the *Great American Songbook*

The two forms of choruses that show up in standard-form songs are the AABA and the ABAB'. Sometimes in this later form, when the B' section strays too far from the original B section, it is labeled C instead of B'.

Most of these choruses are four balanced sections; each section is eight measures long with the entire structure equaling thirty-two measures. Although thousands of songs have been written in this ridged, formulaic structure, the many song gems that remain are a testament to both the sturdiness of this form and the creativity of the composers who successfully worked within it.

The AABA chorus

The form of the AABA chorus often outwardly resembles the verse/refrain, verse/refrain, bridge, verse/refrain form already written about. Titles for AABA choruses usually occur at the beginning or at the end of the A section. "These Foolish Things" by Eric Maschwitz, Jack Strachey, and Harry Link, and "As Time Goes By" by Herman Hupfeld are two well-known choruses that end with the title. Just as many verse/refrain songs begin with a list, so too does "These Foolish Things": "A cigarette that bares a lipstick's traces, an airline ticket to romantic places; Still my heart has wings, these foolish things remind me of you."

Many choruses begin with the title or have the title stated within the first line or soon after the first line. I'm referring to songs like "Somewhere Over The Rainbow" by Arlen/Harburg or "What Is This Thing Called Love" by Cole Porter.

The B section of an AABA chorus is a contrasting section called the bridge. The bridge within the chorus functions in the same way as the bridge found in verse/refrain, verse/

refrain, bridge, verse/refrain songs, i.e., as a contrasting section. The third A section of an AABA song often has a slight change that provides a climax or suitable ending to the song.

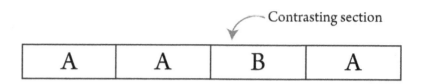

The AABA form demands that the A section be worth repeating. If you are writing in this form, the A section had better be good, because it takes up three-quarters of the entire song!

The ABAB′ chorus

The ABAB′ form of chorus is subtler than the AABA form, in that it contains no obvious contrasting section. This type of chorus is also broken into eight-measure sections, but the B section is often a development of the materials exposed in the A section and, because of that, contrasts in more subtle ways than the B section (the bridge) found in the AABA form.

There are many standards that appear in this form, including, e.g., Berlin's "White Christmas" and Gershwin's "But Not For Me."

The simplicity of the musical ideas in the charming ABAB′ song "But Not For Me" are developed with such facility that the techniques employed can easily slip by undetected. Ira Gershwin's ability to match his lyrics to his brother's musical gestures is so empathetic it seems telepathic. What a terrific title and concept he created for a musical phrase that sounds like an afterthought! The first phrase of the A section is truncated and made into the b-phrase and then the entire four measures are repeated producing an a, b, a, b order of the phrases (Ex. 11.25).

Ex. 11.25 "But Not For Me" the A section, music by George Gershwin, lyrics by Ira Gershwin

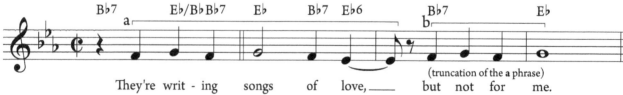

The first phrase of the B section begins with the same rhythm that began the first phrase of the A section, but that phrasal rhythm is now repeated three times, rendering the order of the phrases: a, a, a, b (Ex. 11.26).

Ex. 11.26 "But Not For Me" order of the phrases in the B section

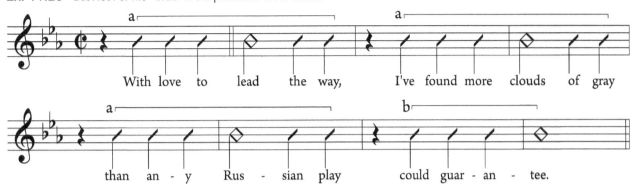

The B section undergoes many tonal changes—melodically and harmonically—with chromatic notes that move the song from a place of musing to a place of yearning. This type of transformation is developmental in nature. And that is the reason you may not easily discern this section when it arrives or even realize it has occurred—until you hear the A section heralding its return with different lyrics. The B′ section often contains a melodic climax and a repetition of the title.

The song as a performance vehicle

The following paragraph may appear to be a history lesson. It's not. It is a prime example of how function determines form.

Before Broadway shows became the main source of popular songs in America, the most popular entertainment format was called vaudeville. Vaudeville shows were prevalent throughout the United States. They were variety shows that featured, e.g., an acrobatic troupe, followed by a comedian, followed by a ballet duo, followed by a vocalist, followed by an animal act.

The vocalists from the vaudeville era had the same problem that today's popular music performers have in introducing a song. A vocalist always feels uncomfortable and is reluctant to introduce a song with a spoken, "This song is about . . . " It is much easier for the vocalist to have the song speak for itself, to have the verse section of the song serve the function of telling the story or setting the scenario and then have the chorus of the song provide the central idea/payoff. This is the reason why the verse section of verse/chorus songs in both vaudeville songs and in today's popular songs is so important, and why the verse/chorus form remains the most popular song form.

Other chorus-only songs

There are some songs other than those derived from Broadway shows that act as choruses throughout. Many of these songs are in one or two sections and often use the blues as their foundation, e.g., Wilson Pickett's "In The Midnight Hour" or Stevie Wonder's "Superstition." These are blues-derived songs that simply elaborate on the central theme. Stevie Wonder seems to gravitate to chorus-only songs sometimes written in two sections;

"You Are the Sunshine Of My Life" is in an A/B form; "Isn't She Lovely" is in a truncated A/A/B/A form.

Contemporary treatment of form

In recent times the prevalence of loop-based songs, songs that contain the same chord sequence and groove throughout, or at least, in a couple of different sections, has fostered as many as four or five different sections in a song, each section usually lasting eight or sixteen bars. Obviously, if a song is based around a chord pattern that repeats, one of the most potent elements of contrast, harmonic contrast, is not available. This places the function of contrast on melody and on texture. These and other means of creating contrast between sections are examined and explained in chapter 16, "Tonal and Rhythmic Strategizing." Another important element used to create contrast is texture. The current trend is toward making the production as seductive as possible. Texture has moved up in the hierarchy of the elements that draw listeners into a song. Ingenious production choices such as broken drum patterns or dropping out the drums completely, propelling the groove with rhythmic synthesizer figures, and using exotic sounds are common devices that keep recordings interesting and enticing. Many of these production devices had their origins in EDM (electronic dance music) but you now find them in recordings by numerous artists in pop and hip-hop as well. Because of the consistency of harmonic movement and groove in these songs, it is also possible to move each section around with more freedom and/or to juxtapose a melody from one section over the melody from another section.

The object of many pop songs is to hook the listener as soon and as often as possible. A fairly recent addition to song form is the *postchorus*—a section immediately following the chorus that uses the same chords as the chorus, but with a different melody, often a chant or a melodic segment of the chorus melody—in order to add yet another hook to the song. Examples include "Poker Face" performed by Lady Gaga and "Last Friday Night (T.G.I.F.)" performed by Katy Perry.

Summary

Song form is often the result of the function of what the song is attempting to express and the way the author has chosen to express it, rather than simply a vessel to be filled. Song forms tend to morph into one another. The inner form—what goes on in the phrases within a section—is as important as the outer form.

Questions to ask yourself when you think that you have completed a song are:

• Does the form of the song fit its function?
• Does the song feel good, with no section sounding either too long or too short?
• Is there a central idea or payoff in the song, and is your chosen song form highlighting it?
• Is there enough contrast between sections to keep the song interesting, but not so much that it is distracting?
• Is the song satisfying in both its form and its content?

If the answer to these questions is "yes," then you have succeeded.

Activities

1. Listen intently to songs you admire and wish you could have written.

   Ask yourself:

   • Where is the central statement located?
   • How long is one section in comparison to another section? (E.g., the verse section, in relation to the chorus section.)
   • How is contrast created between sections?
   • What is similar in these sections?
   • What is the inner structure of each of the sections?
   • How does the form of the song enhance its function and appeal?

2. Compose a verse/refrain song that highlights the refrain line in one or more of the techniques exposed in this chapter under the heading "Verse/refrain form."
3. Compose a multiple verse song that begins with the title or in which the title appears in the first line. Based on the first phrase, develop the ideas both musically and lyrically throughout.
4. Compose a verse/prechorus/chorus song. Compose a verse structure that is rhythmically symmetric (fragmented) and, therefore, calls for a prechorus. Then compose a prechorus that is one half the verse's length, is harmonically unstable, avoids the I chord, and leads to the chorus. Compose a chorus that is about the length of the combined verse/prechorus.
5. Compose a three-section song using a loop-based harmonic progression throughout that contrasts each section by changing either the melodic phrase lengths, the rhythmic content, the tessitura of the melody, or the texture (or a combination of these elements).
6. If you tend to compose songs mainly in one song form, make it a point to study other song forms and attempt to write in those forms.

PART IV

Harmonic Considerations

12

Chords

Chords are not simply chords—discovering chords through voice leading

Chords are not simply conglomerates of notes that sound good together. Chords are made of the very same materials and have the very same tonal dynamics as the scales that we've closely examined in chapter 4, "Tone Tendencies." Chords are made up of separate voices that are singing together. Each voice follows its own path, usually to its closest neighboring voice. If two adjoining chords have some of the same notes, then those notes, called *common tones*, usually stay where they are in the same voice or line. In traditional harmony courses this practice is called "good voice leading"; it is simply the most musical and natural way to treat each voice in a chord. When you allow yourself to think of the individual voices in each chord, then you can discover "new" places for your chords to go.

Here is an example: In the key of C, I want to progress from a I chord, C, to the VIm chord, Am, but I want a chord that occurs in between those two chords, one that leads there in an elegant way. What are my choices? In Example 12.01, tied notes indicate that there are notes in common in adjoining chords and dotted lines indicate where smooth voice leading occurs (▶ AUDIO 12.01).

Ex. 12.01 Movement from a C chord to an Am chord

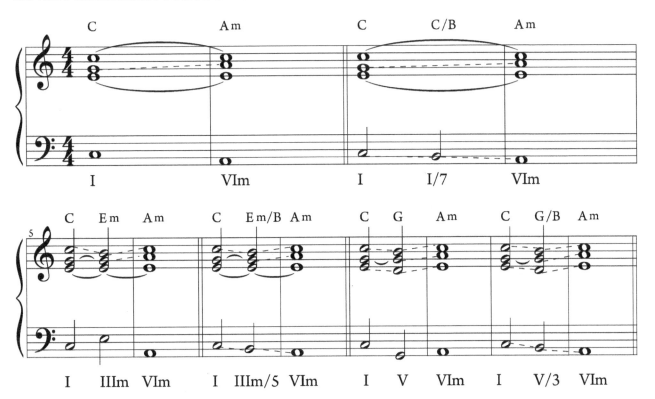

Ex. 12.01 Continued

Since Am is only a minor third down from C, I could make a smooth connection through the important bass part with any chord that contains a B. I look for diatonic triads that contain a B and have tones in common with those two chords. But before making that choice, I realize that the smoothest connection—the least obtrusive choice—would be to retain the C triad and simply place the B, the 7th of the C chord in the bass as a passing tone. In the next examples, I use two diatonic chords that contain a B, Em and G (I could also have used Bdim). They are shown first in their root position and then in their inversions with B in the bass, demonstrating how this voice-driven method is an excellent way to connect chords smoothly.

My next choice is to find chromatic notes that would work with B in the bass. Chromatic chords call attention to themselves, so before making this move you would first have to decide if the use of a chromatic chord works within the style and the lyric of the song you are writing. The G+/3 works well, and since the idea of an augmented chord has surfaced, I decide to also try C+ because G♯ is the leading tone to A. In this case, I did not need to use a B in the bass. The V7/VIm in first inversion also works great in making the sought-after connection, as does the ♯V^dim7.

I decide to try ♭VII as a connecting chord, since B♭ is a half step away from the root of Am and finally, adding the ♯5 of the key, G♯, to the ♭VII chord, I now have two chromatic tones leading to the Am chord, the G♯ leading to A and the B♭ also leading to A. This chord is called an *augmented sixth* chord in traditional harmony and a subV7/VIm chord in jazz harmony (in the short-hand of jazz terminology, the G♯ is considered an A♭, ♭7 of the ♭VII7 chord.) This heavy chromaticism may be more than we need, but it is good to know that it is available.

These chord choices have come about through a consideration of each voice in the chord, rather than simply choosing one blob of sound moving to another blob of sound. I have found this method of conceptualizing chord movement to be the one that is the most musical as well as the one that allows for the greatest creativity in chord choices. I believe that, e.g., The Beatles' and Stevie Wonder's approach to harmonic progression is based on this concept. This accounts for the original and yet completely natural sounding movement of their chords.

The turnaround in "Hey Jude" is an example of The Beatles ability to hear a blues chord in a different way (Ex. 12.02).

Ex. 12.02 "Hey Jude" John Lennon, Paul McCartney

The F7, the I7 chord in F usually leads to the IV chord, B♭ in the key of F. Here, instead, it leads to a C7, the V7 of F! I believe that the Beatles heard the E♭, the 7th of the F7, as a D♯ and let it naturally resolve to the E of a C7, the V7 in the key to lead back to the tonic chord, F, that begins the second verse (Ex. 12.03).

Ex. 12.03 "Hey Jude" chord movement for the turnaround figure to the second verse

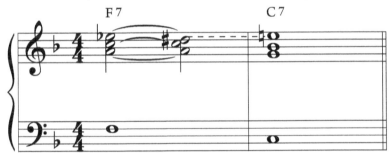

Stevie Wonder has an acute ear for piquant harmonies. His enormous 1973 hit "You Are the Sunshine Of My Life" uses the jazz harmonic vocabulary in an original way (Ex. 12.04).

Ex. 12.04 "You Are the Sunshine Of My Life" Stevie Wonder

The second measure contains a simple but quite original move: the V7 chord is placed in third inversion, with the 7th in the bass, which leads beautifully to the IIIm7 chord in the third measure. The fourth measure houses a secondary dominant chord, the V7/IIm, containing chord extensions, 13, E♯, and ♭9, A♮, that are perfectly voice-led to the C♯m7, the IIm7 in the key of B. In this case, enharmonic thinking (E♯ = F♮) allows the smooth movement to occur. As demonstrated in Examples 12.03 and 12.04, voice leading can have positive and original repercussions in the chord choices you make for your song (Ex. 12.05).

Ex. 12.05 "You Are The Sunshine Of My Life" voice leading

Chord progression

An important connotation of the term "chord progression" is that chords move with an implied directionality toward a tonal goal area. This is the basis of chord movement in styles that involve functional harmony.

A general definition of a chord progression is: *the movement of one chord to another with the amount of change between adjacent chords measured by the number of notes that change in each of the voices of adjoining chords.* If one note changes in two adjacent triads, then a slight progression is realized. If two notes change in adjacent triads, then more of a progression is realized, and if all three notes change, then the greatest progression is realized. A tritone between two adjacent chords in the progression usually increases the dynamic thrust of the progression. The introduction of a chromatic note further increases its momentum forward (Ex. 12.06).

Ex. 12.06 Chord progressions, from slight to great

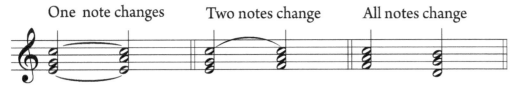

One note changes   Two notes change   All notes change

Tritone   Chromatic note   Tritone

resolution   resolution

If you use voice-leading principles, you have greater freedom to move from one unrelated chord to another without it sounding too abrupt. For example, a C triad moving to an F♯ triad is a tonally radical move. The two triads have no notes in common and the roots are a tritone apart. Even these two chords, seemingly worlds apart, can be made into a logical sounding progression if voice-leading principles are followed. As demonstrated in Example 12.07, in order to move in a fairly smooth way from C to F♯, I place the C chord in first inversion, with its third, E, in the bass. The rest of the progression is closer to a diatonic progression in the key of C. The ♭VII chord (B♭ in the key of C), a modal interchange chord borrowed from the parallel minor, is one that is now used so frequently in major keys that most songwriters treat it as a diatonic member of the major key tonal environment. I choose to use it here because a common tone exists between the F♯ and B♭ (in the F♯ triad, A♯ = B♭ enharmonically). I keep the A♯ and B♭ in the same voice to assure smoothness. All the chords in this example can be understood within an expanded C major context.

The progression that I create, employing simple voice-leading principles, is smooth, usable and original.

Ex. 12.07

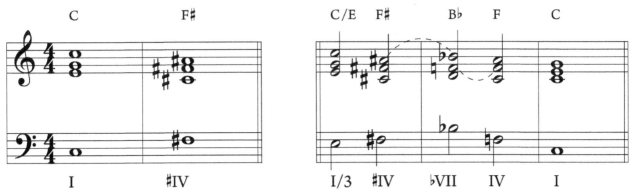

Of course, even with good voice leading, you can't move from chord to chord haphazardly without losing a sense of tonality. To remain within the same key, it is best to stay within a diatonic setting, with only an occasional foray outside of it.

215

The importance of the bass line

The most important two voices in a song are the vocal line and the bass line. Thinking about the bass as a voice, rather than simply as the lowest note of a chord can lead to more choices and to the creation of interesting music. In a photo I've seen of Cole Porter working on a manuscript to one of his songs, the manuscript contains just the melody, the lyric and the bass line. That was enough information for Porter to know what he was dealing with in his composition.

There are many vocal melodies that have been composed to the bass parts. Often the bass part is a scale and, more often than not, a descending one. The direction of the bass line often affects the main vocal melody, especially its direction and contour, as it does in Irving Berlin's "How Deep Is The Ocean" (Ex. 12.08).

Ex. 12.08 "How Deep Is the Ocean" Irving Berlin

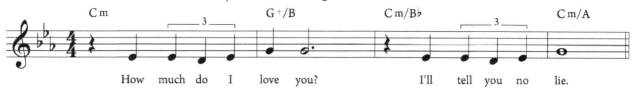

Notice that the ascending contour of each of the melodic phrases reinforces the lyrics' questions while also providing a nice contrast with the descending bass line.

This beautiful example of word painting by Lennon/McCartney uses a descending bass line in 12/8 time (Ex. 12.09).

Ex. 12.09 "Lucy In the Sky" John Lennon, Paul McCartney

Notice that the vocal melody is centered around C♯, while the bass descends, creating an oblique motion between those two outer voices. The desired linearity—the need to have the bass "sing" its own melody— also accounts for the chord inversions found in this song.

Chord inversions

Chord inversions have several different functions. Putting a chord in an inversion affects the stability of a chord and significantly alters the way we hear a chord. Beginning with root position, the most stable position, inversions are then listed here from the most stable to the least stable.

- Root position with the root in the bass
- First inversion with the third in the bass
- Second inversion with the fifth in the bass
- Third inversion chord with the seventh in the bass

It is no wonder that songs in rock, heavy metal, and funk styles—styles that relate directly to the body and, therefore, must be grounded—tend to contain chords mainly in root position. Conversely, chords found in songs from the *Great American Songbook* tend to be loftier and more romantic in nature and, therefore, often contain chords in inversions, as do some pop and contemporary country songs.

A chord in an inversion is a bit more ambiguous, less grounded, and less stable than a root position chord. In Sia's "Chandelier" the I chord appears in the metrically strong third measure. If the I chord had been placed in root position, it would have sounded too stable, but placed in first inversion it furnishes the necessary instability and movement (Ex. 12.10).

Ex. 12.10 "Chandelier" Sia Furler, Jesse Shatkin

An inversion of a chord also provides a way for the bass to move more smoothly while adding propulsion from one chord to another.

The chorus of Billy Joel's "Honesty" has an ascending bass line that begins on the IV chord, E♭, moves to the dominant, F, and then employs a secondary dominant, D, with its 3rd, F♯, placed in the bass, acting like a leading tone to the VIm chord, Gm (Ex. 12.11).

Ex. 12.11 "Honesty" Billy Joel

"A Song For You" is another example of a great song with a descending bass line that engenders many chord inversions (Ex. 12.12).

Ex. 12.12 "A Song For You" Leon Russell

I've been so ma-ny pla-ces in my life and time. I've sung a lot of songs, I've made some bad_rhymes.

Dm: Im   V7/3   ♭III/5   VIm7(♭5)

Because of its instability, a second inversion chord often acts like a suspension, suspending both the 3rd and the 5th of the next chord. This produces the type of "amen" progression found in many R&B songs such as "The Way You Do The Things You Do."

Ex. 12.13 "The Way You Do the Things You Do" Smokey Robinson, Robert Rogers

You got a smile so bright,   you know you could-'ve been a can - dle.

The movement of the A♭ to E♭ In Example 12.13 acts as a kind of embellishment of the E♭ chord.

Elton John begins his setting of Bernie Taupin's lyrics in a very original way: with a chromatic chord in third inversion (Ex. 12.14a).

Ex. 12.14a "The One" Elton John, Bernie Taupin

(a)

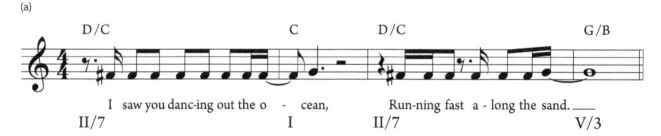

I saw you danc-ing out the o - cean,   Run-ning fast a - long the sand.____

II/7   I   II/7   V/3

The chord is a II7 chord, with its seventh in the bass, a chord that often functions as V7/V that would normally resolve to the V chord in first inversion. In this case however, capitalizing on its instability, it is treated as though the entire II chord is a suspension with all its members resolving to the I chord. In measure 3, the II7 chord in third inversion occurs again. This time it behaves as it usually is expected to and resolves to the V chord in first inversion (Ex. 12.14b).

Ex. 12.14b "The One" chords, showing voice leading

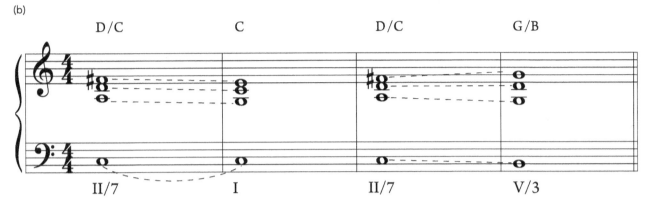

Implied chords

Only one voice other than the melody, usually the bass voice, is needed to imply a harmony. The benefit of doing this is that the function of the chord is implied while the texture becomes cleaner and more transparent. In the first verse of Kelly Clarkson's big hit, "Since U Been Gone," the bass line alone implies the harmony (Ex. 12.15).

Ex. 12.15 "Since U Been Gone" Luke Gottwald, Max Martin

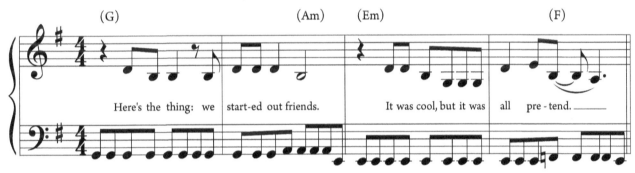

Each section of this song builds texturally; each section adds more notes of the triads until the chorus arrives with doublings of instruments playing full triads.

Many productions today contain incomplete chords or implied chords. This is due to a number of factors: (1) electronic sounds can take up quite a lot of sonic space and full chords tend to clutter the production; (2) a counterline that implies the harmony is often more interesting and elegant than a complete chord; and (3) initially leaving out a note or two of a triad in a verse or prechorus, especially the third (which tends to make the chord sound full), allows another section of the song, usually the chorus, to use complete chords in order to contrast with previous sections that have lighter textures.

Radical textural contrasting of sections was a trademark of the group Nirvana (Ex. 12.16), and is now common in many styles ranging from country to EDM.

Ex. 12.16 "Smells Like Teen Spirit" Kurt Cobain, Dave Grohl, Krist Novoselic

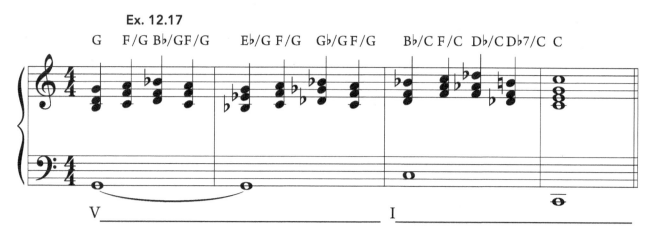

There are no stated chords used in the first verse of this gigantic hit. Instead, the melody, the guitar, and the bass parts imply the chords. This texture is one of three separate textures used in the production—one for each section of the song—that helped make this song a stereotypical model for bands and productions that followed.

Pedal point

Pedal point, the term used to designate a sustained or repeated note that acts as a kind of tonal anchor for the other voices, can appear in any voice, but is usually found in the bass. When used in the bass, it provides the main harmonic function for a passage, over which other harmonic functions occur. This technique, found in many popular songs, has predecessors in classical music from Bach through Richard Strauss.

The harmonies that occur over a pedal point are subservient to the harmonic function implied by the bass pedal point.

Ex. 12.17

The function of the elaborate harmonies that occur above the pedal point in Example 12.17 is the basic progression, V to I.

A pedal point works especially well at the beginning of a song, where the tonic can be implied for a great length of time while different harmonies occur above it (Ex. 12.18).

Ex. 12.18 "Change the World" Gordon Kennedy, Tommy Sims, Wayne Kirkpatrick

If I could reach the stars, ____   Pull one down for you, ____

Other chord structures

There are ways of enhancing the basic sound of a triad without changing its function or making it too dissonant, e.g., adding a 2nd (or 9th, but without the 7th) or 6th to the triad, or suspending the 3d of the triad with the 4th. The following example shows a C major chord and other structures that can be used (when appropriate) in its place (Ex. 12.19).

Ex. 12.19

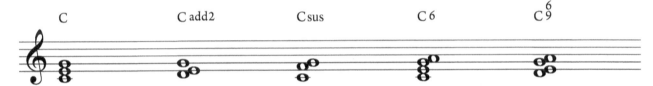

Chords without thirds

Chords have traditionally been built in thirds, and for good reason: the first tones in the overtone series render the major triad. But there are other ways of building chords. Since electric guitars and synthesizers are so potentially powerful and are capable of producing strong overtones, they often obviate the need for triadic structures. Most often, the third of the chord is omitted.

You can substitute a triad with a dyad by removing the third from the triad, leaving only the root and the fifth. This open type of chord gives you many more melodic choices and lessens concern about what kind of third appears in the melody. It is found in much blues-based rock such as heavy metal, where the major and minor thirds are used interchangeably in the melody, and is frequently used in present-day pop and country music. It is referred to as a *power chord* (Ex. 12.20).

Ex. 12.20

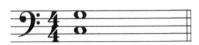

Chords without thirds occur as substitutes for either major, minor, or dominant 7th type chords. The ambiguous nature of these structures can be very useful to you. The chart below first shows a traditional I, IV, V, I progression and then presents the same progression with alterations and additions (Ex. 12.21).

Ex. 12.21

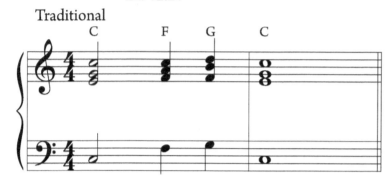

222

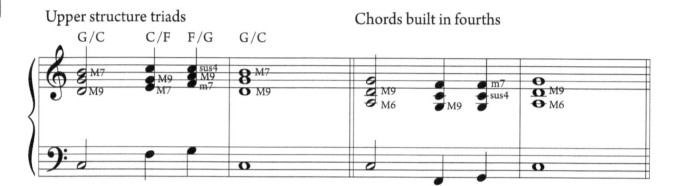

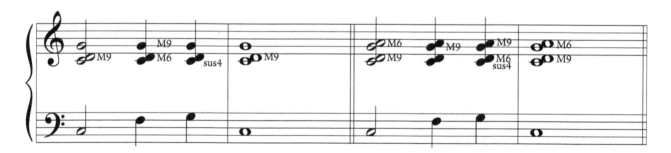

- Upper-structure triads, found in many pop songs, are built from both chord tones and available nonchord tones (see chapter 13) but with the exclusion of the third. By omitting the third, these structures retain their brightness while having less of the voluptuous sound usually associated with older jazz styles. The I chord in C major can be expressed as G/C. The chord still functions as a I chord, but with an added M7th and M9th. Likewise, the IV chord now contains both a M7 and a M9; the V chord now appears with its m7th, making it a dominant 7th chord with a sus4 and an added M9. If a slightly fuller sound is preferred, the 5th of the V chord may be added (In the key of C, this would produce Dm7/G.)
- Chords built in 4ths: These structures also furnish tonal ambiguity without changing the function of the progression.

• Ambient structures allow for multiple notes to be held while the bass note changes. Notice that just a change in the bass note changes the function of the chord.

The physicality of chords

Chords provide a physical connection to listeners. Although the following is a generalization, I have found it helpful: *melody mainly carries intellectual/emotional information; chords mainly carry physical/emotional information.*

Chords provide substantial weight to the music, defining the meter and influencing the groove. Every time a chord changes, a certain amount of weight or stress is felt. The weight of a chord has repercussions on the listener's body and influences the emphasis placed on a word or a phrase in a lyric.

When you choose a chord pattern, you are creating a tonal environment but, since chords affect the physicality of your song, you are also creating a rhythmic environment that can support and invigorate your lyric. Chords seldom appear as simply half notes or whole notes; instead they act, along with the bass and drums, as a driving force in creating the rhythmic groove. When choosing harmonies, find a rhythm and groove that inspire you and instead of a bland statement of the harmony, strive to create something vibrant and inspiring.

Here is a usable chord progression in a setting that is rhythmically bland (Ex. 12.22; ⏵ AUDIO 12.22):

Ex. 12.22

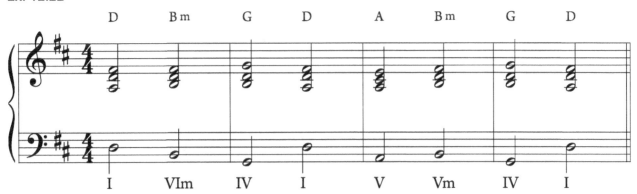

The same chord progression set in motion can create an infectious groove (Ex. 12.23; ⏵ AUDIO 12.23).

Ex. 12.23

This is the basic groove used in John Mayer's hit song, "Waiting On the World To Change." The difference between Examples 12.22 and 12.23 is seismic!

223

Try playing the first two measures of this groove from John Hiatt's "Slow Turning," repeating those two measures over and over again until your body starts rocking (Ex. 12.24).

Ex. 12.24 "Slow Turning" groove, John Hiatt

If you haven't ever really dug into a groove, I advise you to do it as soon as possible. Start enjoying the sheer physicality of music—because many terrific songs emerge from that feeling. If you play piano or guitar well enough to play in time and create a groove for yourself, then great! But today's technology provides for those who don't play a harmonic instrument. You can create a decent sounding, credible track using a simple program like GarageBand, with its library of drum loops and sampled sounds. Or, if you can play an instrument well enough and are drawn to a particular groove in a recording, try to reproduce it and then, using a different set of chord changes, attempt to write an original song.

Chords for dance music

Pop songs that have a dance orientation demand few chords and use repetitive chord patterns that do not cadence, or that cadence infrequently. Most of James Brown's songs do not contain more than four chords. There is a good reason for this: The more that harmonies change, the greater the chances are that the groove will also change. That is something you do not want to happen in a funk or groove-based dance song. What creates the groove in James Brown songs, obviously, is not the changes of harmony; it is, instead, the matrix of propulsive highly syncopated rhythms made by the interaction of drums, bass, guitar, keys and horns, as well as Brown's vocal rhythms and explosions (Ex. 12.25).

Ex. 12.25 "Cold Sweat" horns and electric bass parts, James Brown, Alfred Ellis

The A section of "Cold Sweat" lasts for sixteen measures and contains just one chord, D7. (The movement of the B minor triad to the A minor triad is an elaboration of D7).

Chords can be also be rhythmicized in order to create a propulsive groove, as they are in the chorus of Madonna's hit "Vogue" (Ex. 12.26).

Ex. 12.26 "Vogue" chorus, Madonna, Shep Pettibone

The placement of the chords in this chorus demonstrates how the physical attributes of chords can affect the groove as well as create a counterrhythm to the vocal melody. These chords change quickly in a very defined dance rhythm that adds propulsion to the groove. Placing chords in a very rhythmic setting is prevalent today and has occurred in hit songs, e.g., Rihanna's "Only Girl (In The World)," Adele's "Rolling In the Deep," and Zedd's "Clarity."

Zedd created a tonally subtle chord pattern that runs throughout his mega-hit "Clarity" (Ex. 12.27).

Ex. 12.27 "Clarity" chord pattern, Anton Zaslasvski, Holly Hafermann

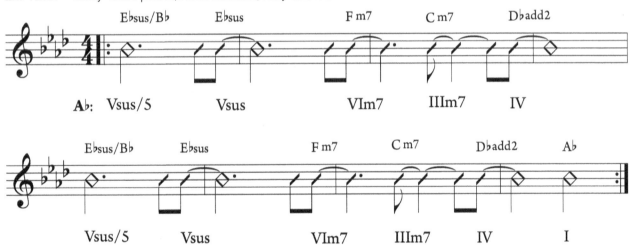

One of the unique qualities of this song is the rhythmic placement of the chords, most of which occur as anticipation of the beat. This chord pattern begins on V7^{sus}, an unstable, rather ambiguous sound. At the fourth measure, the progression ends on IV, also an unstable function. (The second iteration of this pattern does end on the tonic chord, but it appears on the third beat in the metrically weak fourth measure.) The tonal ambiguity of the progression helps the song to take on its mysterious, mythic quality.

This eight-measure chord pattern remains the same throughout the song, while textural changes, along with four distinctly different memorable melodies, one for each section of the song, provide "Clarity" with enough interest to be fascinating.

One of the most popular songs of 2016 (twelve weeks at #1 on the Billboard charts) was "Closer" by The Chainsmokers. The infectious chorus melody is made up of a steady stream of eighth notes, which is offset by the rhythmic treatment of the chords occurring on the downbeat of beat 1 and on the upbeat of beat 3 in each measure (Ex. 12.28).

Ex. 12.28 "Closer" Andrew Taggart, Ashey Frangipane, Shaun Frank, Fredrick Kennett, Isaac Slade, Joe King

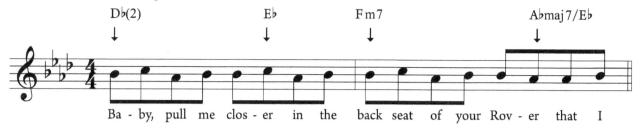

Chord progression's effect on the lyric

There is often a correlation between the lyrics of a song and the accompanying chord progression. A chord progression that cadences on the tonic chord at the end of a balanced section implies a lyric that sums up the movement that came before it. This type of chord progression implies some sort of narrative with the arrival of a tonal goal usually reflected in the lyric.

Ex. 12.29 "King of the Road" second part of verse 1, Roger Miller

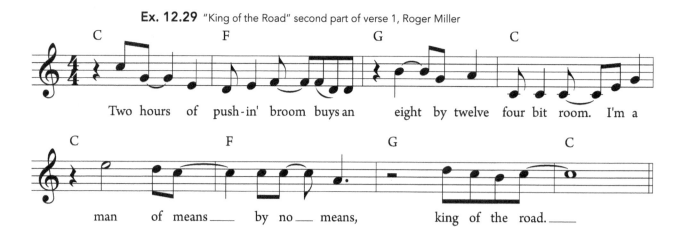

Roger Miller's "King of The Road" is a verse/refrain song with the refrain/title at the end of the second verse. The eight-measure plus eight-measure two-verse structure is perfectly balanced, and the chord pattern could not be more simple and straight-ahead. The first verse ends with a V chord, while the second verse, shown in Example 12.29, serves to balance it and uses the same chord progression as the first verse except for the final tonic chord. This effectively *closes* the section, both tonally and rhythmically, providing a strong cadence and the perfect position for highlighting the title. Lyrics that make a declarative statement, as this one does, usually have a chord pattern that reflects them by being more stable and by cadencing on the tonic chord.

Another good example of a song that makes a strong declarative statement is "We Are The World," the anthem created by Michael Jackson and Lionel Ritchie. The chorus begins with a full tonal statement, IV, V, I, reiterated to reinforce the positive feeling that the writers wanted to imbue in their listeners (Ex. 12.30).

Ex. 12.30 "We Are the World" Michael Jackson, Lionel Ritchie

Often, a full tonal statement is saved for the final cadence in a chorus in order to underline the title and the message of the song, as it does in "For Once In My Life" (Ex. 12.31).

Ex. 12.31 "For Once In My Life" Ron Miller, Orlando Murden

The choruses of "We Are The World" and "For Once In My Life" both end harmonically *closed*, as befits a lyrical statement being made. But there is a difference in their cadences.

Example 12.30 exposes only the first half of the chorus of "We Are The World," where the melodic cadence ends on *sol*, an indication that there is something more to come (it does). *Sol* is a stable tone, but it is not as stable as *do*, the note that melodically ends "For Once In My Life." Compare the two examples and notice the difference in the sense of finality that you experience. The ending of "For Once In My Life" sounds more final because both the harmony and the melody are tonally closed.

Prosodic implications of chord progressions

Since both melody and lyric define in a more detailed way what a song is trying to communicate, is there any reason to look at chord progressions regarding lyrical meaning? I believe there is—because a chord progression plays a major part in creating the tonal environment for your song as well as a syntax that you will further define as you write your melody and lyric. In this way, your chord progression can act as a kind of outline for the architecture of your song. If you begin by writing the lyrics first, your choice of chords can mirror the lyrical syntax that you've created. The choice of whether the song will be a narrative or one that is meant to capture an emotional/psychological moment will also affect the chords and chord movements you choose.

Prosody is ultimately the driving force behind every well-written song. "The Streets Of Philadelphia" uses a chord progression that changes minimally and produces the effect of enervation needed to depict feelings of devastation brought on by the AIDS epidemic depicted in the film *Philadelphia* (1993). Bruce Springsteen was awarded an Oscar for this song (Ex. 12.32).

Ex. 12.32 "The Streets Of Philadelphia" Bruce Springsteen

The prosody in this song is exceptional; not only do the chords change minimally from F to Am, with only one note difference between them; they change slowly, one chord every two measures. The melody also reflects the effects of this grave illness as it keeps repeating in eloquent simplicity, *mi, re, do,* in a hesitating rhythm that makes the protagonist sound as if he were gasping for each precious breath.

A gigantic disco hit, "I Will Survive" (1979) makes very strong lyrical statements that are reinforced by strong harmonic cadences. The song, beginning with "At first I was afraid, I was petrified / Kept thinking I could never live without you by my side," is sung in direct address to a former lover who has shown up very unexpectedly. Each lyrical statement in the verse is one or two measures long, punctuated by a harmonic cadence on every fourth measure. The song, in A minor, first cadences to its relative major, C, and then to the dominant harmony in A minor, E7. The progression then returns to the tonic, Am, where a new group of verbal diatribes begins. A litany of abuses piles up, chord after chord, cadence after cadence, and verse after verse, as the memory of each hardship is recalled (Ex. 12.33).

Ex. 12.33 "I Will Survive" chord progression used in the verse section

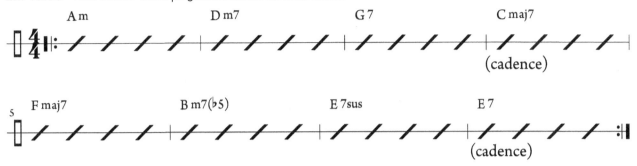

The accusatory lyric ultimately culminates in the chorus in an affirmation of the individual's ability to get past hard times, to not give in to temptation or to repeat mistakes made in the past. When a strong verbal statement such as this is made, an equally strong musical statement is demanded. In this case, traditional minor is used, its forceful leading tone pinning the strong lyrical statement to its musical equivalent. The repetition of the title is sung over V7^{sus}, V7, and finally the tonic chord, Am (Ex. 12.34).

Ex. 12.34 "I Will Survive" Freddie Perren, Dino Fekaris

In contrast to the strongly aggressive lyrics of "I Will Survive," the complaining lyrics of Drake's 2016 hit, "Hotline Bling" project a cooler attitude, one that is reflected in the chord pattern used to house his hurt feelings (Ex. 12.35).

Ex. 12.35 "Hotline Bling" Aubrey Graham, Paul Jeffries, Timmy Thompson

The key of F major is implied in the melody but is never stated by the loop-based chord pattern (two measures of B<flat> followed by two measures of Am). The melodic phrases set the leading tone against the tritone in the bass. This leading tone doesn't initially

resolve up to *do*, but moves dejectedly down to *sol*—a gesture that mirrors the singer's badly bruised ego, as the chords reflect his ambivalent psychological state. A comparison of the effect of harmony on our perception of the lyric in these two well-written songs is very telling:

"I Will Survive"
• Many strong harmonic cadences
• Tonic chord appears
• Tonality stated
• Harmonic rhythm: mainly one chord per measure
• Strong harmonic progressions reflect a lyric that is a declaration and affirmation of self.

"Hotline Bling"
• No strong harmonic cadences
• Tonic chord does not appear
• Tonality implied
• Harmonic rhythm: one chord every two measures
• Weak harmonic progression reflects a self-indulgent complaint.

"Neither One Of Us (Wants To Be the First To Say Goodbye)," a great song written by Jim Weatherly, was a tremendous hit for Gladys Knight and the Pips in 1973. It is a first-person narrative, an internal monologue that is a painfully honest confession to oneself. The movement in the chord progression mirrors the lyric narrative (Ex. 12.36).

Ex. 12.36 "Neither One Of Us" verse 1, Jim Weatherly

The narration informs the listener of the troubled state of two people who still love one another but have come to the realization that the relationship must end, yet neither of them has the courage to say it. The song starts out very leisurely, with chords placed comfortably two measures apart as the narrator explains, "It's sad to think we're not gonna make it" (not shown). As the narrative moves into an explanation of why this is happening (Example 12.36), the chords take on more movement—one per measure—and become increasingly unstable, including a chord borrowed from parallel minor, IVm, making that moment very poignant ("we just won't let it die"), affecting the melody in the way an adjective affects a noun.

The conclusion of the first verse places the title over a group of chords that are part of a strong cadence, the I chord in second inversion (acting as a suspension of the V chord), moving to the V chord and ending on the I chord in root position. This strong cadence musically underlines the lyric's statement that there really is no hope left, even though both parties can't admit to it. Here, the melody ends on *do*, the harmony ends on the tonic chord, and the lyric ends on a perfect rhyme, *die/bye*. All three elements cohere in making this statement as closed and final as it can be.

Unbalanced harmonic phrases and their effect on lyrics

Most of the time we want to make our listener's bodies feel comfortable, so we create music and sections of music that are balanced. When one harmonic phrase grouping does not balance another phrase grouping it makes our bodies feel uncomfortable. Since balance is the norm, you should be aware of any section of music that feels uncomfortable to your own body, and right the problem—but only if it is a problem. You may want to use imbalance strategically or prosodically. Imbalance can provide a welcome surprise in a song and it can also act as a wake up call to your listeners because, by creating tension, imbalance can focus attention on the next thing to occur. As already discussed in chapter 11, "Form and Function," this occurs in most prechoruses or as an added line to an otherwise balanced verse section.

Since chord patterns have such a strong connection to the body, it might be interesting and fun to look at a couple of songs that mess with our sense of balance and instead dish up some asymmetrical phrase structures.

There is great prosody in Adele's "Chasing Pavements," a song that reflects her sense of loss. She shares her thoughts with us as she walks the streets, in a kind of a stupor, in search of her lost love. This state of mind is reflected in the chosen chords (the song is in E♭, but the tonic is not stated until the very end of the chorus) and by the placement of the chords. The irregularity of this placement is, at first hearing, a bit strange but ultimately very satisfying because of its prosody with the lyric. The A♭maj7 chord, that appears on the third beat of measure 2 on the word "pavements," sounds like the first beat of a new measure. One measure later, a 2/4 measure appears, which adds to the imbalance and to the sense of stumbling along, as the protagonist finds nothing but dead-ends. The lyric "nowhere" fittingly appears at this juncture as a G7, an interesting chord choice that leads nowhere except back to where it started, the A♭(9) (Ex. 12.37).

Ex. 12.37 "Chasing Pavements" chorus, Adele Adkins, Eg White

The first half of the chorus is six-and-a-half measures in length; Adele doesn't balance this section of the chorus; instead, she moves on for another five measures, somehow making the whole chorus work and sound natural until she has achieved the song's perfect awkwardness.

The sense of displacement that is the theme of Hal David's lyric "Do You Know The Way To San Jose" is reflected in the music with its unusual five-measure phrase structure (2+3 measures). That Burt Bacharach can keep this phrase structure consistent throughout the entire song except for the coda, where it finally slips into a more familiar four-measure structure, is a sure indication of the man's inventiveness and genius. Before I studied this song, I didn't know why the song made me feel the way it did. I initially had felt that something was not quite "normal"—this unease was caused by the asymmetry of the five-measure phrase (two measures plus three measures). Yet, it had felt physically satisfying to me—due to each five-measure phrase being balanced by another five-measure phrase. Hal David's highly developed sensitivity to music allowed him to use the slightly uncomfortable imbalanced 3+2 structure to write: "I may go wrong and lose my way." Serendipity? Genius? Maybe a little of both (Ex. 12.39).

Ex. 12.38 "Do You Know the Way To San Jose" music by Burt Bacharach, lyrics by Hal David

Summary

Chords function in multiple ways.

- Chords play a major part in creating the tonal environment.
- Chords are not simply vertical structures, but have horizontal, melodic components that help steer the chord progression. Much of the beauty of chords is to be found in the way each of the voices moves.
- Chord inversions are used for several reasons: to make the chord itself less stable; to create a smoother bass line; to create a more consonant or dissonant relationship between melody to bass. (This last aspect is examined in depth in chapter 13, "Melody—Harmony.")
- Chords group measures together forming the harmonic phrase. Chords, therefore, affect structural balance.
- Chords are physical: they organize time and are an important factor in the creation of meter and groove.
- Chord progressions or patterns can be used to engender or reflect lyrics either as a narrative or as a psychological/emotional moment.
- Chord choices can affect the emotional perception of a melody and lyric in the way that an adjective can affect a noun.
- Harmonic groupings are most often used to create balance; however, they are occasionally used to create imbalance to either work strategically and/or prosodically with lyrics.

Activities

- Create a chord progression by playing the first chord, then singing each voice and, while listening very carefully, allowing one of the voices to invoke the next sound/chord. Experiment with the direction each chord takes, allowing each individual voice to either remain in place or to move to a neighboring note.

- Create a melody to either a descending or an ascending scalar bass line. After this is accomplished, fill in the implied chords.
- Create a four to eight-measure bass line using inversions (e.g., move from the I chord to the IV chord by connecting them with a I/3 chord). Once completed, write a vocal melody to it.
- Write a chord progression employing chords without thirds and then compose a melody to it.
- Create a dance groove by using a repetitive, rhythmic chord pattern.
- Create a chord pattern that contains a unique rhythmic placement of some of its chords.

13

Melody—Harmony

Tonally dependent melody

Melodies that mainly consist of stable tones have little tonal tension or melodic interest. They are considered *tonally dependent melodies*. These melodies are dependent on either harmony or on another melody occurring simultaneously such as a riff or a counter line in order to become musically interesting or satisfying. But once appropriate harmonies are added to a dependent melody, it often becomes vibrant or interesting, much the way rather bland foods come to life when the right condiments are added to them.

Melodies that are full of stable tones are readily found in children's songs because children respond to their simplicity, directness, and memorability. Adults also enjoy melodies that contain many stable tones for the same reason. However, if the music is to reflect the level of maturity and complexity that occurs in the adult world, it must be reflected in musical relationships that contain those complexities. These are often found in the relationship of melody to harmony.

Here is the melody to the first eight measures of the chorus of George and Ira Gershwin's "'S Wonderful." The melody alone resembles a children's chant or a bugle-call because it contains nothing but stable tones (Ex. 13.01).

Ex. 13.01   "'S Wonderful" melody, music by George Gershwin, lyrics by Ira Gershwin

But given its rich harmonies and unique lyrics, it becomes the romantic charmer we know it to be. The melody/harmony relationship in measures 3 and 4 takes the music out of childhood innocence and moves it into adolescence and beyond in one gesture (Ex. 13.02).

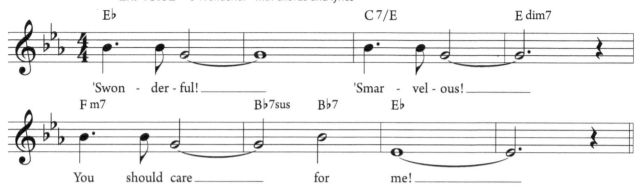

Ex. 13.02 "'S Wonderful" with chords and lyrics

The melody is harmonized initially with the tonic chord. The second chord, C7/E, however, contains a chromatic note, E♮, ♯1, that forms a tritone between ♯1 in the bass and scale degree, 5, *sol*, in the melody. The next chord, E^dim7, adds another chromatic note, D♭, that contains a tritone relationship to the melody note, G (Ex. 13.03).

Ex. 13.03 Tritones

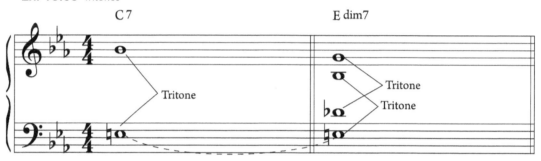

The next chord, IIm7 in measure 5, also creates a dissonant relationship between *re* in the bass and *sol* in the melody, a P11th (an octave + a P4th) (Ex. 13.04). A complete chart of intervallic dissonances is given in (Ex. 13.22).

Ex. 13.04 P11th

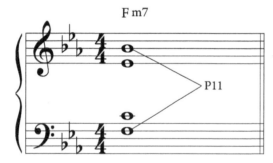

There is a lessening of tension in the relationship of melody to harmony in measure 6 with the introduction of the V7 chord that prepares us for a return to the tonic on the last note of the melody. The song's melodic simplicity coupled with the chromatic chords and the dissonances created by their relationship to the melody sparked Ira Gershwin to create lyrics that incorporate a humorous childlike attitude with a heavy dose of adult romanticism.

Melody's primary and secondary relationships

The Gershwin excerpt provides us with an example of a significant musical/psychological phenomenon that occurs between melody and harmony. Gershwin's melody without its harmonies appears bland because we are hearing it only in relationship to the tonal center—its *primary* relationship. But as soon as harmonies are added, it's as if a mesmerizing perfume has filled the space, clouding the primary relationship. The melody's relationship to its harmonies—its *secondary* relationship—is considerable, causing the total music to become much more interesting and vibrant. Understanding how this phenomenon works provides you, the composer, with ways to conceptualize and find appropriate harmonies that work best for your song. It allows you to work with two layers of relationships that mirror the complexities and subtleties to be expressed in order to make your music more interesting and meaningful. For example, if you realize that your melody contains a lot of stable tones, you can choose to use unstable harmonies that cause the melody to give the impression that it has an innate energy that, in fact, it doesn't possess.

Accord and contradiction between melody and harmony

So that you may further grasp what is taking place in the relationship between melody and harmony, you must realize that there are a number of ways in which these two entities behave with one another. An *unstable* note in your melody can sound more consonant than a *stable* note, or a *stable* note in your melody can sound more dissonant than an *unstable* note, due to the choice of harmony.

Example 13.05 explores how a melody that can easily be heard in relationship to its tonal center can muddle our perception of that relationship when harmonized with chords that help disguise that relationship. The same four-note melody in F major is set against four different diatonic chords.

Ex. 13.05 Same melody, four harmonizations

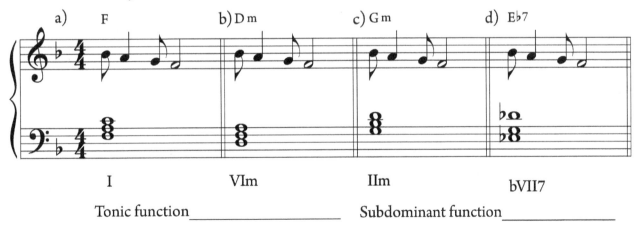

Example (a): The melody's relationship to the tonic F is clear. The first note, Bb, is a dissonant nonchord tone that resolves to the stable A, then moves to the unstable G, which resolves to the stable F, the tonic.

Example (b): Since the VIm chord is often used to substitute for the I chord, it provides us with a similar perception of the melody.

Example (c): This harmonization provides us with a different perspective of the melody; the B♭ is no longer dissonant to the chord, but the A and F (both stable tones in the key of F) are! We've entered into Alice in Wonderland's *Through the Looking Glass* world, where everything that was dissonant now is consonant and vice versa.

Example (d): The "Through the Looking Glass" effect is even more pronounced; the last melody note, F, the tonic note, is heard as a dissonance, causing the music to sound open or unresolved.

Example 13.06 illustrates that *when a harmony contradicts the stability or instability of a melody note, dissonance is increased.* In the key of C, the leading tone B, the most unstable and dissonant note, sounds much more dissonant when it is pitted against a C triad or an A minor triad, tonally consonant chords, than when it is harmonized by either an E minor or G major triad, more dissonant chords in the key.

Ex. 13.06

238

When B is harmonized by either the E minor chord or G major chord, melody and harmony concur with one another and act like a conspiracy of thieves, producing the effect of consonance, even though both melody and harmony are dissonant or unstable to the tonal center.

This then is our playing field: stable tones that are consonant to the tonal center, but are either consonant or dissonant to the chord, and unstable tones that are dissonant to the tonal center, but are either consonant or dissonant to the chord.

You, as a songwriter, must be constantly cognizant of these two relationships: (1) melody's primary relationship to the tonal center, and (2) melody's secondary relationship to the chords. These two relationships cause many of the complexities and subtleties that we, as listeners, find delectable. I find this duality so intriguing because of its analogies to so much of what we know within the human experience and, hence, to the prosody that exists between lyrics and music. All the subtleties of our emotional life are available in music, and because songwriting combines words with music, these subtleties can be most fully realized in song.

The setting of the refrain line in Paul Simon's "Still Crazy After All These Years" exemplifies how well-chosen harmonies can inform the listener of the subtle feelings experienced by the singer. Notice that this melody is full of stable tones that are enlivened or activated by the choice of harmonies. While the melody closes twice on *do* on the word "years," the harmony remains open. Especially poignant is the tonic in the melody with the minor IV chord in the harmony (measure 7); hearing it with the lyrics, we sense a darkness hinting at regret in this one musical gesture. The delayed closures caused by the tonal contradictions between the melody and harmony make this setting of the title very poignant. Simon finally allows the instruments to close the section (Ex. 13.07).

Ex. 13.07 "Still Crazy After All These Years" Paul Simon

Many pop and country songs through subtle manipulation of diatonic harmonies cause a blurring of the tonality, yet enable the music to be both appealing and comprehensible in its simplicity. (Both melody and harmony remain diatonic, so the listener can still easily sing along with it.) A good example of a simple diatonic melody harmonized by simple but contradictory harmonies is found in "Hard To Love," a song sung by Lee Brice that reached #1 status on the country charts in 2014. Upon hearing this chorus, the listener feels completely comfortable with the melody, yet there seems to be some hidden ingredient that makes the music beckon. It's an itch that can't quite be scratched; there's something sensual about it.

Ex. 13.08 "Hard To Love" Billy Montana, John Ozier, Ben Glover

The cause of this phenomenon is the melody's relationship to the harmony. The first beat of the chorus has the stable C♯ in the melody pitted against a D chord, producing a dissonant major seventh interval between the root of the chord in the bass and the melody note. The last two notes in (Ex. 13.08) make a common melodic gesture in tonal music, one that is often found in Mozart's music, sometimes called a "sigh motive." Usually the first note in a sigh motive is dissonant to the chord with the second note providing its resolution. In this example, just the opposite occurs: the first note is consonant and the second one is dissonant to the chord. The effect is like tasting a familiar food, but with some exotic spice added to it.

239

I've reharmonized the melody with a more "correct" harmonization in (Ex. 13.09). In this rewrite of the harmonies I've made most of the melody notes into chord tones and, in doing so, have taken most of the bite and beauty out of the music.

Ex. 13.09 "Hard To Love" reharmonization

When we compare these two harmonic settings of the same melody, it is easy to conclude that an informed use of dissonance between melody and harmony can spell the difference between creating a hit or a miss.

Process

If you've written a melody that may seem to have too many stable tones and may seem tonally uninteresting, you have a choice to make. You may either alter your melody by changing some of the stable tones to unstable ones, or you may retain your melody and seek out interesting harmonies that can enliven your entire music. I suggest that you first try to retain your melody and try using harmonies that create more interesting, dissonant relationships when placed with your melody.

The following examples (Exs. 13.10–13.13) demonstrate how your ability to grasp the stability/instability of your melody in relationship to the tonal center can inform the harmonic choices you make as well as influencing the effect your melody and lyrics have on the listener.

This melody appears to be tonally dull. The stable tones are marked with an "st" above them.

Ex. 13.10 Original melody

Harmonized in the following way, the music remains fairly dull; this is due to the tonal agreement between melody and harmony.

Ex. 13.11

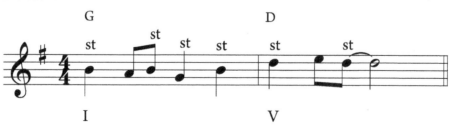

With new choices of chords in (Ex. 13.12), the melody is more dissonant to the chords and becomes more interesting. Notice that certain nonchord tones (B in measure 1) simply do not resolve because they are *supportable* dissonances and sound perfectly fine. *An explanation of supportable dissonances appears in this chapter under the heading "Supportable nonchord tones" and in a chart, (Ex. 13.37).*

Ex. 13.12

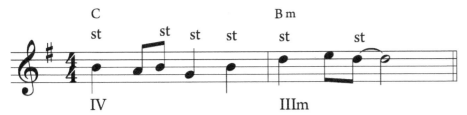

This third harmonization, (Ex. 13.13), is even more transformative.

Ex. 13.13

Now try singing the following lyric, "You never hear a word I say," with each of the given harmonic settings in (Exs. 13.10–13.13; ⊙ AUDIO Exs. 13.10–13.13).

- The first setting is so bland that you may be left wondering why those words are being sung.
- The second setting feels more valid with a loving but slightly downtrodden tone (most likely due to the final minor chord).
- The third setting is the most biting and sounds the most heartfelt to me. Beginning with the nonchord tone, B, on the word, "You," moving to a chord tone, G, harmonized by a minor chord on the word, "hear" and to the nonchord tone, D, on "word" and "say" in the second measure, this setting seems to capture the intent of the lyric best. These examples should indicate to you the power that harmony possesses to capture subtleties and nuances that affect the listener's perception of both the melody and the lyrics.

The next examples (Exs. 13.14–13.17) demonstrate how a dependent melody can be harmonized in ways that either emphasize its stability or disguise it. This melody consists entirely of stable tones (Ex. 13.14; ⊙ AUDIO 13.14).

Ex. 13.14

The following harmonization is bland because it uses too many chords that are also relatively stable (Ex. 13.15; ▶ AUDIO 13.15).

Ex. 13.15

With well-chosen harmonies, the music appears wistful, delicate, and not without charm (Ex. 13.16; ▶ AUDIO 13.16).

Ex. 13.16

Contradiction between melody and harmony mark many of the popular songs in the early part of the 21st century. Set in a hip-hop groove, the melody in (Ex. 13.17), similar to ones above, employs only the stable notes E, *mi*, and G, *sol*, in C major, while the harmonies create interesting dissonances and tonal ambiguity by totally avoiding the I chord (Ex. 13.17; ▶ AUDIO 13.17).

Ex. 13.17

The prismatic effect

Example 13.17 demonstrates one of the simplest and most natural ways to develop a musical idea: simply restate or slightly vary the melody while changing the harmonies that support it. This technique can be applied to an entire melody, a motive, or a note that appears in the same rhythmic area in similar phrases. I call this technique the *prismatic effect*, likening the musical effect to a visual one in which different moving colored lights (the chords) are directed at a stationary crystal (the repeated melody); as each edge of the crystal catches and reflects the different colored lights, the crystal itself seems to move. This technique provides repetition, a key ingredient to ensure memorability, while it also provides change, a key ingredient to avoid monotony. It is a simple and effective way to employ a basic compositional tenet: *create variety within similarity.*

The Beatles used this technique in their transformative album, "Sgt. Pepper's Lonely Hearts Club Band." (Ex. 13.18)

Ex. 13.18 "Sgt. Pepper's Lonely Hearts Club Band" John Lennon, Paul McCartney

One of the biggest hits of 2013, Daft Punk's "Get Lucky," employs the prismatic effect to a four-chord repeated pattern (Ex. 13.19).

Ex. 13.19 "Get Lucky" Thomas Bangalter, Guy Christo, Pharrel Williams, Nile Rodgers

Katy Perry's tremendous success as a songwriter is partially due to keeping her songs simple and interesting. The use of the prismatic effect helps her achieve this. Notice how the melody emphasizes G, the tonal center, while the tonic chord, G, is completely avoided (Ex. 13.20).

Ex. 13.20 "Last Friday Night (T.G.I F.)" Katy Perry, Lukasz Gottwald, Max Martin, Bonnie McKee

Burt Bacharach, a masterful songwriter with a background that includes study with the composer Darius Milhaud, wrote "(They Long To Be) Close To You" with his longtime lyricist, the great Hal David. It became an anthem during the early 1970s due to the song's deceptively simple melody and delightful lyric, along with a terrific recording of the song by the Carpenters (Ex. 13.21).

Ex. 13.21 *"(They Long To Be) Close To You" last 4 measures of the verse, music by Burt Bacharach, lyrics by Hal David*

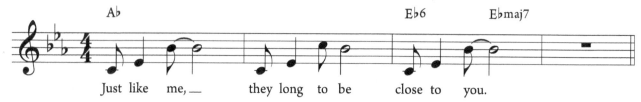

Here we see how the prismatic effect can also be used strategically. The song begins using that same motive with which it ends. The motive is first harmonized by the subdominant harmony and doesn't arrive at the tonic chord until its final two bars, highlighting the title/refrain. This song, like many of Burt Bacharach's songs, is rich in techniques and well worth further study.

The importance of dissonance in the melody/harmony relationship

Dissonance in any art is a catalyst, the main activating force that causes interest and forward motion to take place. What would a mystery be without an incidence of crime, and what would a love story be without a loss or a hint of betrayal occurring? Likewise, in music, dissonance is an activator and a major source of interest and beauty.

The informed use of dissonance in songwriting is important, because dissonance attracts attention to your melody, causes it to progress, and contributes to its emotional power. This is true whether dissonance happens between the melody to its tonal center or between the melody to the chords that support it. Chapter 4, "Tone Tendencies," has already given you some necessary information so that you may knowingly use melodic dissonances in relationship to the tonal center. Measure the melody's relationship to the chord that is supporting it by examining:

- the intervallic dissonance of the melody to the root of the chord
- the intervallic dissonance of the melody to the bass note (e.g., the chord may be in an inversion)
- the dissonances of the intervals within the chord itself
- whether or not the music contains chromatic notes (a chromatic note is more dissonant to the tonal center than any diatonic note.)

The chart below lists intervals from consonance to dissonance into four sets that are easy to remember and that serve as a quick guide to possible choices for chords or bass notes (Ex. 13.22).

Ex. 13.22 Consonance to dissonance chart

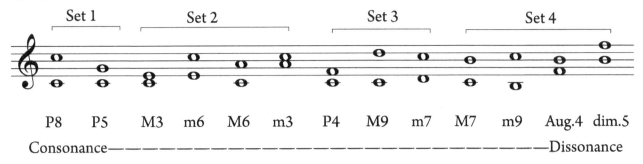

Set 1		Set 2			Set 3			Set 4			
P8	P5	M3	m6	M6	m3	P4	M9	m7	M7	m9	Aug.4 dim.5

Consonance———————————————————————————————Dissonance

- Set 1: The octave and the perfect fifth, the two most consonant intervals, form set 1.
- Set 2: Major and minor 3rds and 6ths form set 2.
- Set 3: The P4th—a dissonant interval because it is always heard as an inversion of the P5th—the m7th, and the M9th form set 3.
- Set 4: The M7th, the m9th, and the A4th/d5th (the tritone) form set 4.

All the notes in this chart are diatonic in C major to facilitate your understanding this concept, but this chart applies to all keys and all modes. This chart only applies to intervals within a diatonic setting; once a chromatic note appears in a diatonic tonal environment, it forms a dissonance that is greater than any found within the diatonic intervallic set.

Here are examples of how I use this information (Exs. 13.23–27; ⏵ AUDIO EXS. 13.23–27). Measured by its relationship to the tonal center, the melody in Ex. 13.23 already has some progression built into it. Its high point, the B in measure 1, has a dissonant relationship to the tonic and acts as expected to a delayed resolution to C in the second measure.

Ex. 13.23

If I choose to have the harmony agree with the melody's tonal implications, it would result in a rather bland rendering, with consonant set 1 and 2 intervals occurring between melody and bass on the strong beats (Ex. 13.24).

Ex. 13.24

To heighten the dissonance of the B, the climax of the melody, I place the dissonant tritone, F, under it (Ex. 13.25).

Ex. 13.25

In Ex. 13.26, I place an A in the bass to form a set 2 interval to begin the piece and D in the bass to form a set 3 interval, a minor 7th, with the melody, C, in measure 2. This provides an ending that is more open.

Ex. 13.26

The next harmonization is the most dissonant and demonstrates a complete contradiction of the melodic tonal implications by the harmony (Ex. 13.27).

Ex. 13.27

To do this, I heighten the dissonance of the first melody note, E, with Dm7, producing a M9 interval between the bass to melody, and harmonize the C in the second measure with a chord that contains a very dissonant chromatic note, F♯, the ♯4 of the key of C. As mentioned, a chromatic note is automatically dissonant to the tonality, and this one produces the tritone, providing an extreme dissonance. The tonic note is now the climax of the phrase, practically screaming for our attention. This rather bland melody now sounds like part of a romantic score from a film noir 1940 Hollywood movie!

Nonchord tones in the melody

When a dissonance occurs between melody and harmony, depending on the style of music, the melody note either (1) will be a nonchord tone that resolves to a note that is found in the chord or (2) will stay there absorbing the dissonance (I call this type of nonchord tone a *supportable nonchord tone*).

When a melodic dissonance resolves to a note found in its harmonic underpinning, it is acting in the way nonchord tones have traditionally been treated in music from Bach through Brahms. These resolutions usually are immediate and move down a step to the note of resolution. Less frequently, the nonchord tone resolves up a step to the note of resolution. When a melodic dissonance occurs that does not resolve to a chord tone, it must be supported by harmonies that are compatible with it and can support the dissonance. (A listing of chords and intervals they can support is found in a chart, (Ex. 13.37.)

Nonchord tones often provide "the juice," the good stuff, and the more interesting notes in a melody. All the academic terms used to name these notes, such as "passing tone," "neighbor tone," "suspension," "unprepared approach tone," "appoggiatura," "escape tone," etc., don't do complete justice to these notes that are often the choicest notes found in a melody.

The nonchord tones, C and E♭, found in (Ex. 13.28), measure 1, resolve to chord members; the C initially resolves up to the D and then more fully resolves to the B♭, while the E♭ resolves down to the D and the C resolves down to the B♭. The only note in measure 2 that is a chord tone is G; the F, found on the downbeat, is an example of a *supportable nonchord tone*, a note that does not resolve to a chord tone but is, instead, supported by a compatible harmony. The F, a stable tone in B♭, supported by a chord, E♭ that does not contain an F, produces a somewhat unresolved or open ending to the phrase. *Throughout the following examples in this chapter, nonchord tones are marked with an asterisk* *

Ex. 13.28

When we reverse the chords in measures 1 and 2, the effect is very different. In (Ex. 13.29), measure 1, the first two notes, C and D, are now nonchord notes. The C doesn't immediately resolve but, instead, moves up to the D and then resolves down to the B♭; the D, in a slightly delayed resolution moves up to the E♭, the root of the chord. The D and C appear again, this time descending to the B♭ chord tone. The only note in measure 2 that is a nonchord tone is G; the F is consonant to both the chord and the tonal center and gives us, the listeners, a tonal closure.

Ex. 13.29

In comparing (Exs. 13.28–13.29), we realize the power of harmony to influence the way we perceive the same melody and harmony's ability to influence our perception of the music's tonal stability and closure.

Examples of nonchord tones found in well-known songs

An analysis of any melody should begin by stripping away the harmony to reveal the relationship of the melody to the tonal center. If we omit doing this, we are willfully ignoring the primary relationship of melody to tonal center and giving all the power of tonal movement in the melody to its relationship to the chords.

The melody of The Beatles' "In My Life" is haunting even without its choice harmonies. The melody in (Ex. 13.30a), heard only in its relationship to the tonal center, B♭, is revelatory. Without chords, this melody still retains most of its beauty because of its relationship to the tonal center. Yes, chords do help refine and beautify the entire music, but chords are an enhancement, not the main generator of interest in this melody. The contour of the overall melody along with the intervallic leaps of a P4th, major and minor 3rds, and especially the M6th, add to this melody's memorability.

Ex. 13.30a "In My Life" melody in relationship to the tonal center

Stable tones abound in this melody (indicated by the dotted lines). The dissonances of the unstable tones moving to stable tones provide interest and melodic progression. The note C, (*re* in B♭) in measure 1 resolves down to *do*, its primary resolution, but when C appears again, it resolves to D (*mi* in B♭) its secondary resolution, imbuing the music with energy, encouraging D to rise to the F in measure 2. The chromatic G♭ in measure 3 naturally moves to *sol* on the downbeat of measure 4 (Ex. 13.30b).

Ex. 13.30b "In My Life" John Lennon, Paul McCartney

This gorgeous melody has its beauty heightened by Lennon and McCartney's choice of harmony. The B♭7 chord, easily could have been used to harmonize the F in the melody on the first beat of measure 2, but the writers wisely chose to use a Gm7 chord. The G in the bass sounding with the F in the melody form a m7th interval, a set 3 relationship that is more dissonant and interesting than one that would have resulted from using B♭, a P5th interval, set 1 relationship. The C, a nonchord tone, appears first on the fourth beat of measure 2 as a nonchord tone that resolves up to the third of the B♭7 chord and then, on the downbeat of measure 3, resolves down to B♭, the fifth of the E♭ chord. The chromatic E♭m chord corresponds to the G♭ in the melody and adds a poignancy that the lyrics demand.

Elton John, one of the best songwriters of this and the last century, often begins his creative process by reacting to a given lyric with harmony. His choice of melody notes is informed by a great understanding of how nonchord tones produce the dissonances needed to express feeling (Ex. 13.31).

Ex. 13.31 "Don't Let The Sun Go Down On Me" music by Elton John, lyrics by Bernie Taupin

Notice how he uses nonchords in word painting in measure 1 and 2, on the words "sun" and "down" and on the words "I" and "my" in measure 3, and especially on the chromatic note, E♭, that forms a m9th, set 4 relationship with the root of the D7 chord on the downbeat of measure 4, in order to create a melody of great emotion and beauty.

The value of knowing how to use nonchord tones comes into focus when beginning a song with a chord pattern. Here is one of the most common chord progressions used during the doo-wop era, one that produced many hit songs (Ex. 13.32):

Ex. 13.32

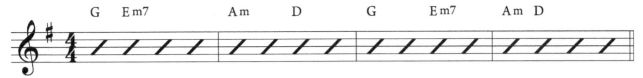

Sam Cooke managed to write a number of classic songs employing this chord pattern. Notice how important the nonchords are in the success of the melody and how these momentary dissonances highlight important words (Ex. 13.33).

Ex. 13.33 "You Send Me" L. C. Cook

The melody of "Let It Be" contains nonchord tones that highlight the important words in its lyrics (Ex. 13.34a).

Ex. 13.34a "Let It Be" John Lennon, Paul McCartney

Can you imagine what this melody would sound like without those dissonances?

Ex. 13.34b "Let It Be" melody without nonchord tones

The results of this rewrite (Ex. 13.34b) should prove to you how necessary dissonances and nonchord tones are in the creation of beautiful and interesting melodies.

Notice how the title word "California" is highlighted in (Ex. 13.35) by the use of nonchord tones.

Ex. 13.35 "Hotel California" Don Felder, Glen Frey, Don Henley

Wel - come   to   the   Ho - tel   Cal - i for - nia.

Most of the nonchord tones that have been demonstrated until now have resolved *down* a step to the nearest chord tones. Although this is the path they usually take, this is not always the case, as demonstrated in (Ex. 13.36), Bruno Mars's hit song, "When I Was Your Man," where most of the nonchord tones resolve *up* to the nearest chord tone. Notice the nonchord tones that end the two phrases. These are *anticipations*, very pronounced syncopated rhythms that occur before the beat, in this instance before the first beat of measure 2 and measure 4, creating strong accents that call attention to themselves and are very enticing to the listener.

Ex. 13.36 "When I Was Your Man" Bruno Mars, Philip Lawrence, Ari Levine

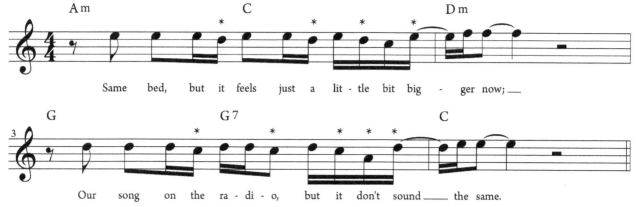

Same   bed,   but   it   feels   just   a   lit - tle   bit   big - ger   now; ___

Our   song   on   the   ra - di - o,   but   it   don't   sound ___ the   same.

Supportable nonchord tones

Melodic dissonances can be treated in any number of ways, depending on the chosen style of music, and are a major factor in defining the style of the music. In current popular song, nonchord tones in the melody do not always resolve to chord tones. This is especially true if the melody note that is dissonant to the chord is consonant or stable to the tonal center.

Dissonances in the melody that don't have to resolve to the nearest chord tone, but instead can be sustained, are what I call *supportable nonchord tones*. The following chart, (Ex. 13.37), will assist you in more fully understanding which nonchord tones are supportable by the various chord types.

Ex. 13.37 Supportable nonchord tones

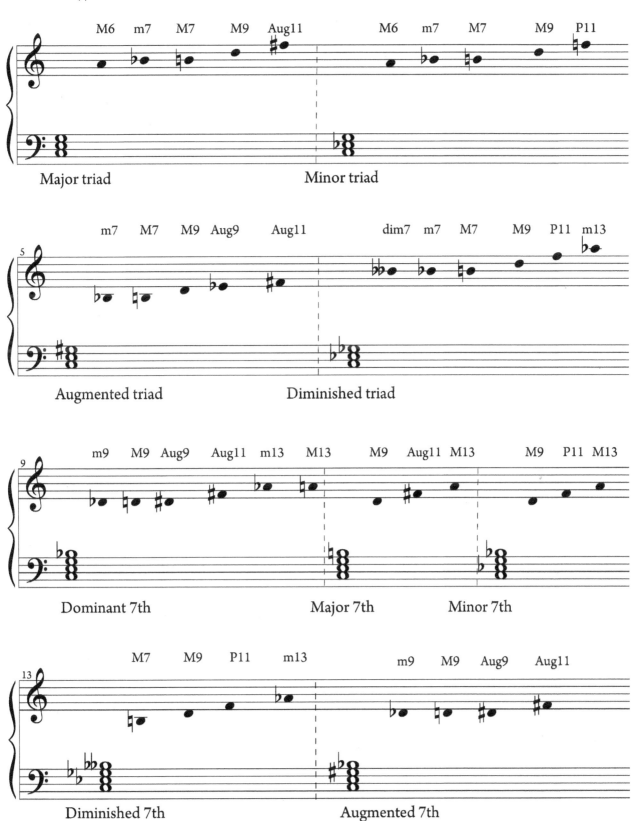

Each chord type listed above supports its own group of nonchord tones (i.e., they do not have to resolve to chord tones). However, you must realize that once a tonal environment has been established, anything outside of that tonal environment (i.e., a chromatic note) is going to sound foreign and dissonant to it. (This doesn't mean that going outside the given tonal environment is to be avoided, but doing so is a move outside of the established environment and will call attention to that event.)

For example, the chart indicates that a major triad can support a M7th. In the key of C major, the C major triad can support B, its M7th, because B (*ti*) is diatonic in the key of C. Likewise, an F major triad can support E (*mi*), its M7th, because E is diatonic in the key of C. Although a G major triad can support F♯, its M7th, the F♯ is foreign in the tonal environment of C major. The use of the chromatic note, F♯, would produce an unexpected dissonance and would indicate that either a move to C Lydian has occurred or a modulation, possibly to G major or E minor, has taken place or is about to occur.

Likewise, in the key of E♭, not all of notes that Cm, the VIm chord, can support are diatonic to E♭. Although Cm can support the M6th, A♮, and the M7th, B♮, neither note is in the key of E♭ and, therefore, would sound dissonant to the key.

When I first heard "I Could Not Ask For More," sung by the country artist Sara Evans, the melody moved me so much that I was compelled to discover why. After hearing the melody only in its relationship to the tonal center, I realized Diane Warren's rather unusual treatment of the melody in its relationship to the harmony caused me to react in such an intense way (Ex. 13.38).

Ex. 13.38 "I Could Not Ask For More" Diane Warren

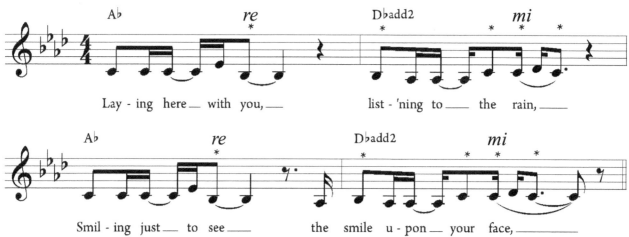

Both notes that end these two phrases, the B♭ and the C, are *supportable nonchord tones*, dissonances that do not resolve to chord tones. But when I listen to these two phrases, I do hear a melodic resolution from *re*, the B♭ that ends the first phrase, to its secondary resolution, *mi*, the C that ends the second phrase. That sense of melodic resolution is caused by the melody's primary relationship being fulfilled. *Re* is resolving to *mi*. However, the unresolved dissonances of those notes to their respective chords produce a haunting, sensual effect that is perfect in its embrace of the feelings the lyrics are generating.

Taylor Swift has been innovative in her use of melodic dissonances and in the use of unstable harmonies that support stable tones in her melodies. Notice how the melody and harmony in this chorus excerpt of "You Belong With Me" contradict one another (Ex. 13.39).

Ex. 13.39 "You Belong With Me" Taylor Swift, Liz Rose

Nonchord tones are used here to underline the biting message delivered by the singer. Notice how Swift uses dissonance to highlight the lyric's important words: "'Cause she **does**-n't get **your hu**-mour like **I do**."

Resolution to the tonal center is achieved in the melody—since the final tone, B, *mi* in the key of G, is a stable tone—while simultaneously the amount of dissonance is increased because B, a M7th, is more dissonant to the root of the C chord than the previous half note, A, a M6th. This tonal contradiction is the perfect choice for the lyric's emotional outburst. It venomously underlines the message: I'm the one you should have chosen! It is no accident that Taylor Swift has had tremendous success. Whether it is by superb natural instincts or schooling in the craft of songwriting (most likely, a combination of both), she is one amazing songwriter!

The extent of tonal contradiction in this song, caused by its many stable tones in the melody accompanied by unstable harmonies or vice-versa, has not been a stylistic trait of traditional country music, but has slowly, over the years, crept in—and now defines the sound of both contemporary pop and contemporary country music. This has occurred as a natural consequence of the need to retain diatonic melodies and mainly diatonic triadic harmonies to keep the simple, straightforward pop and country sound intact, coupled with the need to express the complexities (dissonances) of contemporary life. This is yet another example of the formula "simple and interesting" at work in well written popular songs.

The mixing and matching, agreements, and contradictions between melody and harmony is one of the great joys of all music composition, but especially so in songwriting, where these amalgamations give us the means by which to deepen the meaning of our lyrics and help us mirror the complexities of the human condition.

Beyond tradition

Dissonances that go beyond those listed in "Supportable nonchord tones" appeared noticeably in two major hits in 2015: Omi's "Cheerleader" and Adele's "Hello." These dissonances have been considered by academicians to be too dissonant and therefore "wrong" in any course in traditional harmony. Isolated, these dissonances might be identified as something from Stravinsky's neoclassical period or a creation of the experimentalist composer Charles Ives. One thing that popular songs remind us academicians of—there are no rules in popular music. If it sounds good and feels good, it can and will be used.

Ex. 13.40 "Cheerleader" beginning of bridge, Omar Pasley, Clifton Dillon, Mark Bradford, Ryon Dillon, Andi Muhammed

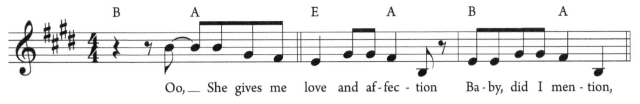

The last measure in (Ex. 13.40), in the gigantic 2015 summer hit "Cheerleader," contains a seemingly bizarre harmonization of the melody: not one note of the melody is part of the harmonies that support it. One note in this example, the E in in the last measure, is usually considered too dissonant: a P4th that should not appear sustained while the major third of the B major chord, D♯, is sounding.

Compare (Exs.13.40–13.41), a "correct" harmonization of the same melody. The "correct" harmonization sounds like the kind of harmonies that are found in a pleasant island-tinged song, perfect for easy listening, but probably not a hit by today's standards, whereas the hit version has a bite and pungency that act as a lure to today's listeners.

Ex. 13.41 "Cheerleader" beginning of bridge, reharmonized in a more traditional setting

One of Adele's great strengths as an artist is her ability to communicate emotionally charged lyrics with equally emotionally charged music. The melody, no doubt composed to the tonal center rather than to the harmonic underpinning (a four-chord pattern that repeats), moves from the nonchord tone B♭ in measure 2 and, in measure 4, to its resolution, A♭. The E♭ chord that appears with the melody as it resolves to the tonal center contradicts the resolution, causing an important dissonance (the clash of the melody's A♭ against the harmony's G, the third of the E♭ chord) to occur, a dissonance that reflects the hurt and pain that the singer is expressing (Ex. 13.42).

Ex. 13.42 "Hello" beginning of chorus, Adele Adkins, Greg Kurstin

Listen to what happens if the E♭ chord does not appear. Although the melody is now correctly resolved, it lacks the tensile strength and beauty of the actual harmonization (Ex. 13.43).

Ex. 13.43 "Hello" beginning of chorus, reharmonized in a more traditional setting

The reason more of these clashes between melody and harmony have occurred in popular songs in recent times has been the preponderance of loop-based harmonies. Repetition of the same chord progression acts as a drone. You can more easily use dissonances against a drone-like repeating harmonic pattern without calling undue attention to the event because only one thing, the melody, is changing, not two things, the melody and the harmony.

Jazz songs

In pop music or country music, the melody is usually diatonic and therefore doesn't present too many notes that are both dissonant to the tonal center and dissonant to the harmony. This, however, is not true of many jazz songs, where a higher degree of dissonance is not only accepted but often sought after.

This expansion of "acceptable" dissonances in melody writing has been part of the jazz treatment of melody/harmony relationships for a long time, and before jazz—in the music of the Impressionists—notably Debussy and Ravel. Unlike pop or country songs, in jazz songs the dissonant melody notes are also incorporated into the harmony—into the underpinning that supports the melody. This has the effect of making the melody and harmony agree with one another, lessening the effect of the melodic dissonance but increasing the harmonic dissonance and the density of the music itself. This accounts for most jazz ballads sounding so lush.

Among the traits that characterize jazz songs are the contradictions that exist between what has come to be expected and what actually occurs. This trait is not so obvious now, long after jazz originated in the early part of the 20th century, when the "new" music produced a negative reaction from conservative listeners, much the way rap does from today's conservative listeners. Now jazz just sounds like jazz; a style of music that appears to the general public as an acceptable, slightly old-fashioned music that has a niche audience and can be heard piped into department stores into malls and restaurants. Nonetheless, jazz is a great American original music, a more complex and demanding music than most present-day popular music styles, and one well worth studying.

We've long heard the question "What is jazz?" My definition is: *jazz is a well-dressed man in patent leather shoes, a dark blue Armani suit with an elegant white dress shirt— wearing a yellow and green polka dot tie.* The musical equivalent of that image occurs in the contradiction of the expected accents of the meter of the music: Instead of **one**, two, **three**, four, we get: one, **two**, three, **four**, a syncopated meter. Much of the melody is heavily syncopated as well—another form of contradiction. Not often analyzed or discussed in jazz are the tonal contradictions that are as important as the metric and rhythmic ones.

The tonally complex landscape that exists in "Lush Life," one of the most skillful and original compositions in the jazz song literature, helps define that style of song. This example also is a reminder of how difficult it is to sing the intervals and the modulations that inhabit this little masterpiece (Ex. 13.44). Go ahead and try it and you'll see what I mean.

Ex. 13.44 "Lush Life" Billy Strayhorn

Jazz musicians have often been attracted to Broadway songs because of their memorable melodies coupled with their complex harmonies that have allowed jazz players a way to showcase their improvisational skills. Because these songs were often originally sung in a fairly rigid fashion on Broadway, jazz players could contrast their looser approach to these songs by adding syncopations and blues notes to the melody and by reharmonizing the melody in order to make the songs "jazzier."

There are two methods of treating tunes that form the modus operandi of jazz. The first approach to "jazzing up" a tune is to choose a simple tune and then add more syncopation and a deeper level of complexity to the harmony. We saw this approach in Gershwin's "S'Wonderful," where the simple melody is in complete agreement with the tonal center while complexities result from tonal contradictions that occur between the melody and the harmony. The choice of a simple melody (sometimes even children's songs have been used to good effect, e.g., Miles Davis's treatment of "Put Your Little Foot," renamed "Fran Dance") allows the jazz composer or arranger a chance to substitute complex, foreign harmonies to accompany it.

Here's one of the best-known children's song, "Twinkle, Twinkle" (Ex. 13.45; ▶ AUDIO 13.45):

Ex. 13.45 *"Twinkle, Twinkle"*

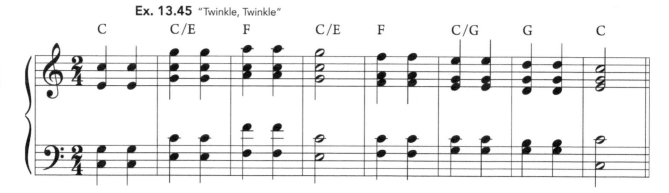

Here is a jazz treatment of what no longer sounds like a children's song (Ex. 13.46; ▶ AUDIO 13.46).

Ex. 13.46

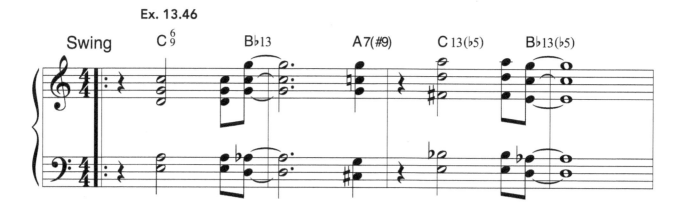

We can partially attribute the success of Steely Dan songs to this approach. Many of their songs have memorable melodies that are often fairly simple but are accompanied by complex or more sophisticated harmonies (Ex. 13.47).

Ex. 13.47 "Deacon Blues" melody

Ex. 13.48 "Deacon Blues" reharmonized with traditional root motion

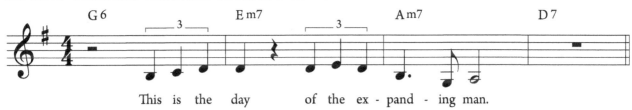

This melody could easily be harmonized in a more traditional way using diatonic chords (Exs. 13.48–13.49).

Ex. 13.49 "Deacon Blues" Walter Becker and Donald Fagen

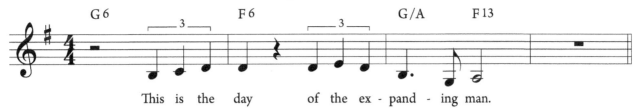

The second approach to creating a jazz song is to use nondiatonic or chromatic notes in the melody and harmonize them with chords that also have a dissonant relationship to the tonal center, as exemplified in (Ex. 13.50), Duke Ellington's "Sophisticated Lady" (Ex. 13.50).

Duke Ellington's music, as the lyricist Mitchel Parish heard it, sounded "sophisticated."

This unique melody seems to be in search of the tonic note, A♭, but is not destined to locate it until measure 16 (not shown), where the tonic in the melody finally appears in the cadence before the bridge. The first melodic phrase begins on ♭7, and ends on the 7th degree; the second phrase ends on the 6th scale degree in measure 5, and the third phrase finally cadences on ♭7 in measure 8. *The numbers above the melody indicate the degrees of the scale and chromatic notes in their relationship to the tonal center.*

257

Ex. 13.50 "Sophisticated Lady" music by Duke Ellington

Because the melody is so tonally ambiguous, the harmonies mainly mirror the melody, except for measure 3, where the leading tone in the melody is contradicted by the tonic harmony. Here, the Imaj7 chord incorporates the dissonance that appears in the melody into the basic harmony. Both the rich harmonies and the tonal contradictions that exist between the melody to the tonal center give this wonderful tune its jazzy flavor (Ex. 13.51).

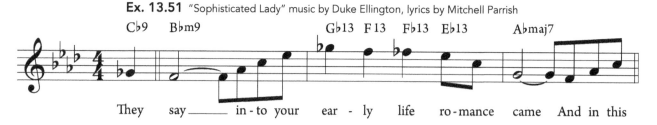

Ex. 13.51 "Sophisticated Lady" music by Duke Ellington, lyrics by Mitchell Parrish

Summary

The beauty of music, much like the beauty of life itself, is often found in its relationships. One of the most interesting relationships is that of melody to harmony, where every aspect of concurrence and contradiction is in play. To deal with this complex relationship, the primary relationship of the melody to the tonal center should always be kept in mind. Once that relationship is recognized, your options in chord choices greatly increase. The secondary relationship, that of melody to harmony, has its own dynamic, one in which a melody note that is dissonant to the harmony either resolves to it or is supported by it. Deciding on the perfect harmony for a melody is critical because of the repercussions that choice has not only on your melody, but on the lyric, and ultimately, on your listeners.

Activities

- Compose a dependent melody. Harmonize it in ways that make it come alive with interest. Write a lyric that works with it.
- Compose an independent melody. Find two different sets of chords that work with it. Write a lyric that works with it.
- Compose a melody that repeats a melodic phrase or the same notes throughout. Create the *prismatic effect* by using harmonies that cause the total music to progress.
- Create a chord progression first, then write melody to it that incorporates nonchord tones; resolve some of the nonchord tones downward and others upward.
- Create a melody that incorporates *supportable nonchord tones*. Write a lyric that works with it.
- (Optional) Syncopate and reharmonize a children's tune, substituting the original harmonies with jazz harmonies.

14

The Melodic Phrase—
The Harmonic Phrase

There are two separate and distinct kinds of phrases that occur in every song: the harmonic phrase and the melodic phrase. This chapter guides you in understanding the symbiotic and fascinating relationship between these two types of phrases. Being able to control this relationship is paramount to your success as a songwriter.

Harmony: the great organizer

One of the main functions of harmony is to organize time. Since harmony has a direct connection to the body, itself a balanced entity that tends to prefer balance to imbalance, harmony too tends to create balanced structures. For example, a two-measure phrase can be balanced by another two-measure phrase or by 2 one-measure phrases; 2 two-measure phrases can be balanced by a four-measure phrase, etc.

The Carole King, Gerry Goffin classic, "Will You Still Love Me Tomorrow?" contains a balanced harmonic phrase structure made up of a four-measure chord progression that repeats.

Ex. 14.01

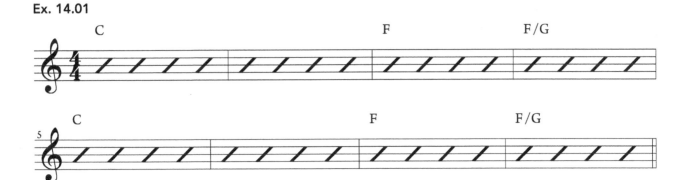

Chords often occur at regular intervals: one chord per measure, two chords per measure, etc. In Example 14.01 the chords last for either one or two measures and are heard here as a four-measure grouping. Heard alone, the chords of a song do not carry a specific message; rather, they—along with the rhythms of the groove— set up a tonal/rhythmic environment.

Rhythmic and tonal independence of melody to harmony

The melodic phrase cannot and should not be equated with the harmonic phrase; it is a separate entity coexisting with the harmonic phrase. There are a number of ways by which a melody achieves its independence from its harmony, as demonstrated in Example 14.02. The melody of "Will You Still Love Me Tomorrow?" establishes its rhythmic independence; it does this by not beginning or ending where the harmonic phrase begins and ends. Instead, it fits into the harmonic phrase; it begins one-and-a-half beats after the harmonic phrase begins, and ends an entire measure before the harmonic phrase ends. Beginning after the first beat gives the melody independence from the harmonic phrase and provides propulsion by providing another point of entry. The second melodic phrase rhythmically mimics the first melodic phrase; each ends on the third beat of the third measure of the harmonic phrase with a perfect rhyme. Although melody and harmony are heard as being in sync with one another, there is a healthy degree of rhythmic independence maintained.

Ex. 14.02 "Will You Still Love Me Tomorrow?" music by Carole King, lyrics by Gerry Goffin

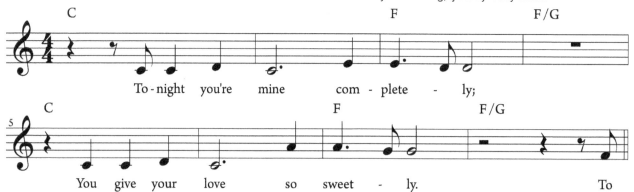

The melody establishes more of its own identity and independence by tonal means as well. Notice that the melody in the third measure of the first phrase is made up of two nonchord tones, E, a M7th, a set 4 relationship from the root of the F chord, which then "resolves" to a lesser dissonance, D, the M6th of the F chord, a set 2 relationship (sets are defined in Example 13.22, consonance to dissonance chart). Keep in mind that the note E, discussed here as a dissonance, is *mi*, the stable 3rd in the key, made more interesting here because of its dissonant relationship to the harmony. Now notice the parallel melody in the second phrase in measure 7. Here the melody lands on a chord tone, A, that resolves to G, *sol*, a stable tone in the key, but one that is a set 3 relationship, a major 9th interval from the bass, F. The melody and harmony are tonally independent of each other, yet have a symbiotic relationship that results in a uniquely beautiful music.

The chord progression and melody from the title song of the great Hollywood movie *Laura* (1944) demonstrate how tonal independence of melody from harmony has the potential of producing extraordinary music. Please note that the song has a key signature of C major (it does end in C), but actually begins in the key of G (Ex. 14.03).

Ex. 14.03 "Laura" chord progression

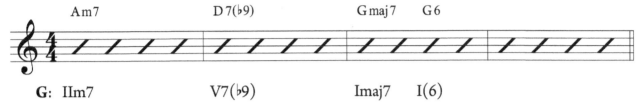

The chord progression follows the traditional SD, D, T movement with added tensions of 7ths, 6ths, and a ♭9. The melody of this famous Hollywood theme rhythmically fits comfortably within the harmonic framework. It is its tonal makeup that gives this melody its independence from the harmony (Ex. 14.04).

Ex. 14.04 "Laura" music by David Raksin, lyric by Johnny Mercer

The harmonic movement in "Laura" begins in an unstable area. In the key of G, Am7 is fairly unstable, moving to dominant chords, D7 and D+7, that increase the instability, and finally resolving to the stable tonic, G. Contrarily, the melody begins in a stable area, on the third of the key, *mi*, moves to a very unstable chromatic area ♭3, B♭), that resolves, not to a stable tone but rather, to the unstable second degree, *re*, that then moves to *la*, another unstable tone (Ex. 14.05).

Ex. 14.05

The harmonic movement is from unstable to stable; the melodic movement is from stable to unstable. What feelings do these musical contradictions produce? Feelings of romance, of uncertainty, the feelings that the lyrics attempt to evoke are now captured by this extraordinary music that presents the listener with a sense of mystery that had motivated David Raksin to write this amazing song in the first place!

How dull music would be if the melody always fit within the harmonic phrase, or, as I often refer to it, *the harmonic box*. As I pointed out in my book, *Melody in*

Songwriting, the most stable metric area in which to end a melodic phrase is exactly halfway through the entire harmonic phrase, because that is the balancing position. If the harmonic phrase is four measures in length, then the halfway point is on the downbeat of measure 3; if it is a two-measure harmonic phrase, then the most metrically stable area on which to end that phrase is on the down beat of measure 2. If you are trying to create forward motion and rhythmic interest in your song, it may be wise to avoid ending on the most stable metric area.

Example 14.06 contains a very simple chord progression, one that most writers would avoid using because it is the most academic, traditional chord progression known in Western music: I, IV, V, I.

The melody I composed over it demonstrates how dull a melody can be when the melodic phrase begins on the first beat and ends at the midway point (the midway point of a two-measure phrase is beat 1 of the second measure.)

Ex. 14.06

My second attempt lessens this fault. Beginning after the first beat and ending on the anticipation of the second beat adds both interest and momentum to the total music.

Ex. 14.07

Since melody guides the listener's attention; both Examples 14.06 and 14.07 are heard as two-measure phrases. In the next example, the listener hears the phrase as a four-measure phrase instead of 2 two-measure phrases (Ex. 14.08)

Ex. 14.08

Here is the same chord progression with a similar melody that now divides the four-measure harmonic phrases into two asymmetric melodic phrases. This example clearly demonstrates the power that melody has to draw the listener's attention and interest. The traditional chord pattern is no longer as much of a controlling factor, because the melody has asserted both tonal independence through the use of nonchord tones and more interesting dissonances and rhythmic independence through its entry and exit points (Ex. 14.09).

Ex. 14.09

Back-heavy and front-heavy phrases

Melodic phrases can be placed in many different areas within a four-measure harmonic phrase. But think outside of the box—the harmonic box. That is what Kris Kristofferson did when he wrote the pop/country classic "Help Me Make It Though The Night" (Ex. 14.10). Study the relationship between the melodic phrase and the harmonic phrase. Take your time in studying it.

Ex. 14.10 "Help Me Make It Through The Night" Kris Kristofferson

265

Notice how the melody begins well before the harmonic phrase begins and is continually out of sync with it. The melodic phrase ends soon after the harmonic phrase has begun. This furnishes the listener with two moments of interest: the melodic moment and the harmonic moment. This interesting back-and-forth activity is retained throughout this masterful song, even in its bridge section (not shown) (Ex. 14.11).

Ex. 14.11

When the melodic phrase precedes the harmonic phrase, as it does in "Help Me Make It Through The Night," the melodic phrase is referred to as a *back-heavy* phrase because the melodic activity mainly happens before the harmonic phrase begins. If the melodic phrase begins with the harmonic phrase or is heard within it, the melodic phrase is referred to as a *front-heavy* phrase.

I've been fascinated in my studies of the songs from the *Great American Songbook* to find wonderfully interesting melodies that somehow thrive within the rigid 8+8+8+8 measure structure often referred to as the "thirty-two-bar chorus," the norm for many songs written in that era. "How do they do it?" I've often asked myself. How did Kern, Berlin, Gershwin, Rodgers and Porter, etc., create interest and beauty time and again within what seems to initially be a structural straitjacket? The following examples are meant to demonstrate how some of that interest and beauty can be created within those rigid boundaries.

Notice that, when heard alone, the harmonic phrase controls our perception of where the phrase begins and ends. In Example 14.12, the harmonic phrase begins on the F chord that appears every two measures. This chord progression could easily be turned into the boring type of vamp figure used to accompany tap dancing:

Ex. 14.12

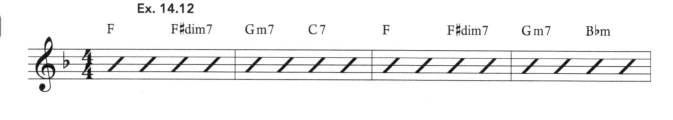

Here is a mundane melody of my own devising set to the above chord progression (Ex. 14.13; ▶ AUDIO EXS. 14.12–14.13):

Ex. 14.13

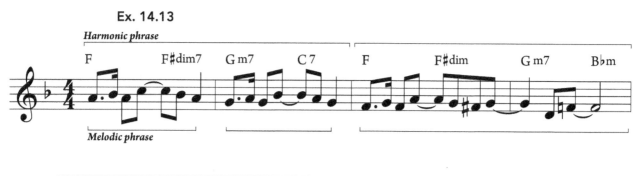

Notice that the melody and harmony are pretty much in lockstep. You will notice that the melody causes us to hear the phrase structure in measures 1–4 as 2 one-measure phrases followed by a two-measure phrase. Measures 5–8 are heard as 2 two-measure phrases. Admittedly, this is a mediocre, mundane scrap of music.

Instead of my tired, clichéd, vamp-like melody, here is the same chord progression with a melody that has become a standard (Ex. 14.14). "A Sunday Kind Of Love" is still sung today and has lasted well over sixty-five years (published in 1946)!

Ex. 14.14 "A Sunday Kind Of Love" Barbara Belle, Anita Leonard, Stan Rhodes, Louis Prima

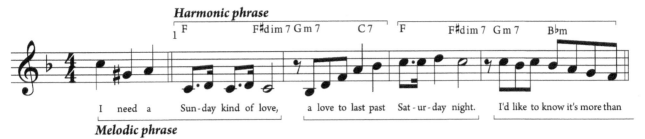

Notice how the opening back-heavy melodic phrase forces your attention onto the melody so that you are oblivious to the rather clichéd harmonies that are its underpinning. After the pickup notes and the first measure, we hear the melodic phrase beginning in measure 2 on the Gm7 chord and ending on the F#dim7 in measure 3. The out-of-sync melody and harmony make alluring music together. This type of activity continues throughout the section.

From this example we can draw an important conclusion: melody, not harmony is the main attention-getter. It is melody that beckons us, not only because it houses the lyric but also because it is rhythmically independent and interesting, not bound by the regularity of the harmony.

Another way to define a back-heavy phrase is as a melodic phrase that begins on a weak measure in a harmonic phrase and ends on a strong measure in a harmonic phrase.

The following chord progression corresponds to a standard song that practically everyone knows. I've indicated in Example 14.15 where the harmonically strong and weak measures occur. Since we already know that a metric grouping of two has a pattern of strong/weak, a grouping of 2 two-measure harmonic phrases also has that same attribute.

Ex. 14.15 Harmonically strong and weak measures

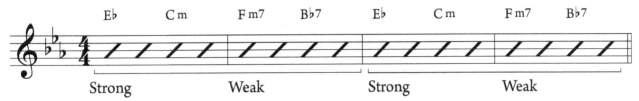

"Blue Moon," the Rodgers and Hart gem from 1934, keeps our interest throughout as the melody and harmony vie for our attention (Ex. 14.16).

Ex. **14.16** "Blue Moon" music by Richard Rodgers, lyrics by Lorenz Hart

Measure strength: Strong Weak Strong Weak

Harmonic phrase: Eb Cm Fm7 Bb7 Eb Cm Fm7 Bb7

Melodic Phrase

Blue moon, ____ you saw me stand-ing a-lone, ____ With-out a dream in my heart,

Because of the relationship of the melody to the harmony in this song, we have two points of interest continually presented to us as listeners, one produced by the melody, one produced by the harmony. The pickup note and the first measure isolate the title, "Blue Moon." The next melodic phrase begins in the weak measure 2 and finishes at the end of the strong measure 3, overlapping the beginning of the next harmonic phrase. The melodic phrase and the harmonic phrase *interlock*, a useful visual term for this type of melody/harmony phrasal relationship. (In Ex. 14.16, see this interlocking activity between the melodic phrases marked with broken lines and the harmonic phrases marked with unbroken lines.)

The importance of back-heavy phrases

Melodic rhythm is one of the most neglected subjects in the teaching of music, and yet it is one of the most powerful and controlling elements in composition, especially in songwriting. The differentiation of the melodic phrase from the harmonic phrase, which includes the use of back-heavy phrases, is one of the most important subjects in this book.

If a melodic phrase begins on the measure before the downbeat appears, the phrase takes on a lot of energy. It is like a windup by a baseball pitcher—Here it comes—ZAP! Right over the plate. Many hit songs use a back-heavy phrase to lead to the downbeat of the chorus so that listeners have no doubt that they are experiencing a new and important event in the song. If a verse section contains front-heavy phrases and the chorus section arrives after a lead in from a long back-heavy phrase, the result is highly effective.

Compare the first few measures of the verse of "Firework" to its chorus (Ex. 14.17). The front-heavy verse melody fits neatly into each of the one measure harmonic boxes.

Ex. **14.17** "Firework" verse, Katy Perry, Mikkei Eriksen, Tor Erik Hermansen, Sandy Wilheim, Ester Dean

Ab Gb

Do you ev - er feel like a plas - tic bag?

The chorus melody begins with a powerful back-heavy phrase and continues that activity throughout most of the chorus (Ex. 14.18).

Ex. 14.18 "Firework" chorus

'Cause ba-by, you're a fi - re work.__ Come on, show 'em what you're worth.

If there is no change in the chord pattern, then the melodic phrase must provide contrast and direct our attention. Marvin Gaye's song "Let's Get It On" has the same harmonic progression throughout its verse and chorus (Ex. 14.19).

Ex. 14.19 "Let's Get It On" Marvin Gaye, Ed Townsend

Each phrase of the blues-inflected verse melody of "Let's Get It On" begins soon after the downbeat or on the downbeat of the harmonic phrase—until the lyric phrase, "Oh! come on. Oh! Let's get it on." The title, "Let's Get It On," begins well before the first beat of the first harmonic phrase of the chorus and lands on the downbeat of the chorus. When we hear the arrival of the title with the tonic chord, our perception of the total music—which had been, up to this event, a kind of a relaxed enjoyment of melody and harmony grooving along in two bar repetitious phrases—completely changes. We hear the message in the song and also feel the form change—we recognize the arrival of the chorus—even though the chords have remained the same.

Repeated chord patterns

Since loops have been used extensively in recent years, the repetition of harmonic progressions presents a problem to songwriters: though repetition may feel great to the body, our minds demand more. Well, why not change the chord progression? Of course, that's been done many times before, and it still works. But, if you do decide to change the harmonies, you run the risk of either losing the groove or losing one of the elements that's making the song a unified piece. The solution to the problem often lies in your ability to create melodies that have a high degree of independence, that have a life of their own, that coexist but do not coincide with the harmonic box.

A repeated four-measure chord pattern has the ability to retain the groove and work very well in pop songs that are also meant to be dance hits. Often, the same four-measure chord pattern occurs in all sections of a song, as it does in Katy Perry's hit, "Last Friday Night" (Ex. 14.20).

Ex. 14.20 "Last Friday Night" chord pattern

Like many songs in this genre, this song does not state the tonal center or cadence on the I chord. A chord progression that does not state a goal area also implies less of a narrative and more of a snapshot of a moment, a moment that may be viewed through a number of different lenses and from a number of different angles. Rather than stating a tonal center, the chord progression may be available in a couple of related keys—keys that contain the same notes but different tonal centers. The progression for "Last Friday Night" contains chords that are found in either the key of G major or the E Aeolian mode, since both of those scales contain the same notes.

The melody is the major factor in determining what tonal center is implied. This minimalist approach to songwriting offers you M. C. Escher–like melodic opportunities to create different tonal perspectives while using the same chords (Ex. 14.21).

Ex. 14.21 "Last Friday Night" prechorus, Katy Perry, Lukasz Gottwald, Max Martin, Bonnie McKee

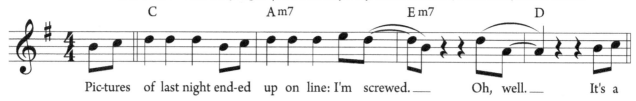

Pic-tures of last night end-ed up on line: I'm screwed. ___ Oh, well. ___ It's a

The first melodic phrase of the prechorus of "Last Friday Night" pauses in measure 3 on the note, B, that is supported by the Em7 chord. The P5th between E in the bass and B in the melody form a strong tonal anchor and momentarily imply E Aeolian.

The last chord in the cycle, D, acts as the support for the back-heavy phrase that begins the chorus and leads to the title. Additional back-heavy phrases employing the prismatic effect rivet our attention on G as the tonal center (Ex. 14.22).

Ex. 14.22 "Last Friday Night" chorus

Have you noticed that the *tessitura* (the range) of the prechorus in this song is higher than the tessitura of the chorus? (See Ex. 14.21.) This breaks the rule of thumb often cited in some songwriting texts that states that the chorus should contain the highest notes of the song. There are three reasons that the lower tessitura works in this chorus: (1) the back-heavy phrases, (2) the greater sense of tonal stability, (G major) and (3) the repetition of the hook. I do find it astonishing how many times *mi, re, do* appears melodically in titles of songs. This works especially well in this song, because those three notes take on a new perspective each time they repeat over a different chord—yet another example of the importance of the prismatic effect, a technique covered in chapter 13, "Melody/Harmony Relationships."

Masterful use of melodic phrasing

"Here, There, And Everywhere," the song that John Lennon felt was Paul McCartney's best, amply demonstrates how effective it can be to keep the melodic phrase free from the dictates of the harmonic phrase. In this iconic song, McCartney's first melodic phrase is a three-measure phrase, (also heard as a one-measure phrase followed by a two-measure phrase). Once McCartney establishes the relationship of the melodic phrase to the harmonic phrase, he miraculously holds to it throughout this transcendent song. Here are the first four measures of the song's chord progression showing the 2 two-measure harmonic phrase structure (Ex. 14.23).

Ex. 14.23

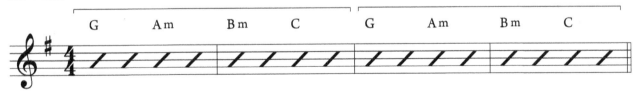

In this song, the melodic phrases and the harmonic phrases coexist but do not coincide; this causes the listener's interest to be continually beckoned by one and then the other (Ex. 14.24).

Ex. 14.24 *"Here There And Everywhere" John Lennon, Paul McCartney*

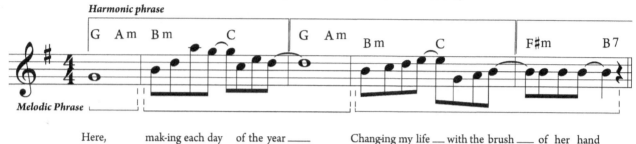

Harmonic phrase

Melodic Phrase

Here,   mak-ing each day   of the year ____   Chang-ing my life __ with the brush ____ of her hand

The title "Here There And Everywhere" reflects what is musically happening; indeed, the music seems to emerge from an eternal fountain of endless melody, with each melodic phrase ending as the next harmonic phrase begins, creating a perpetual flow of beauty—a superb example of prosody. There are many more gems to be found in this song than I can demonstrate here. For example, the introduction of the song makes an allusion to the key of B♭ that is fulfilled in the bridge. The bridge alone is a small miracle of composition. Purchase the sheet music or transcribe the song and reap the benefits it offers.

There's no need to show you the sister song to "Here, There and Everywhere"; I'm sure you know it. It's one of the most recorded songs in history, "Yesterday." And in it, Paul McCartney uses the same technique, the one word, one measure utterance, "Yesterday," followed by a two-measure melodic phrase, "all my troubles seemed so far away." In "Yesterday" the melodic phrases and harmonic phrases are more in sync with one another. It is the one-measure plus two-measure beginning that makes these two songs "sister songs" or, at the least, kissing cousins.

I don't know whether Paul McCartney, a man of musical genius, ever thought about the melodic phrase as opposed to the harmonic phrase, or if he simply has a natural proclivity to go there because it appeals to his immense musicality. It honestly doesn't matter; the technique is one of the most important techniques used by contemporary professional songwriters.

John Shanks and Kara DioGuardi have had lots of songwriting success as cowriters with other people, but when they collaborate with each other they form a very special team. "Pieces Of Me," written by them and Ashlee Simpson, contains one of the most amazing uses of melodic phrasing that I am aware of.

The chords used in the progression in the chorus, I, IV, IIm, V, are the tired and true (yes, "tired" is right, it's not a typo). This is a difficult progression to make sound fresh; that's the reason why this melody is so outstanding; it miraculously makes the cliché sound of this progression completely disappear (Ex. 14.25).

Ex. 14.25 "Pieces Of Me" Kara DioGuardi, John Shanks, Ashlee Simpson

The exclamation "Oh" that occupies measure 1 allows the main impetus of the melodic phrase to begin on the harmonically and metrically weak second measure. Here, this measure sounds anything but weak, because the melody sounds like it is starting in earnest on it. We, therefore, do not hear this chord progression in the way we normally would; in fact, we are gripped by the melody that now winds around the beginning of the next harmonic phrase and ends on the IV chord, G, on the third beat of measure 3. This allows the next melodic phrase to begin again on the IIm chord, Em, situated in the middle of the harmonic phrase. Quite amazing! The harmonic phrase structure is 2+2; the melodic phrase structure is 1+1.75 +1.25; a rather interesting way to break up four measures, don't you think? When we look at the pitch content we realize that the element of pitch is also distancing us from the chords, because so many of the pitches are nonchord tones (e.g., the D in the melody in measure 2 that occurs with the A chord). "Pieces Of Me" is a very original song with great prosody, one worth studying because every section contains songwriting techniques waiting to be exposed.

Summary

The relationship of melody to harmony is one of the hidden areas of complexity that has a great effect on the listener. An understanding of what actually occurs between these two important elements furnishes you with many more powerful tools to enable you to write simply and interestingly. The fact that you know within a given amount of space and time that there are two phrases occurring: the harmonic phrase and the melodic phrase— either in sync or out of sync with one another—gives you options and choices unavailable without this knowledge.

273

Activities

- Compose a four-measure chord progression that starts in a stable area and moves to unstable area. Compose a melody to the same chord progression that begins in an unstable area and moves to a stable area.
- Write a song that contains a two-measure harmonic phrase throughout. (This does not have to be a repeating chord pattern.) Compose a melody to it that retains its independence tonally and rhythmically by the various techniques demonstrated in this chapter.
- Write a song that mainly contains front-heavy phrases in the verse or verse/prechorus sections. At the end of the prechorus, compose a back-heavy melodic phrase that leads into the chorus. Continue to use back-heavy phrases in your chorus.
- Create a four-chord pattern that repeats throughout (one chord per measure). Compose four different melodies to it that contrast with one another.

PART V

Deeper into Technique

15

Riff-Based Songwriting

Before harmony took on its substantial role in Western music, most notated music combined two or more melodies at the same time. This musical activity, called *counterpoint*, hardly plays a role in the *Great American Songbook*. There are exceptions: some nice examples of double melodies by Irving Berlin ("Play A Simple Melody"), and Frank Loesser ("Inch Worm," "Baby, It's Cold Outside," and "Fugue for Tinhorns") and some beautiful counterpoint in the songs and arias from Gershwin's "Porgy and Bess." The relationship of bass to melody in songs of that era is important and can be understood as a relationship of melody to melody, with the vocal melody more varied and interesting and the bass part more harmonically functional. However, the beauty of the music in those songs is mainly found in the relationship of melody to harmony presented in a homophonic texture. Professional arrangers of standards also often provided excellent "filler" type melodic lines that sometimes acted as a striking counterpoint to a main vocal melody, but those lines were not part of the actual composition.

Counterpoint is alive and well in much of rock, R&B, and pop music; in fact it is intrinsic to many song in those genres. Many rock and funk songs are based on either a guitar or a bass *riff*. A riff is a short, rhythmic melody that is repeated, usually throughout a section of a song, and over which a more elaborate melody is sung or played). Much of rock and funk is dependent on two melodies taking place at the same time, an instrumental riff and the melody sung by the vocalist. This type of songwriting technique evolved from early blues singers, who often accompanied themselves on the guitar with a riff instead of chords.

A riff provides an implied harmony and can also provide a fill between vocal phrases, producing a call-and-response type of activity, one of the traits of African-derived music. Excellent examples of riff-based songs abound in the blues-influenced music of The Rolling Stones, Aerosmith, and AC/DC and in funk tunes by James Brown, Stevie Wonder, and Sly Stone. Usually the guitarist or bassist in a band creates the riff and another band member, often the lead singer in the group, then creates a melody that rhythmically fits in—that works with the riff, and the song emerges.

Counterpoint

The term "counterpoint" seems totally out of place in the realm of popular music, yet it is the compositional activity that occurs when creating riff-based music. Maybe the name is a bit stodgy, but the music that is made this way is anything but. Some of the same basic general guidelines that are used to teach 17th- and 18th-century counterpoint apply to pop music. The goal of these guidelines is to allow two or more voices to be both independent of each other and complementary to each other.

The guidelines for creating viable counterpoint are:

• When one voice is active, the other voice is either not active or is less active. This implies that if one voice moves, e.g., the other voice either rests or holds a note, or if one voice moves in eighth notes, the other voice could move in slower moving values, e.g., quarter notes and half notes, or in faster moving values, e.g., sixteenth notes or eighth-note triplets.
• Entrances and exits are key areas in which to establish independence of voices; if one voice enters on the downbeat of a measure, the second voice is better heard if it enters either before the downbeat (as pickup notes) or after the downbeat. Likewise, both voices should not, in most cases, stop in the same place.
• The motion or direction of each voice is very important in establishing independence of voices and in creating interest, so you must be aware of the contour of each voice. If you want the two voices to be very distinct from one another, contrary or oblique motion provides the most contrast.

Melodic motion and direction between two voices

Melodic motion and direction between two voices—demonstrated (below) from the most contrasting to the least contrasting are:

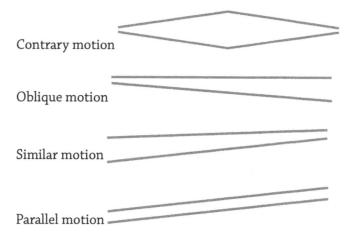

Contrary motion

Oblique motion

Similar motion

Parallel motion

Contrary motion and oblique motion are the most effective in establishing independence of voices, but all types of motion are available and can be used effectively. Sometimes, after independence of the voices has been established, bringing the voices together—by having them do the same thing or something in parallel or similar motion—produces a welcome contrast.

In the teaching of traditional counterpoint, much time is spent in how to treat intervallic dissonances between the voices in order to ensure stylistic cohesiveness to 17th- and 18th-century practices. This focus on style causes the study of traditional counterpoint to dwell as much on harmony as on the relationship of one melody to another. Fortunately, in today's music there is greater acceptance in the use of dissonance and, therefore, much greater freedom available in how voices move in contemporary songwriting. You, of course, still must be aware of the intervallic consonances or dissonances that take place between the melodic lines, but you are not bound by rigid rules; all sorts of dissonances may take place. You must also be aware of the harmonic implications, especially of the lowest voice. My best advice is simply to use what sounds good to you. Listen carefully to the two voices. If they each sound independent and they also complement one another, you've made the right choices. "If it feels good, it's alright," a phrase from Sly Stone's song, "Life And Death In G &A," applies especially well to writing popular music.

One of the benefits that technology brings to present-day songwriting is that no longer do two or more people have to be involved in writing a riff-based song. Now it is easy to simulate an entire band using drum loops and MIDI-based instruments or a combination of MIDI-based instruments and real instruments. You may start by recording a bass or guitar riff to a drum loop and then, on another track, attempt to sing a melody that works with it. You don't even need to sing the vocal line; just play it on another track using a synthesized sound. You can also see how the melodic lines are interacting via the computer-generated music notation, now a capability of most DAWs (Digital Audio Workstations). This allows you to see the details of your counterpoint and to make small adjustments.

The rhythmic relationship between two lines

When composing a riff-based song, the rhythmic relationship of the two separate lines (usually the bass and vocal lines) is of paramount consideration. The two-measure riff in the lower voice in Example 15.01 simply repeats throughout. In order to amplify its separate role, the upper voice begins and ends in different metric areas than those of the lower voice (▶ AUDIO 15.01).

Ex. 15.01

Notice that the upper voice begins on the second beat, after the riff has begun. The overall shape of the top voice consists of a long arch contour that lasts four-and-a-half measures and contrasts with the repetitious two-measure riff in the lower voice.

If a riff figure produces a closure (marked "dead spot" in Ex. 15.02), the upper voice must supply motion and interest. Notice that the upper voice is made up of eighth notes, sixteenth notes, and sixteenth-note syncopations in order to contrast with the riff that is made up of quarter notes and eighth notes (▶ AUDIO 15.02).

Ex. 15.02

Not all counterlines are riffs, nor are they always found in the bass. The synthesizer part in Justin Bieber's hit song "What Do You Mean" is in the middle register and provides a counterpoint that is active when the vocal is not, incisively fitting into whatever spaces the vocal melody provides (Ex. 15.03).

Ex. 15.03 *"What Do You Mean?"* Justin Bieber, Jason Boyd, Mason Levy

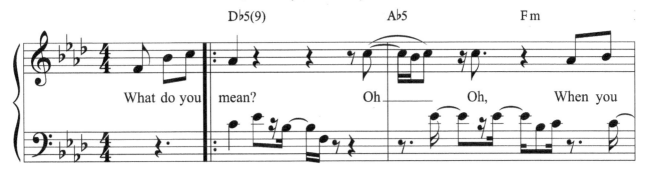

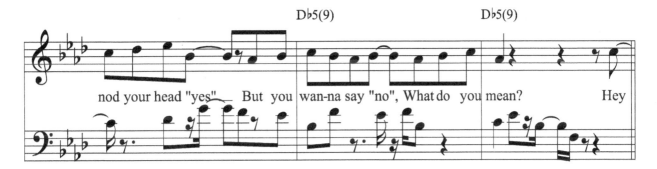

The use of two or more melodies occurring at the same time creates musical interest, half of our winning formula: simple and interesting. The other half, the simple part of that equation, also benefits because substituting melody for chords makes the texture more transparent. Chords, as important and evocative as they can be, take up a lot of aural space. I've often noticed in recordings of hit songs how the sparseness and transparency of the production allow the lyrics to be heard and the emotion to be felt. More transparent textures become available to you when you choose to use counterpoint rather than the *homophonic texture*, i.e., of melody accompanied by chords.

An alluring transparent texture was created in the hit song "Somebody That I Used To Know."

Ex. 15.04 "Somebody That I Used To Know" Wally De Backer

In Example 15.04 notice that:

- The bass line implies the harmonies and supports the other two lines.
- The registers of the three melodic lines do not interfere with one another, allowing each of the lines to be heard.
- Each of the three melodic lines has its own independence and phrase length.
- Contrary motion is important in establishing the relationship between the vocal line and the bass line.

Bill Withers has written some great songs built on riffs. Among them is "Who Is He And What Is He To You?" The riff that runs throughout the piece creates a mood of anticipation and stealth that correspond to lyrics that are rife with questions of infidelity. The vocal melody enters on the last note of the riff, with the back-and-forth action between the riff and the vocal line adding to the tension (Ex. 15.05).

Ex. 15.05 "Who Is He And What Is He To You?" Bill Withers

Keith Richards composed the most famous riff in popular music. It runs throughout the verse section of "(I Can't Get No) Satisfaction" while Mick Jagger issues one complaint after another all sung to a nearly stationary melody. The listener can enjoy this litany of complaints because while Jagger is singing a nearly static melody, Richards's riff keeps humming along, creating enough melodic and rhythmic interest between the vocal line and the guitar line to keep us happy. This is a good example of the effectiveness of *oblique motion* (Ex. 15.06).

Ex. 15.06 "(I Can't Get No) Satisfaction" Keith Richards, Mick Jagger

When I'm   driv-in'   in my   car ___   and the

man comes on   the ra - di-o, ___   He's tell-in'me more and more ___ a - bout some

Notice how effectively this riff works with the vocal melody. The ending of the riff also forms its beginning (this type of event is called an *elision*), creating an endless loop. The riff keeps the forward motion of the song going as the vocal line stops and starts. The bass duplicates most of the guitar riff, but down an octave and a 5th or an octave and a 4th, establishing the roots of the implied chords.

Writing from a riff or using counterpoint as the main way of composing a song is not confined to blues or blues/rock songs. In recent years, pop songs have made use of counterpoint to great effect, as already demonstrated in "Somebody That I Used To Know" and in Katy Perry's hit, "California Gurls" (Ex. 15.07).

Structural use of the riff

The riff for "California Gurls" provides melodic forward motion and rhythmic interest as well as a unique identity element for this song. The riff that is used throughout the verse section is abandoned in the prechorus and comes back, more fully fleshed out and harmonically embellished, in the chorus. In this way, it acts as a part of the architecture of the song form.

Ex. 15.07 "California Gurls" Katy Perry, Lakasz Gottwald, Max Martin, Benjamin Levin, Bonnie McKee, Calvin Broadus

Notice that the riff occurs when the vocal melody is either resting or is not too active, providing the listener points of interest throughout.

Michael Jackson's infectious bass line for "Bad" is first introduced alone and is then joined by the verse melody. The bass line moves in quarter and eighth notes, while the vocal melody contains various rhythmic values ranging from sixteenth notes to half notes that produce the necessary contrast.

After the twelve-measure verse section repeats, a four-measure prechorus introduces contrasting material, and then the riff returns in the chorus section. This song uses the same strategy as "California Gurls," exposing the riff in the verse, removing it in the prechorus, and then reestablishing it in the chorus (Ex. 15.08).

Ex. 15.08 "Bad" Michael Jackson

The independence of each line allows the listener to enjoy both the vocal line and the bass line because they act so symbiotically with one another. The eighth-note pickup, the sustained notes, and the syncopated sixteenth notes all help differentiate the vocal melody from the insistent quarter-note and eighth-note bass line riff. Notice how the vocal line overlaps the riff, never beginning or ending with it.

Sometimes a riff is so catchy that to ignore doubling it with the vocal line would be a mistake. A case in point is the powerful riff found in Queen's "Another One Bites the Dust" (Ex. 15.09).

Ex. 15.09 "Another One Bites the Dust" John Deacon

An interesting riff can capture and satisfy listeners' attention for great chunks of time, as it does during the entire verse of Rhianna's hit (Ex. 15.10).

Ex. 15.10 "Only Girl (In the World)" Crystal Johnson, Mikkel Erikson, Tor Erik Hermansen, Sandy Wilhelm

A vocal melody doesn't have to be wildly ear-catching when a riff is as melodic and memorable as this one is and, in addition, serves as a complement to the vocal melody. The relationship between the riff and the vocal melody in "Only Girl In the World" works because:

- While the synthesizer riff is busy with sixteenth notes, including a sixteenth-note anticipation of the third beat, the vocal melody enters right on beat 3 and consists of straight eighth notes that contrast nicely with it.
- As the vocal melody ends, the riff begins. In this way, constant musical interest is maintained.
- The nearly stationary vocal melody creates oblique motion to the ascending bass line until contrary motion between the two voices occurs, as the last two notes of the vocal line descend while the riff ascends.
- The vocal melody, helped by the lyric, is heard as a four-measure phrase, while the riff is a one-measure repeated phrase.

Summary

A riff provides melodic, rhythmic, and harmonic material to your song. A riff helps set the groove, and almost always implies a harmony, but expresses it horizontally as well as vertically. Beginning with a riff provides you with another way to begin a song and the possibility of creating a unique one, since there are fewer songs that use this technique.

Your understanding of how counterpoint is used today is vital, because many contemporary songs are built starting with a track, self-composed or written by someone else. The track often contains a riff or a repeated figure, and, if you are a top-line writer, your task is to write a melody that works with it. Your ability to write a vocal melody to a riff or a track demands that you identify where the track is rhythmically active and where there are "dead spots" (rests or held notes) that are available areas for your vocal line to become more active. You must be aware of the direction of the riff, so that you can use a melodic shape that contrasts with it. You must be able to hear where dissonances between the vocal line that you are attempting to create and the riff are working and

287

where they are not. Your ability to notate what you hear can be very helpful and is practically a necessity. The ability to compose a melody to a riff may open vast new areas of creativity to your songwriting.

Activities

- Either create an original drum pattern or find a drum loop that you like. Then create a bass or guitar riff that leaves enough space for your vocal melody to thrive. Finally, compose a vocal line that is independent yet functions synergistically with the riff that you've created.
- Use the Justin Bieber song "What Do You Mean" as a model; create a vocal melody that has spaces within it to be "filled in" by another voice. Keep the texture as transparent as possible.
- Create a very melodic bass, guitar, or synthesizer riff and then compose a rather stationary vocal melody that works with it. In the next section of your song, you may choose to abandon your riff and create a more memorable vocal melody. Use "(I Can't Get No) Satisfaction" as your model.

16

Tonal and Rhythmic Strategizing

Tonal strategizing

Tonality is one of the most potent elements in music. All people, not simply musicians, respond to tonality; like gravity, its importance is often not acknowledged. We feel the tonal center—even if we are not able to single it out while listening to a song—and when we move from it, we sense it.

If you can control your tonal moves, you will be one step closer to controlling how your song affects your listeners. If you are cognizant of a tonal direction when writing a song, you are more likely to provide the listener with a journey that leads to a satisfying conclusion and one that provides continual delights along the way.

Strategy #1

- Start your song off in a stated key, forming a stable area, one that establishes the tonal center and allows your listener to be comfortable in it. This section is usually rhythmically balanced.
- Next, move away from the tonic area, leaving the listener with a desire to return to the tonal center, to what had originally been established. Often, but not always, the section in which this occurs also rhythmically unbalances the previous section or sections.
- Finally, give the listener what s/he craves: the return to the tonal center and a restoration of rhythmic balance.

This strategy is psychologically similar to a "now you see it, now you don't" game that is played with children and usually delights them. It goes like this: show them that you have some candy in one hand, and then hide both hands behind your back; then ask them to guess which hand the candy is in. They invariably yell out their guesses. You keep them waiting, but finally you expose which hand holds the goodies, and when you do they are usually delighted—especially when you allow them to have the candy.

Use in verse/prechorus/chorus songs

Strategy #1 can be found within most song forms, but the most obvious use of this strategy is found in verse/prechorus/chorus songs. The *verse* establishes the key, and if it is a balanced section or, even better, a symmetric section, it almost demands a prechorus. The purpose of the prechorus is to create tension both tonally and/or rhythmically. The chorus, the goal area, is where the tonal center and rhythmic balance are reestablished.

The simple scheme is:

- **Verse**: Establishes the tonal center and creates a balanced section.
- **Prechorus**: Moves away from the tonal center and creates imbalance.
- **Chorus**: Returns to the tonal center and establishes balance between the chorus and combined verse/prechorus sections.

Each song in the following examples uses strategy #1.

"How Deep Is Your Love" is one of the huge hits written and performed by the Bee Gees from the blockbuster film "Saturday Night Fever" (1977). The verse section is a balanced eight measures that fully establishes E♭ as the key (Ex. 16.01).

Ex. 16.01 "How Deep Is Your Love" verse, Barry, Robin, and Maurice Gibb

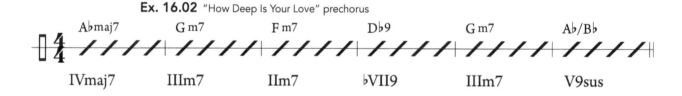

The verse leads to a prechorus whose six measures unbalances the front section of the song. (The "front section" of a song consists of the combined verse and prechorus that lead to the chorus.)

The prechorus avoids the tonic chord, the chord that finally appears at the beginning of the chorus supporting and reinforcing the title (Ex. 16.02).

Ex. 16.02 "How Deep Is Your Love" prechorus

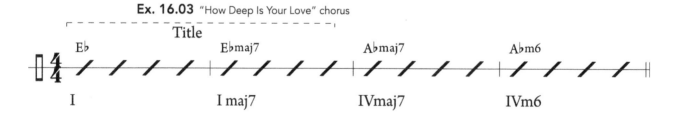

The chorus immediately states the tonal center in measure 1 (Ex. 16.03).

Ex. 16.03 "How Deep Is Your Love" chorus

```
            Title
 Eb                  Ebmaj7         Abmaj7         Abm6
|4/ / / / | / / / / | / / / / | / / / /||
 4
  I                  I maj7         IVmaj7         IVm6
```

"How Deep Is Your Love" tonal strategy:

- Verse (eight measures): establishes the tonal center.
- Prechorus (six measures): moves away from the tonal center and creates a rhythmic imbalance.

- Chorus: states the tonal center and is eleven measures long, not quite balancing the two previous sections' fourteen measures, but close enough to have the listener feel that balance has occurred.

In using this tonal strategy, avoid cadencing on the tonic chord within your prechorus. Since the tonic is usually the goal area in the chorus, overuse of the goal area before the actual tonal arrival is a poor strategy; it's like being told the ending of a movie midway through it.

"Someone Like You," Adele's gigantic hit in 2011, presents us with a good example of strategy #1. The tonality (key of A) is stated in the verse section of the song without the help of the dominant. This four-measure chord progression repeats three times, creating an unbalanced twelve-measure verse (Ex. 16.04).

Ex. 16.04 *"Someone Like You" verse, Adele Adkins, Dan Wilson*

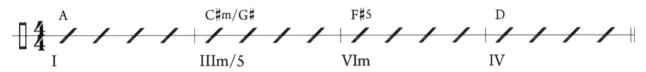

The prechorus begins on the V chord, a chord that has been strategically saved for this section. Notice that the V chord does not lead to the I chord, but, instead, to the VIm. The length of this section also creates asymmetry between the two sections (twelve- measure verse; four-and-a-half-measure prechorus). This provides the necessary rhythmic tension to set up the chorus (Ex. 16.05).

Ex. 16.05 *"Someone Like You" prechorus*

The same progression repeats throughout the chorus, stating and restating the tonal center (Ex. 16.06). The chorus to this emotionally charged song is ten-and-a-half measures long. After the chorus establishes a balanced eight measures, two additional measures housing the potent last line, "Sometimes it lasts in love and sometimes it hurts instead," are tacked on, ending the section. The repetition of these lyrics causes the form of the chorus to be elongated and made more interesting, but more importantly, this gesture also highlights the feeling of painful separation that is at the very center of this highly emotional song.

Ex. 16.06 *"Someone Like You" chorus*

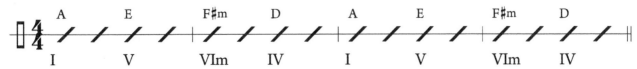

291

"Someone Like You," tonal strategy:

• Verse: firmly establishes the tonal center while omitting the V chord.
• Prechorus: begins with the V chord and avoids the tonic chord, producing a less stable section than the verse. It contains faster harmonic rhythms (two chords per measure as opposed to the verse's one chord per measure), and it does not balance the verse section, i.e., the verse section is twelve measures in length while the prechorus is four-and-a-half measures in length.
• Chorus: begins with the I chord, restoring tonal stability and is more balanced and rhythmically stable than the other two sections.

Tonal strategy #1 is also used in "Drive," a song that was a huge hit for Incubus in 2000. The song begins in E Aeolian (or natural minor) with a two-measure progression that is repeated four times for a total of eight measures (Ex. 16.07).

Ex. 16.07 "Drive" verse

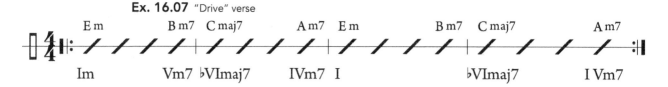

The next section, the prechorus, is very original in creating the necessary tension to build to the chorus, tension that is built here through tonal means by using only two chords, Cmaj7 and A7, and by avoiding the tonic chord. The note that differentiates the Aeolian mode from the Dorian mode is the 6th degree; C is the ♭6th degree of the E Aeolian mode, while C♯ is the 6th degree of the E Dorian mode. The sound of these two notes juxtaposed in adjoining measures is intriguing and, as the lyric states, "seems to have a vague, haunting mass appeal." The lyrics, of course, are not specifically referencing these tonal delights, but are referencing society's acceptance of conformity; nonetheless, the musical equivalent is present (Ex. 16.08).

Ex. 16.08 "Drive" prechorus, Brandon Bond, Mike Einziger, Chris Kilmore, Alex Katunich, Jose Pasillas

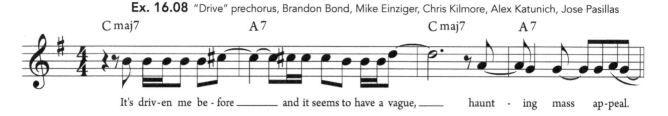

The ambiguous chromatic activity between these two chords continues for the next four measures, building listeners' need to hear the tonic harmony once again. This song's prechorus breaks the rule of thumb concerning the usual length of a prechorus. Here, the prechorus is the same length as the verse, balancing it and, in turn, creating balance for the entire front part of the song (verse = eight measures, prechorus = eight measures). What allow metric balance to work in the prechorus are the tension-building unstable harmonies.

The opening line of the chorus, "Whatever tomorrow brings, I'll be there with open arms and open eyes," arrives using the same harmonic pattern as the verse, restoring tonal stability while the chorus melody outlines the stable tones in E minor, firmly rees-tablishing the tonal center. This unique song has a chorus that does not contain the title.

It does, however, contain the central idea, the singer's vow that he is not going to follow the herd but instead, be open to whatever may happen in the more creative path he chooses to live.

Use in the AABA song form

Strategy #1 appears in nearly every chorus written in an AABA form found in the *Great American Songbook*. The B section or bridge usually involves moving away from the tonality that was established in the A section, only to return to it in the last A section.

In Gershwin's iconic "I Got Rhythm," the A section firmly establishes the key (B♭). The eight-measure section is then repeated, further hammering home the B♭ tonality (Ex. 16.09).

Ex. 16.09 "I Got Rhythm" the A section, music by George Gershwin, lyrics by Ira Gershwin

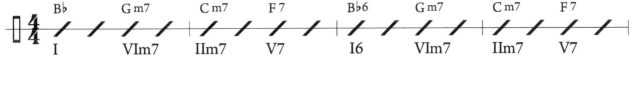

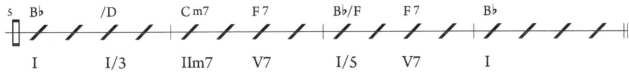

The B section, the bridge (sometimes referred to as the "release") provides a very welcome tonal relief by moving to a group of secondary dominant chords: D7, G7, C7, and F7. These chords contain chromatic notes: F♯ in the D7, B♮ in the G7 and E♮ in the C7. Each chord lasts for two measures and moves in the circle of fifths right back to the original key, B♭ (Ex. 16.10).

Ex. 16.10 "I Got Rhythm" bridge

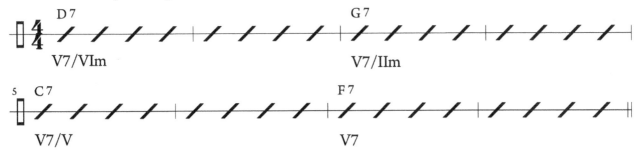

Tonal strategy #1 works naturally with this song form.

- A, A sections: The tonality is firmly established, and the repetition of the first A section assures rhythmic balance.
- B section: This section tonally distances itself from the two A sections that preceded it, while rhythmically, the eight-measure B section imbalances the previous sixteen measures created by the two A sections.
- The last A section restores both tonal stability and balance to the total form.

Many early Beatles songs employ the same kind of tonal strategizing used by the composers of the previous era, and for good reason: the Beatles studied many of those songs and used them as models. "I Want To Hold Your Hand" is written in the standard's form of AABA. The A section, which houses the central statement, is twelve measures long, ending with a strong cadence where the title is reiterated for the third time (Ex. 16.11).

Ex. 16.11 "I Want To Hold Your Hand" John Lennon, Paul McCartney

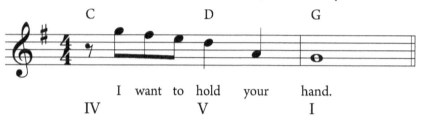

I want to hold your hand.
IV   V   I

The A section of "I Want To Hold Your Hand" is in the key of G, while the B section or bridge begins on a Dm7 chord, the IIm7 in the key of C, which is immediately established, providing a welcome tonal contrast to the A section. In measure 7 of the B section, the C chord switches from functioning as the I chord in C to functioning as the IV chord in G (a *common chord modulation*). It is here that the Beatles extend the IV-to-V progression by three additional measures, repeating it as they plead, "I can't hide, I can't hide, I can't hide," beckoning not only the lover they hope to have but also to the I chord in the key of G that begins the last A section. Naturally, when the A section reappears, tonal satisfaction comes with it (Ex. 16.12).

Ex. 16.12 "I Want To Hold Your Hand" bridge

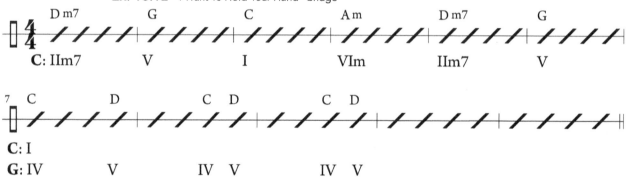

Modulation is one option for moving away from the original tonal center, but it is not a necessity. (E.g., "I Got Rhythm" doesn't modulate in the bridge, but simply moves through a group of chromatic chords.)

Chorus beginning in a tonal area other than the tonic

Strategy #1 may also be at play if your verse begins and ends on the tonic chord. If that is the case, your chorus initially can provide tonal contrast by starting in any area other than the tonic and wend its way back to the tonic at the end of the chorus. This use of strategy #1 may seem unusual, even contradictory, because we assume that the chorus, being the arrival point, should state the tonality at its outset. Choosing to delay the statement of the tonality, the goal area, until the end of the chorus may make the song less commercial because of the length of time it takes to get there. It is best to consider the individuality of each song and ignore formulaic songwriting that gets in the way of artistic expression and prevents the song from fulfilling its own path.

John Mayer's evocative "Slow Dancing In a Burning Room" has two verses that end on the tonic chord, E. In order to create contrast, the chorus begins on the V chord and slowly leads back to the tonic chord and the title (Ex. 16.13).

Ex. 16.13 "Slow Dancing In a Burning Room" chorus, John Mayer

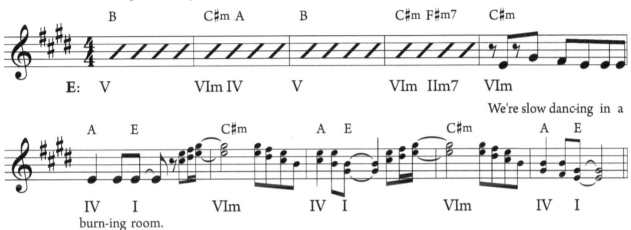

The greatest point of tonal tension is at the beginning of the chorus, making the form of this song analyzable as a verse/verse/prerefrain/refrain form with the arrival of the chorus sounding like a prerefrain and the arrival of the title resembling the arrival of a refrain. This is a good example of the way song forms can easily transmute from one to another.

Strategy #2

• Begin your song in an unstable tonal area, one that is related to the primary tonal center but does not state the primary tonal center.
• As you get closer to your goal area (refrain or chorus), slowly introduce stronger hints of the primary tonal area.
• Provide the listener with a satisfying tonal payoff when you reach your goal area.

In this strategy, avoid a strong cadence on the I chord in the verse and/or prechorus—the section or sections that precede your goal area. As you compose your song, listen with your body and emotions as well as your mind. The purpose of this strategy is to make the music that leads to your central statement or title feel tonally ambiguous. Only at your chorus or refrain, where the title and central idea appear, should the tonality of the song be stated and felt by the listener.

Many of the songs that employ this strategy begin either on a secondary chord or a chord from a different tonal area than the tonic area. Granted, most popular songs do begin on the tonic chord and don't use this strategy, but beginning in a different tonal area is a viable alternate way to travel.

There are a few precedents for this strategy in the *Great American Songbook*. One of them is the standard "Body and Soul" written in 1930, a song that hints at the tonal center but doesn't cadence fully on it until the last measure of the A section. From the beginning, you feel the song reaching for something, and when it finally arrives it is absolutely satisfying. This standard has been recorded numerous times including the Tony Bennett and Amy Winehouse recording in 2011, one of Amy Winehouse's last (Ex. 16.14).

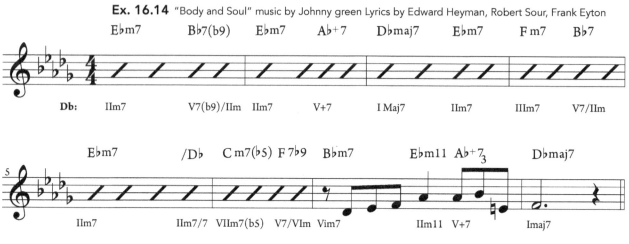

Ex. 16.14 "Body and Soul" music by Johnny green Lyrics by Edward Heyman, Robert Sour, Frank Eyton

During the period between 1965 and 2000 certain songwriters, especially Burt Bacharach and those influenced by him, incorporated some fairly sophisticated tonal moves using this tonal strategy.

One of the first of Barry Manilow's hits (1976) "I Write The Songs," has a harmonic progression that begins quite far from the tonic, but slowly wends its way there and fully embraces it in the chorus (Ex. 16.15).

Ex. 16.15 "I Write the Songs" Bruce Johnston

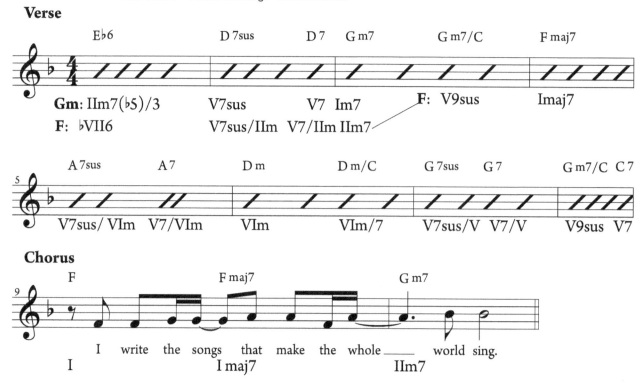

296

This song, written by Bruce Johnston, a member of the Beach Boys, begins on a chord that is only peripherally related to F major, E♭6, the ♭VII6 in F, but in this harmonic context, it is actually Am7(♭5) in second inversion, the IIm7(♭5) chord in G minor. Once the G minor chord arrives, it transforms from a Im7 in G minor to the IIm7 in F major. There is a cadence on I chord, F, in measure 4, but because of the complex harmonic activity that leads to it, there is still an appreciable sense of tonal ambiguity at its arrival. The next four measures build harmonic tension by employing two secondary dominant chords (A7 and G7). In measure 9, the chorus explodes with the power of a newborn baby as the I chord arrives in all its glory along with the title of the song.

Burt Bacharach seems to have been fascinated with tonal ambiguity and with this particular strategy, and has penned some great songs that use it. We are two-thirds of the way into "Walk On By" (measure 13) before we feel we've arrived at the main tonal center.

The analysis in Example 16.16 demonstrates how Bacharach probably conceived the tonal relationships, thinking in two keys at the same time, knowingly plotting to fully embrace F major later on, but having his listeners perceive the song in A minor at first. The chords, Am to D, seem to indicate that the song is in A Dorian, as does the B♮ in the melody in measure 3. In measure 5, Gm7 cancels the F♯ with an F♮ and introduces the B♭, and the gradual movement toward F major gets underway. The IV chord in measure 12, leading to the V chord in measure 13, firmly establishes F as the tonal center. Do not be confused by the analysis below that seems to indicate that the song is heard in both A minor and F. Be assured, the song is heard initially in A minor or is heard as tonally ambiguous, and only at the chorus is the complete arrival in the key of F major felt by the listener (Ex. 16.16).

Ex. 16.16 "Walk On By"

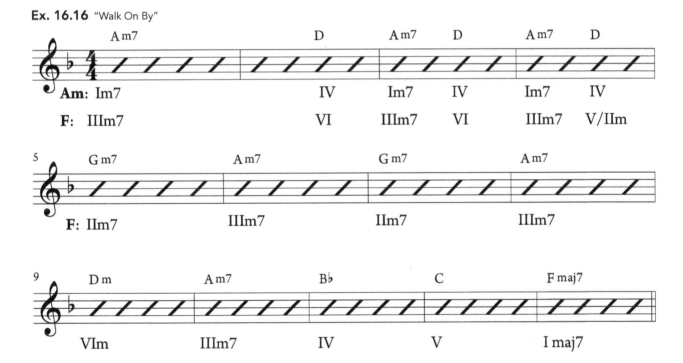

Bacharach begins his melody on E, the leading tone to the key of F, but heard here as the stable 5th scale degree in A minor. Both the A minor harmony and the melody that outlines the A minor triad in Example 16.17 indicates to us that the key of the song is A minor.

You might assume that the average listener could not possibly enjoy or appreciate such a complex treatment of tonality. Since this song was a gigantic hit (by both Dionne Warwick and by Isaac Hayes) and recorded by many other artists, that assumption has staunchly been disproved. I believe the average listener simply experiences the feeling of the song because it is so perfectly reflected in both the music and the lyrics. That the song begins in a minor key is very relevant to the emotions expressed and is an indication that the singer's state of mind is one of regret and anger.

Ex. 16.17 "Walk On By" opening measures, music by Burt Bacharach, lyrics by Hal David

As the song progresses, the singer's attitude becomes more adamant and aggressive in denying her former lover any access to her, assertively highlighted by the full tonal arrival of F major, biting syncopations, accented tritones, major sevenths, and the repetition of the title (Ex. 16.18).

Ex. 16.18 "Walk On By" chorus

This music underlines a message that expresses both anger and personal empowerment, speaking strongly and deeply to many. This is an innovative and original song.

The use of strategy #2 with modes

We all are familiar with the relative minor, the minor key built from the sixth degree of a major scale. This familiar relative is also called the Aeolian mode. Other *relative modes*, i.e., those modes that contain the same notes as the Ionian but whose tonics are different from the Ionian tonic and, therefore, have different hierarchal structures, also exist. If you want to control your tonal materials, it is vital for you to get to know the other relatives intimately.

There are six usable relative modes. They are the Ionian, Dorian, Phrygian, Lydian, Mixolydian, and Aeolian modes (the Locrian mode, built off of the 7th degree of a major scale, does not contain a dominant; instead, it contains a tritone from its tonal center and is, therefore, not useful in this context because it is too tonally ambiguous and volatile for our purposes.)

Modes are usually taught based on their placement in relationship to the Ionian mode because it is the most popular and common scale we use. Basing the Ionian on C, the Dorian mode would be on the 2nd scale degree, D; the Phrygian on the 3rd scale degree, E; the Lydian on the 4th scale degree, F; the Mixolydian on the 5th scale degree, G; and the Aeolian on the 6th scale degree, A (Ex. 16.19).

Ex. 16.19

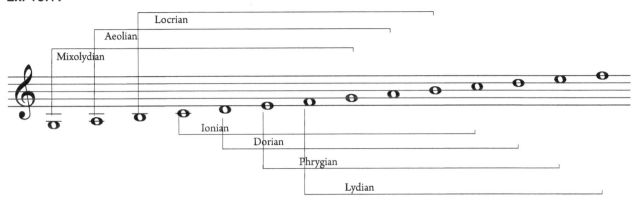

It is easy to fall into the trap of considering each of these modes shown in the chart above as simply offshoots of the Ionian mode. In doing so however, you would miss the importance of realizing each of the individual mode's characteristics and individual hierarchal structure. You would also miss the fact that these modes, because they share the same notes, are all relatives of one another. In order for you to grasp the individual characteristics of each of these "relatives," it is best to think of them as individuals in a family, and to give each one detailed study so that you can fully understand and appreciate their individuality. (See a more complete explanation of modes in chapter 8, "The Blues, Rock, R&B and Modal Environments," under the subheading "Modes").

Strategy #2 uses two or more modes that contain the same notes in different relationships to one another. This means that, while retaining the same notes, a modulation (i.e., moving from one tonality to another tonality) must occur to create contrast and to heighten the arrival of the central statement. The easiest and most prevalent use of this technique is the movement from the familiar Aeolian mode in a verse to the Ionian mode in the chorus. This movement, from a minor key to its relative major appears in many songs, e.g., the Beatle's "Girl" and Paul Simon's "Richard Cory." More recent examples include Bruno Mar's "Locked Out Of Heaven" and John Legend's "All Of Me."

Each mode creates its own emotional atmosphere. In fact, in ancient Greece, each mode was designated for certain ceremonies or activities and was forbidden in others. In writing a verse/chorus song using this strategy, you receive the benefit of having an element that remains the same: the notes in both sections remain the same, and the benefit of achieving contrast: the modes change, as does the tonal center. When this strategy is successful, the resulting impact that occurs when the chorus arrives in the relative major key can be extraordinary.

Once you attempt to write your verse in any mode other than the Aeolian and try to move to the related Ionian in the chorus, things become a bit more interesting and tricky. Remember, when using this strategy, it is not the notes themselves that change but their relationship to one another. The way in which you treat the notes causes the listener to perceive them in totally different keys.

Let me give you an example: If your song's verse section is in the key of F Lydian with the chorus in the key of its relative Ionian, C, your job as a composer is to make F, not C, the tonal center of the verse and C, not F, the tonal center of the chorus (Ex. 16.20).

Ex. 16.20

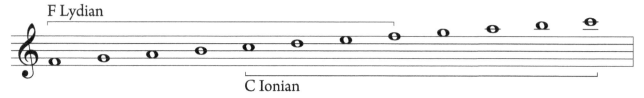

The Lydian mode is quite unstable, so some means must be found to indicate the song is in F Lydian, not C Ionian.

Here are some techniques for tonally anchoring an unstable mode:

- Create a pedal point or an *ostinato* (a repeated figure, like a riff) in the bass that centers on the tonic note.
- Use the stable tones (1, 3, 5 of the mode) in the melody, especially the dominant to tonic (*sol* to *do* or *do* to *sol*) axis in the melody to help define and stabilize the tonality.
- Use the characteristic notes of the mode either in the melody or in the harmony or both.
- Be aware of how you treat the tritone; if you resolve the tritone in an unstable mode to the stable tones in the relative Ionian, you will probably modulate out of the mode and into the relative Ionian. You must save this move for the strategically appropriate moment.

"Keep On Loving You," Kevin Cronin's #1 pop song in 1981, performed by REO Speedwagon, moves from an F Lydian verse to a chorus in C Ionian. It uses the strategy and techniques I've outlined above (Ex. 16.21).

Ex. 16.21 *"Keep On Loving You" verse, Kevin Cronin*

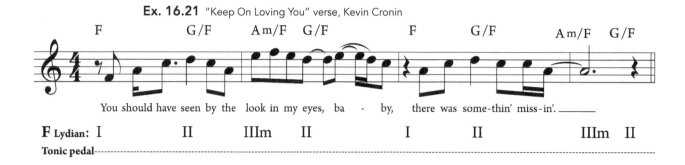

The ambiguous, unstable sound of the Lydian mode in this first section of a two-part verse, moving to an ambiguous, unstable, second part reinforces a lyric that contains the feeling of devastation expressed by the singer.

Whenever I heard this song on the radio I was immediately drawn to it. Only after making a lead sheet and studying it did I realize how masterfully the tonality had been treated. The pedal F in the bass anchors the first part of the verse in F Lydian. The melody also helps define the tonality with its many stable tones in F; the verse melody begins with all three stable tones. Notice that the characteristic note (B in the key of F Lydian) does not appear in the melody, but instead, in the harmony (The second part of the verse [not shown] abandons the use of the pedal tone and hints at tonal movement, but then leads us right back into a second verse).

Only after the verse with its big lead-in created by a descending scale bass figure (G, F, E, D) do we finally arrive at the chorus in C major, the relative Ionian to F Lydian (Ex. 16.22).

Ex. 16.22 "Keep On Loving You" chorus

Notice how the first note, F, on the downbeat of the chorus, is no longer heard as the tonic, but as a nonchord tone that submissively resolves to E, the third of the C chord. The song is now totally in C major, with the strong functional harmonic progression of the I, IV, and V chords in C major stated and restated. This tonal commitment matches the singer's overwhelming act of forgiveness, acceptance (or, more cynically, capitulation), and commitment to his lover that is found in the lyric. This is a good example of how a well-chosen tonal environment reinforces prosody.

Faith Hill's #1 country and top 10 pop hit "This Kiss" (1998) begins in C Mixolydian and moves to F, its relative Ionian, in the chorus. The verse melody and harmony indicate that the tonal center is C Mixolydian, not F Ionian. When writing in unstable modes, the melody itself plays an important role in defining the key. The verse melody in "This Kiss" outlines the C major triad in the first measure, while the repeating two-measure chord progression containing the defining characteristic note in the Mixolydian mode, ♭7, B♭, leads right back to C (Ex. 16.23).

Ex. 16.23 "This Kiss" verse, Beth Neilsen Chapman, Robin Lerner, Annie Roboff

The chorus is in F Ionian, the relative Ionian to C Mixolydian. The chorus melody is practically built around the melodic outline of an F triad and the harmony's I, IV, V, I progression in the key of F Ionian firmly establishes F as the new tonal center (Ex. 16.24).

Ex. 16.24 "This Kiss" chorus

It's ___ the way you love me.   It's a feel-ing like this: It's cen-trif-u-gal mo-tion;   it's per-pet-u-al bliss.

The problems inherent in using unstable modes (those other than the stable Ionian and Aeolian modes) in a verse section often stem from the difficulty encountered when you attempt to establish a sense of tonality in modes that have very weak cadencing attributes. But remember: you do *not* have to establish the key of the mode in an obvious or complete way, especially in a verse section, because most verses are meant to be narratives that carry fluid verbal material that asks for unstable tonal material, not declarative statements which occur in the chorus section and ask for more stable tonal material. You can use the tonal ambiguity of any of the unstable modes to create a sense of forward motion in the verse section so that when you arrive at your chorus in a more tonally stable mode it feels natural and very satisfying. This strategic use of modes to reinforce the function of the form and the lyrics is very powerful.

302

Strategy #3

Tonal strategy #3 is simpler than tonal strategy #2, but equally effective. When you use tonal strategy #3, you do not modulate to another key to create a tonal contrast, as you do in strategy #2. Instead, you remain in the same key, but simply change one or more notes. This technique is called *modal interchange*. Changing just one note derived from one mode to another can have a dramatic effect on your song. It creates interest and is used to differentiate one section of the song from another. Traditionally, the term, "modal interchange" connotes "modal" to simply mean major or minor and, more specifically, the traditional major and minor scales, not all the modes listed above. The following example is the more traditional approach.

Cole Porter was so fascinated with the interchangeability of major and minor that it even shows up in one of his lyrics: "How strange the change/from major to minor" (from "Every Time We Say Goodbye"). Many of his well-known songs contain great examples of this technique (Ex. 16.25).

Ex. 16.25 "I Love You" Cole Porter

"I   love   you" ___   hums   the   A - pril breeze. ___   "I

This song is in the key of F major, and in the very first phrase, Porter borrows from F minor, the parallel minor. The D♭, in measure 1 in both the melody and the harmony, is a borrowed note from F minor. The G♯ (♯2 in the key of F), in measure 3 hints at the minor third (G♯ = A♭) of F minor, but sinuously leads to the major third instead.

The present-day use of the term "modal interchange'" is inclusive of all parallel modes, i.e., all modes based on the same tonic are available. It is helpful to know the hierarchal stability of modes because it allows you to create feelings of stability or instability from section to section or even within the same section.

Here is a listing of modes from most stable to least stable:

- Ionian—most stable
- Aeolian
- Mixolydian
- Dorian
- Phrygian
- Lydian—least stable

"You've Lost That Loving Feeling" is an iconic song that has been a hit multiple times because of its uniqueness, its powerful message, its tonal ingredients, and its memorable melody. It retains the same tonic, D, throughout. The verse, in D Mixolydian, contains compelling prosody. The tritone in the melody immediately implies something is askew, and the lyric defines what that something is: "You never close your eyes anymore when I kiss your lips" (Ex. 16.26).

Ex. 16.26 "You've Lost That Loving Feeling" verse, Phil Spector, Barry Mann, Cynthia Weil

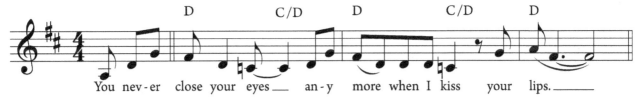

The prechorus yields a change of mode with the introduction of the leading tone of D Ionian, C♯, in the melody. The chords strategically avoid use of the tonic and move diatonically upward. The prechorus is often referred to as "the climb," and here it does just that in the ascending line in the bass (Ex. 16.27).

Ex. 16.27 "You've Lost That Loving Feeling" prechorus

The chorus makes the statement that sums up what the verses have already implied. The chorus begins on the I chord in D Ionian, underlining the admission of love that has ended, but the song reverts to Mixolydian at the end of the chorus (not shown) as the lyric bemoans: "now it's gone, gone, gone, whoa, oh, oh" (Ex. 16.28).

Ex. 16.28 "You've Lost That Loving Feeling" chorus

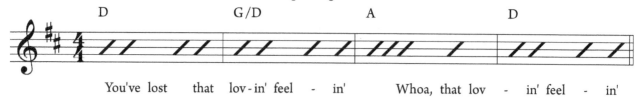

The turnaround figure in the bass actually uses F♯, the minor third of D, beckoning the even deeper sadness of the blues (Ex. 16.29).

Ex. 16.29 Turnaround figure

"What I Wouldn't Do (For the Love Of You)," a hit song in 1980 recorded by Angela Bofill, that I cowrote with the lyricist Denise Utt, is a good example of the use and power of this strategy. This song has a twelve-measure verse. The first four measures are in the key of F Aeolian, a stable mode that presents strong cadential possibilities, but the next six measures, measures 5–10, are in F Dorian, a less stable mode that increases the tension and propels the song toward the chorus (Ex. 16.30).

304

Ex. 16.30 "What I Wouldn't Do (For The Love Of You)" verse, music by Jack Perricone, lyrics by Denise Utt

D♮, the characteristic note of the F Dorian scale, appears in measure 6, not in the melody, but in the harmony of the B♭7 chord. There is a conscious use of repetition as a tension-creating device in this section (measures 5–10); causing an uneasiness in the listener. This tension is heightened with the appearance of two unstable chords in the Aeolian mode at the end of this section in measures 11–12. The yearned-for resolution appears at the beginning of the chorus in measures 13. Here we have strategy #3 combining with strategy #1. The tonal movement is from stable (Aeolian) to less stable (Dorian), back to stable (Aeolian), accomplished by changing the modalities, but remaining in the same tonality (Ex. 16.31).

The Aeolian mode is more stable than the Dorian mode, hence, the movement in the song is:

• first part of the verse, measures 1–4 (Aeolian)—stable
• second part of the verse, measures 5–10 (Dorian)—unstable
• measures 11–12, two chords reintroduce the Aeolian mode and lead to the tonic chord that begins the chorus.
• chorus, measure 13 in F traditional minor—stable; tonicization to D♭, leading back immediately to F traditional minor.

Ex. 16.31

The chorus makes its strongest tonal statement in traditional minor, enhanced by a tonicization to D♭ major. Since both chords, D♭ and Fm, are diatonic in both D♭ and F minor, moving back and forth between the two tonal centers is easily accomplished. The chorus tonizations to D♭ major strengthen the statement but, because of the return to the minor mode, do not take away from the disconsolate emotion of the lyrics.

Ex. 16.32 Harmonic analysis of the first four measures of the chorus

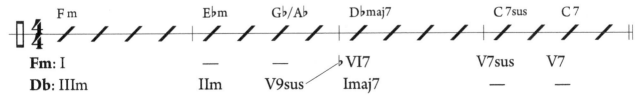

Many techniques beyond tonal strategizing were used in this song and helped lead to its success. Especially important are the phrase structures, the use of front-heavy phrases in the verse and prechorus, and the strategic use of a back-heavy phrase in measure 12, leading to the chorus.

The entirety of Michael Jackson's "Billie Jean" is in the key of G minor and contains a brilliant use of modal interchange resulting in a tonally interesting song. The introduction and first four measures of the verse are in the Dorian mode (the E♮ in the Am/ G harmony is the defining note) but the verse moves to the Aeolian mode in measures 5 and 6 (here, the defining note is the E♭) in order to produce a stronger cadence (the Aeolian mode has much stronger cadencing possibilities than the Dorian mode). Then it's back to the Dorian mode for two more measures, followed by another two measures that cadence again in the Aeolian mode, and, finally, a return to two introductory measures in the Dorian mode that lead to the second verse (Ex. 16.33).

Ex. 16.33 "Billie Jean" verse, Michael Jackson

The prechorus (not shown) is completely in the Aeolian mode. However, just before the chorus arrives, the leading tone of G minor, F♯, along with the V7 chord, appears—acting as a wakeup call to the listener that the chorus is about to arrive. The chorus uses the same harmonic progression as that of the verse section, but with a melody in a much higher tessitura. This is a song worthy of deep study.

Strategies using loop-based chord patterns

You would hardly imagine that as simple an idea as using the same four chords throughout two or three sections of a song or throughout an entire song would constitute the basis for a strategy but, in fact, it does. Since the chords do not change, contrast between sections must be acheived mainly by melodic means, both rhythmically and tonally.

Contrast can be achieved rhthmically:

• by varying the rhythm of the melody.
• by varying the placement of the melody in relationship to the chord pattern.
• by varying the length of the melodic phrases.

Contrast can be achieved tonally:

• by writing the melody to the tonal center rather than writing the melody to the chord pattern.

This allows the melody increased independence. The writer must be aware of the scale generated by the main tonality and the supportable dissonances to each of the chords used in the pattern.

• by writing the melody to the modal/tonal implications of each of the chords (see Ex. 16.34).
• by varying the tessitura of the melody in each section.
• by the use of different textures in order to to contrast one section from another. This is an arranging and production device, but especially in the pop, hip-hop, and dance areas, a songwriter must be aware of these devices and, ideally, be able to execute them.

The positive reasons for using the repetitiveness of same harmonic progression throughout are:

• it allows the same groove to be retained throughout, which unifies the piece.
• it allows for more pronounced and differentiated motivic ideas or melodic hooks to occur.
• it allows for the order of sections to be easily changed.

Your first consideration in writing a song with a limited number of chords is most likely to be what chords to choose. Create a chord pattern that:

• has a sense of endless momentum and interest, not one that cadences too obviously.
• can work in more than one tonal center.
• is diatonic, but implies rather than states the tonality.
• contains a mixture of major and minor chords; this allows for modal variety.

Example 16.34 is a chord pattern that is tonally ambiguous and has been used innumerable times, yeilding many hit songs. Based on each the four chords stated in the pattern, the two most obvious tonalities are A minor (Aeolian) and C major (Ionian), and G Mixolydian is possible. F Lydian, though possible, is less likely to occur.

Ex. 16.34

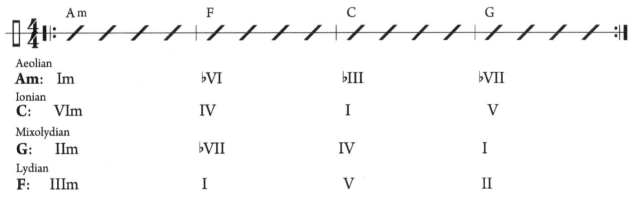

	Am	F	C	G
Aeolian **Am:**	Im	♭VI	♭III	♭VII
Ionian **C:**	VIm	IV	I	V
Mixolydian **G:**	IIm	♭VII	IV	I
Lydian **F:**	IIIm	I	V	II

The primary tonalities implied in this progression are A minor or C major, the two most stable modes and chords that fall on the strong first and third measures. But since the chord pattern is tonally ambiguous, melodic choices you make can veer the listener's attention toward one implied tonal center or another.

It is here that the power of conceiving your melody to a tonal center is invaluable. Since the tonal center is somewhat ambiguous, you may choose to center your focus on the tonal center generated by each of the individual chords for separate sections of a song. The following three melodies attempt to define the tonal center by either stating a *do/sol* axis or by employing an abundance of stable tones in the chosen key.

Example 16.35 is conceived in A minor. Stable tones in A minor are highlighted throughout this melody. Notice the last E, *sol* in A minor, supported by a G chord (▶ AUDIO 16.35).

Ex. 16.35 A minor (Aeolian)

Example 16.36 is conceived in C major (Ionian). The stable tones in C form the melodic outline in measures 1–2 and 5–8. The resolution and cadence in measure 3 help define C as the tonal center (▶ AUDIO 16.36).

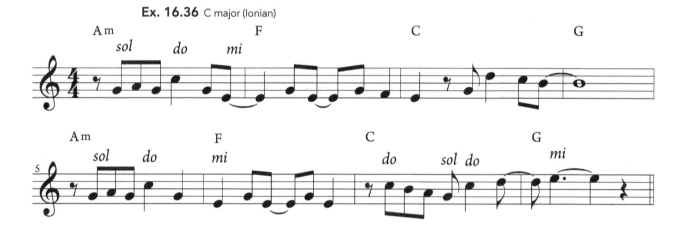

Ex. 16.36 C major (Ionian)

The next melody attempts to define the tonal center as G by using a preponderance of stable tones in G and by beginning the second melodic phrase on the fourth measure containing the G chord.

Ex. 16.37 G Mixolydian

The disruption of the four-measure harmonic phrase in Example 16.37 by a 3+3+2 melodic phrase structure not only helps define the key but also provides another way to create melodic interest. The choice of using a tonally ambiguous chord pattern that can be heard diatonically in three or four different keys, depending on the treatment of the melody, is an exciting creative option (▶ AUDIO 16.37).

In the hit "Radioactive," by Imagine Dragons, the chords used throughout the song are Bm, D, A, and E. These chords exist both in A major and in B Dorian, E Mixolydian, and D Lydian. The two most stable tonal centers used in the melody of this hit song are B Dorian and A Ionian. Heard in the key of B Dorian, the progression is Im, ♭III, ♭VII, IV; heard in A major, the progression is IIm, IV, I, V.

The portion of the verse melody shown in Example 16.38 defines the key of A major. The dominant-to-tonic axis, E to A, stated in the melody and reinforced at the melodic cadence in measure 3, implies A as the tonal center.

Ex. 16.38 "Radioactive" heard in A major, Ben McKee, Dan Platzman, Dan Reynolds, Wayne Sermon, Alexander Grant, Jay Mosse

The chorus melody shown in Example 16.39 implies that the chorus is in B Dorian. Notice the dominant to tonic axis, F♯ to B, that defines B as the tonal center for this portion of the song.

Ex. 16.39 "Radioactive" chorus, heard in B Dorian

Wel-come to the new age,   to the new age. Wel-come to the new age,   to the new age.

Although we can definitely state that the overall song is in B minor Dorian (since the chorus is in that mode and the song ends on B), there are moments within the song where the melodic cadences point to A major or even to to E Mixolydian.

The tonal ambivalence that this type of chord pattern supplies is a definite asset. This is a cybernetic music that interacts with itself and produces itself from itself.

This type of repeated chord pattern with tonally ambiguous chords is the perfect vehicle for expressing a state of mind. In this way, contemporary writers have extricated themselves from past practices of using chord progressions that start in one place and take the listenener through a journey that reaches a goal in another place. Chord progressions that more obviously cadence are perfectly suited for narrative, storytelling, or depicting literal or linear events, whereas chord patterns that are somewhat tonally ambiguous and repeat are perfect vehicles for capturing states of mind.

"Clarity," the gigantic hit by Zedd in 2013, employs one more of the benefits of this using loop-based chords: two melodies that originally appeared separately in earlier sections of the song now appear juxtaposed in the same section. This is possible because the harmonies are the same in both sections. One of the two melodies is a chant, "Hey, ay," that avoids the possibility of verbal confusion that normally occurs between two different melodic lines with two different sets of lyrics sung at the same time. Notice how the two voices achieve rhythmic independence, not only in the way long notes in one voice are set against short notes in the other voice but also where each voice enters and exits (Ex. 16.40).

Ex. 16.40 "Clarity" Anton Zaslavski, Holly Haferman, Matthew Koma, Porter Robinson

If our love   is   tra-ge-dy why are   you my rem-e-dy?

Hey   -   ay, _____   Hey   -   ay, - ay. _____

Rhythmic contast is one of the most important elements in creating contrast between sections. Taylor Swift, who frequently writes songs that use the same chord progression throughout, has much to teach us. In "We Are Never Ever Getting Back Together," the verse melody is close to rap because of its machine-gun-like rhythms. It centers most of its melodic activity around the note, D, the 5th of the key (the implied tonality is the key of G). These fast-moving rhythms and short, caustic, slightly broken phrases are perfect in capturing the way a person who is angry and upset speaks to her former lover (Ex. 16.41).

Ex. 16.41 "We Are Never Ever Getting Back Together" verse, Taylor Swift, Max Martin, Shellback

The next section, the prechorus, is more melodic and contains a wider tessitura and intervallic leaps, more balanced one-measure phrases, and more playful, relaxed rhythms. This section gives the listeners a chance to hear and sing along with a memorable hook (Ex. 16.42).

Ex. 16.42 "We Are Never Ever Getting Back Together" prechorus

The chorus is a gem of creativity. The rhythms are jagged, perfect for this angry statement. The repeated syncopated notes, B, A, on "never, ever, ever," are inspired, displaying a wonderful use of rhythmic displacement. Reinforcing the arrival of the chorus, the two-measure melodic phrase now perfectly matches the two measure harmonic phrase (Ex. 16.43).

Ex. 16.43 "We Are Never Ever Getting Back Together" chorus

After the title line repeats, another melody appears with shorter phrases that provide relief as well as a little more melodic and lyric information. And then it's back to the title line again, which ends the chorus. The form of the chorus, AABA, is the same configuration found in many choruses of the *Great American Songbook*, but miniaturized.

After the second chorus, the song references the prechorus by adding a bit more melody built from the musical ideas already stated in the prechorus. After some choice spoken words by Taylor Swift over the same chords, the chorus makes a final appearance. This is the kind of structural freedom that is available when you choose to use a loop-based chord pattern.

Summary

The professional songwriter uses every technique available to make the song as inviting and as tantalizing as possible to his or her listeners. Sometimes a strategy is precompositional, i.e., the songwriter decides to use a certain strategy before beginning the song. But just as often, in the midst of writing, a need for a strategy becomes apparent in order to gain listeners' attention.

Some of the strategies demonstrated in this chapter are ones that were relevant in the past but are out of fashion today. Nonetheless, I decided to show these strategies because they may be used—possibly in an altered way—in some yet-to-be-discovered style. Studying these strategies also will prove valuable when you attempt to analyze songs that employ these techniques.

Activities

Attempt to write a song using each of the tonal strategies demonstrated in this chapter. Details concerning each of these tonal strategies are exposed within the chapter and should be used as guidelines.

Although all the strategies exposed in this chapter are worthy of study, the current state of songwriting indicates that working with loop-based chord progressions is important to achieve commercial success. Working with a repeating chord pattern also provides a simple corridor into an understanding of melody/harmony relationships, since elaborate harmonic knowledge is not needed.

• Create a four-chord pattern that implies or allows for at least two different tonal centers.
• Using your four-chord pattern, create a melody for your verse that implies one of the possible tonal centers within the harmonic pattern. Then create another melody for your chorus that implies another tonal center.
• Create three or four different sections of your song using various techniques listed and demonstrated in this chapter as contrasting devices.

PART VI

Final Results

17

Prosody

Every well-written song contains functional prosody. This chapter, however, focuses on some exceptionally well written songs that go beyond a healthy use of prosody; these songs combine words and music in extraordinary ways.

Instead of the general dictionary definition of *prosody*: "The study of versification and especially of metrical structure," most professional songwriters understand prosody to mean all the compositional aspects of the song that allow words and music to conjoin into a whole. The combination of music and lyrics is very potent because each of the two disciplines has the possibility of strengthening the other. Expanding the definition of prosody allows us to examine the relationship of words to music at a micro level, e.g., the relationship of the metric and rhythmic setting of the syllables of a word or a phrase, and at a macro level, e.g., whether the form of the song or the tonal environment are the appropriate vehicles to house the message of the song. Although our main concern and focus is on the song itself, we allow the term "prosody" to include elements that allow for enhancement of the song: production, arrangement, and performance. Each of the elements that constitute prosody have unique properties that contribute to making the whole greater than the sum of its parts.

Lyrics

Because lyrics are more discrete and less abstract than music, they provide an answer to the question "What is the music saying?" Although many different lyrics could work with a given music, a palpable sense of rightness occurs when the accent of each syllable corresponds to each musical accent and when the choice of verbal language corresponds to the rhythm, harmony, and melody of the music. The content of the lyrics defines the feeling or feelings the music is only implying.

Music

Music provides a lyric with a stream of abstract information that enhances the lyric in many subtle ways while giving it a specific rhythmic and tonal context that amplifies its meaning.

Prosody occurs between music and lyrics in many areas, from the most basic and mundane—accenting syllables properly, placing important words on strong metric or rhythmic areas, etc.—to more subtle musical relationships: the choice of a musical environment for the lyric, the relationship of melody to the tonal center and to the harmony, the choice of one melodic pitch over another and the exact amount of space designated between phrases.

Stravinsky was right in saying, "Music only expresses itself in its own terms." But when music is combined with words that correspond to the music's internal dynamics, the combination produces a very powerful cocktail, a heady mixture, like the right mixture of excellent gin mixed with a fine dry vermouth and a lemon peel.

Production, arrangement, performance

Even after a song is completed, the choice of arrangement and the type of production given the song, the attire the song is dressed in—how naked or elaborately adorned the song is in its public appearance—has a tremendous effect on how the song is perceived. Most important is the choice of a vocalist, either for a demo, in a public performance, or in a commercial release of a recording. This is an element of prosody that cannot be overlooked, because without the right vocalist—one who not only has the right voice for your song but also whose sensibility is right for it—all the hard work that has gone into writing it may be for naught.

The subject of prosody is so vast that it cannot be covered in one chapter; that is why I have referenced prosody throughout this book.

Examples of exceptional prosody

Every well-written song contains prosody (like the word, "health," prosody is assumed to be good unless an adjective like "poor" is put in front of it). But there are some songs in which the prosody is so interesting and enlightening that it would be a shame not to offer them to you.

Burt Bacharach and Hal David, who had numerous hits together, wrote "Raindrops Keep Fallin' On My Head" for the motion picture *Butch Cassidy and the Sundance Kid* and won an Academy Award for Best Original Song in 1969. The song also was a #1 record sung by B. J. Thomas, arranged by Bacharach, and produced by both writers.

The origin of the title is known: it was a title that Burt Bacharach, the composer, came up with along with the music for the song. We can readily hear why Bacharach felt that the title was perfect for the opening musical phrase of the song, with its dotted-eighth followed by a sixteenth-note rhythm, reminiscent of raindrops bouncing off of a pavement or a window. The difficult job was finding the right words for what followed that opening two-measure phrase. Here's why: the next melodic phrase is two-and-a-half measures long, followed by a one-measure phrase and another two-and-a-half- measure phrase that finally completes the first eight measures. That phrase structure is 2 + 2½ + 1 + 2½ = 8! This is the music that Bacharach presented to his lyricist (Ex. 17.01).

Ex. 17.01 "Raindrops Keep Fallin' On My Head' Music by Burt Bacharach

I can just imagine Hal David, the lyricist, listening to these opening phrases as they were played to him time and again, thinking to himself that no matter what he tried nothing seemed to fit this awkward but charming music.

And "nothin' seems to fit" gave him the perfect lyric for the third phrase as well as the lyric idea for the second phrase. That awkward two-and-a-half- measure melodic phrase that didn't match the two-measure first phrase, but instead barreled its way over the bar line, now had a perfect lyric to go with its oversized self: "And just like the guy whose feet are too big for his bed." Hal David rhymes "head" with "bed" and the puzzle created by the music has found its happy solution (Ex. 17.02).

Ex. 17.02 "Raindrops Keep Fallin' On My Head' music by Burt Bacharach, lyrics by Hal David

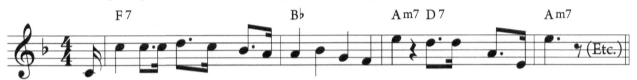

The title, "Raindrops Keep Fallin' On My Head," seems to imply a depressed state of mind, but the music is quite happy-go-lucky, full of quirky moves. So, the sensitive Mr. David centers his lyric from a contrarian's point of view and has his protagonist speak in the first person optimistically and courageously to the sun about not liking how "he got things done." Later on, in the bridge, he makes us aware that the raindrops mentioned earlier are not necessarily literal, but metaphorical, when he writes, "The blues they send to greet me won't defeat me. It won't be long 'til happiness steps up to greet me." The song is certainly worthy of all the honors it received.

"Against All Odds" is a very emotional song. It emanates from a deeply personal place, a place that most writers would find too difficult to deal with. Phil Collins lays it all out there, not holding anything back, baring all the pain in his soul. This is apparent in both his singing and his writing.

In order to explain the beauty of Phil Collins's choices in the song, please allow me to take a path that is slightly diversionary but totally relevant to understanding the prosody of this song. The verse of a verse/chorus song is supposed to lead the listener to the crux of the matter, the central idea of the song, the reason the song is being sung. Because of this, most verses have a built-in element of tonal instability and the payoff, the restoration or statement of tonal stability, usually resides in the chorus.

The verse of "Against All Odds" is unstable; it does not contain the tonic chord and its last measure, with a IIm7 followed by a V^{sus}, combined with a back-heavy melodic phrase that leads to the first beat of the chorus, perfectly sets up the listener for a satisfying arrival of the stable chorus in the tonic key of C major. When the chorus is reached, the listener should have a sense of, "Aha, we've arrived, this is it." Here is the problem: the lyric for the first line of the chorus is, "Take a look at me now, 'cause there's just an empty space." The arrival of the central statement occurs in empty space, in the middle of nowhere! Phil Collins needed to find a way to musically express an arrival—but in the middle of nowhere!

Ex. 17.03 "Against All Odds (Take a Look At Me Now)" chorus, Phil Collins

Amazingly, Collins achieves the sense of arriving—in a void (Ex. 17.03). This is how he does it: The chorus does arrive on the tonic chord, C, but the 5th of the chord, G, is placed in the bass, acting as a pedal tone. The tonic chord in 2nd inversion, C/G, is in the most unstable position in which a triad can be placed! And the magical effect of arriving in a void is experienced by anyone listening. On the words "empty space" Collins uses a D7/G, a V7/V chord placed over the same dominant pedal tone. Collins has perfectly translated the sense of arriving in an empty space into actual music. This is one of the most fantastic prosodic moments I've ever experienced in song.

So far, we've realized that prosody has been affected musically by phrasal imbalance ("Raindrops Keep Falling On My Head") and brilliant use of harmony ("Against All Odds"). Now, I'd like you to experience an example of how prosody is affected by tone tendencies.

"The Long And Winding Road" by Paul McCartney is a unique song that sounds from its inception like it is in the middle of a journey. The lyrics indicate abandonment, being left alone, and attempting to get back to a safer haven but continually being frustrated, ending up in the same God-forsaken place. The music mirrors the lyrics. The song is in E♭, but not until we reach the fourth measure does the music seem to arrive at a very temporary resting place; the melody rests on C (*la*), not E♭ (*do*), and the chord is unstable, the subdominant, A♭. We continue on this pilgrimage, pausing at resting places that keep us hungering for a more final resolution. This effect is achieved not only through harmonic choices, but through melodic choices as well. Notice how each melodic pause is on C, *la* in E♭, the mildest of unstable tones. There is a slight respite on "I've seen that road before," as *la* resolves to *sol* and even to *do*, but alas, the chord that appears with the melodic resolution is the V7sus/IV chord, so the possible arrival is again thwarted. The next phrase, "It always leads me here" (what perfect prosody!) pauses again on *la* in the melody sounding with Cm, the VIm chord. Not until measures 11–12 does *la* move to *ti* and finally to *do*, arriving on the tonic chord with the lyric, "Lead me to your door," and then it's back to the beginning to continue its Sisyphus-like journey (Ex. 17.04).

Ex. 17.04 "The Long And Winding Road" John Lennon, Paul McCartney

Ex. 17.05

"What Goes Around Comes Around," Justin Timberlake's hit song in 2006, creates great prosody by connecting its lyrical concept to its treatment of the melodic phrase to the harmonic phrase.

"What Goes Around Comes Around" uses a four-chord pattern, one chord per measure (Ex. 17.05).

One of the most available techniques for strategizing between sections of a song—the tonal arrival at the chorus—is nullified when you choose to use the same chord pattern in all sections. Since the chorus section should be the most stable section of a song, and since the chord pattern in this song, by design, doesn't change, stability in the chorus section must be achieved by some other means. This feat is achieved in this song through the treatment of the relationship between the melodic phrase to the harmonic phrase. The perfect prosody in this song ranks it as one of the finest songs written in the past decade.

The song is written in four different sections. The melodic phrases in sections #1, #2, and #3 are out of sync to the harmonic four-measure phrase. When section #4, the chorus, arrives with its melody in sync with the harmonic phrase, it achieves the needed stability we associate with the arrival of the chorus section of a song.

The opening melodic phrase in section #1 sets up a series of 2-measure back-heavy phrases that are out of sync with the harmonic phrase. Notice how the last melodic phrase spills over into the next harmonic phrase (Ex. 17.06).

Ex. 17.06 "What Goes Around Comes Around" section #1, Justin Timberlake, Timberland, Tim Mosley, Nate Hills

Section #2 contrasts with section #1 by employing one-measure melodic phrases that begin an eighth note after the downbeat. In the final phrase of section#2, a three-measure melodic phrase imposes itself on the first measure of the harmonic phrase of section #3, causing its melody to be out of sync with the harmonic phrase (Ex. 17.07).

320

Ex. 17.07 Section #2

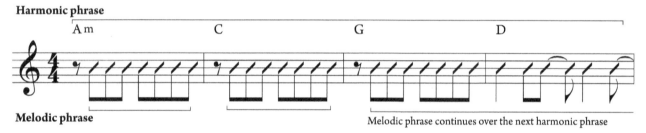

The harmonic phrase beginning section #3 houses the melodic phrase ending of section #2. This causes the listener to hear the melody in section #3 begin on the C chord, rather than on the A minor chord. The melodic phrase and the harmonic phrase are now totally out of sync with one another yet sound great together (Ex. 17.08).

Ex. 17.08 Section #3

The title of the song and the central idea appear in section #4, the only section where the melodic phrase and harmonic phrase come close to coinciding (Ex. 17.09).

Ex. 17.09 Section #4, chorus

All the lyrics up to this point in the song have been of a personal nature, such as "Hey girl, is he everything you wanted in a man?" but in the chorus the lyrics are of a philosophical nature (as well as supplying a commentary on the structure of the music itself): "What goes around, goes around, comes all the way back around," creating the song's stupendous prosody. When the chorus does arrive, with its lyric's central idea and its melody conforming to the four-measure harmonic pattern, listeners grasp intuitively that this, indeed, is the chorus.

Prince was an amazing musician and songwriter touched with genius. A song he wrote for his movie *Purple Rain* describes the mental state experienced when he felt out of control with his lover. The music is stark, as befits a near psychotic state, and the setting is rife with sexual imagery (Ex. 17.10).

Ex. 17.10 "When Doves Cry" Prince

At the time when "When Doves Cry" was recorded (1984), every record, especially R&B and rock records, had electric bass prominently featured in the rhythm section. Prince's spare, nearly naked production practically leaves out the electric bass (it is mixed way, way back). Only voice and drums are heard, with a sparse percussive synth figure counterpointing the voice. The song, written in A minor, has only four notes in its melody, A, G, E, and an occasional G♯; this stark minimalist approach was startling when this song was recorded. There are no chords, no harmony accompanying the vocal melody, just as there is no emotional harmony in the relationship depicted.

The lyrics go well beyond describing the physical attraction and mutual abuse these two lovers are experiencing; Prince wants us to feel their sexual passion, which he achieves with his music and with his visually driven lyrics:

Dream if you can a courtyard
An ocean of violets in bloom.
Animals strike curious poses;
They feel the heat,
The heat between me and you.

The combination of this stark music and the emotionally driven lyrics, is what makes this song so riveting.

321

Rhythm and texture are elements that can greatly affect the impact your lyrics have on listeners. Taylor Swift and Jack Antonoff created a leisurely reflective verse for "Out Of the Woods" (Ex. 17.11).

Ex. 17.11 "Out Of the Woods" verse, Taylor Swift, Jack Antonoff

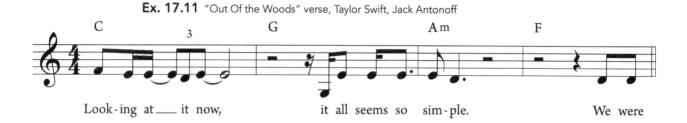

The rhythms in the chorus change radically, they are dense, reflecting a crowded or tortured state of mind. Even as she asks her lover, "Are we out of the woods yet?" we know that they are far from being out of the woods. We know it—because the music tells us so (Ex. 17.12).

Ex. 17.12 "Out Of The Woods" chorus

The importance of the concept of "open" and "closed" in prosody

An overriding concept that you should keep in mind in combining the various elements of your song is whether an event is ending open or closed or half-open/half-closed. These terms can apply to song form or to tonal and/or rhythmic components of a phrase. A section ends either open or closed or half-open/half-closed depending on the last melodic note in a phrase, or on the metric and rhythmic placement of the last melodic note, or on the choice of the last harmony. The combination of elements conjoining throughout a song, especially at cadences, makes working with them so interesting and challenging.

For example, a section of a song may close rhythmically and melodically and remain open harmonically. These contradictory activities are crucial to all music, especially songwriting, in that they provide subtleties that parallel our emotional lives and, in doing so, provide the listeners with feelings that cannot quite be duplicated in any other art form. They also provide for us, the songwriters, one of the great joys in the actual process of creating songs. Even a word that is expected to rhyme because it is a matched phrase in a balancing position—but doesn't rhyme—can keep a section open when all the other elements are closed.

A good example of this is found in a #1 pop song in 1974, "Laughter In The Rain." The matched phrases in the first verse call for rhyme. The listener, therefore, is momentarily jarred by the lack of rhyme in the cadence, where s/he expects to hear "pour" answered by a rhyme like words such as "core" or "door," but instead is confounded with the word "spine." The listener is amply compensated for this interruption by the accommodating next line, "I feel the warmth of her hand in mine," that rhymes "spine" with "mine." This added line not only supplies the needed rhyme but also provides a delightful element of surprise that is a perfect entrée into the chorus (Ex. 17.13).

Ex. 17.13 "Laughter In The Rain" music by Neil Sedaka, lyrics by Phil Cody

The carefree sense of young love permeates this entire song, helped by the jaunty rhythms and the major pentatonic tonal environment. No dissonant half steps here to get in the way of the lovers having a good time—even in a downpour.

Cadences are the areas where you may ask yourself if the song is moving in the way you want it to move, if the feelings generated by the words (e.g., "Is it better to have a perfect rhyme or to use assonance?") and music (e.g., "Would it be better to have a stable tone in the melody while the harmony is unstable, or should both melody and harmony be unstable?") are being optimized.

The first two phrases in "Always On My Mind" are matched and rhyme. Both parameters are, therefore, closed (Ex. 17.14).

Ex. 17.14 Melodic rhythm

The four-measure melody repeats and ends tonally open both times on the unstable *la*. The prosody in these repeated four measures is enhanced by the descending melody's overall contour (Ex. 17.15).

Ex. 17.15 Melodic pitch

Phrase two ends harmonically open (measure 4) on an unstable diatonic chord, while phrase four's ending (measure 8) increases that openness with E7, a chromatic chord. This heightens and slightly changes the depth of the emotion, amplifying the feeling of guilt and regret while also enticing the listener to look forward to what is to follow (Ex. 17.16).

Ex. 17.16 *"Always On My Mind"* Wayne Carson, Johnny Christopher, Mark James

The eight measures are:

- rhythmically closed (matched phrases)
- lyrically closed (with perfect rhyme, "could/should")
- melodically tonally open (on *la*)
- harmonically open (a chromatic chord ends the structure)

Another beautiful example of how harmony affects the openness of a cadential area and the implied meaning of the lyrics is found in Paul Simon's "Still Crazy After All These Years" (see Ex. 13.07).

As in all things, prosody can be abused. When this occurs, it is called "Mickey-Mousing," after the cartoon music that underscores every slight and gross movement made by cartoon characters. Just because a lyric references something going higher, doesn't mean the melody necessarily has to go higher—although it might. As in all artistic endeavors, whether or not prosody is overdone is measurable only by the judgment of the creative artist and later, by the public and the critics. Just keep in mind that as important as prosody is, it too can be exaggerated and become a parody of itself.

Summary

Great prosody is the result of music and lyrics conjoining, creating the perfect child of two lovers meant to be together. It sometimes happens when writing a song that the music and words come together simultaneously because the songwriter is so tuned in to what is to be expressed that the perfect exposition of that feeling emerges spontaneously. But just as often, great prosody is the result of rewriting and, then, rewriting.

Activity

- Listen for prosody in songs. When a song moves you, don't simply enjoy the feeling. Listen again and again. Notate what you hear and analyze why it affects you. The answer is almost always found in the way the elements of music, words, and performance and production have coalesced to create the experience. If you do this on a regular basis, the knowledge you have accrued will gradually seep into your own writing and you too will be able to create songs containing prosody that will move others.
- Rewrite your songs until every lyrical and musical gesture amplifies each other.

18

Process

The process of creating a song is one of the most difficult subjects to teach. My process may not be yours, yet I believe that there is much to be gained by taking you through the kinds of choices and decision-making that occur when I am writing a song. I'll use two of my songs as examples, one of which I've already referenced in chapter 1, Examples 1.03 and 1.04, a ballad entitled "Out Of My Dream." The other song is "Goodbye Again," a moderate up-tempo song built from a repeated four-chord pattern that required a different approach.

Since I am introducing you to a song you've never heard before, I advise you to listen to it before reading the detailed process I went through composing and writing lyrics for it. The entire song may be heard at ⏵ AUDIO "Out Of My Dream" (complete). Here are the first two verses and chorus of "Out Of My Dream" (Ex. 18.01; ⏵ AUDIO 18.01).

"Out Of My Dream"

Ex. 18.01 "Out Of My Dream" verses 1and 2 and chorus, Jack Perricone

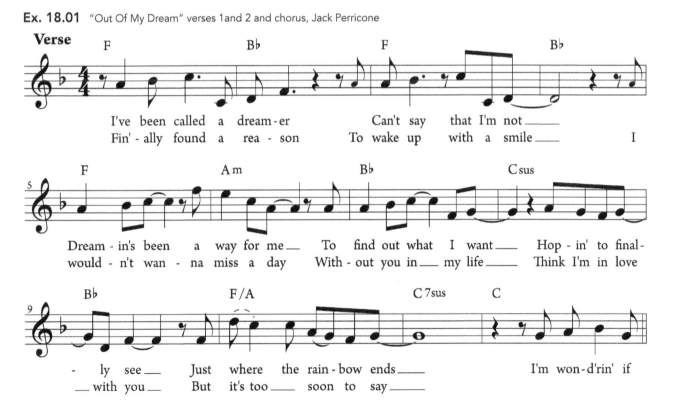

Verse

I've been called a dream-er   Can't say   that I'm not ___
Fin' - ally found a rea - son   To wake up with a smile ___   I

Dream - in's been   a   way for me ___ To   find out what I want ___ Hop - in' to final-
would - n't wan - na miss a day   With - out you in ___ my life ___   Think I'm in love

- ly see ___ Just   where   the rain - bow ends ___   I'm won-d'rin' if
___ with you ___ But   it's too ___ soon to say ___

Ex. 18.01 Continued

you dream of me ___ The same way that I dream of you ___ 'Cause late-ly when-ev-er ___ I think ___ of you ___ I want you by ___ my side ___ Out of my dream In-to my ___ life. my life. Each

Music for the verse

The music for the verse came first; I heard a six-note motive in my mind while away from an instrument. I then went to the piano, my main instrument, and started to compose. Here is the initial idea (Ex. 18.02):

Ex. 18.02 motive #1

I chose to repeat the opening motive—but inexactly. I altered the second phrase rhythmically by beginning the melodic phrase on a pickup note leading to the downbeat, and I truncated the phrase by taking away the last note. The first phrase has a feminine ending; the second phrase has a masculine one (Ex. 18.03).

Ex. 18.03

I had created 2 two-measure phrases using an a, b, phrase structure. I liked ending the second phrase on *la* because it left the phrase open, sounding expectant and whimsical.

After studying these two phrases, I started the next phrase with the same motive. I knew that doing so might cause the song to become dull unless I made other changes. I copied the first four notes of the second melodic phrase and created a four-measure phrase that would both contrast with the first 2 two-measure phrases and balance them. I also increased the range of my melody to the high F, but made E, *ti*, my main target note within the phrase. This note called attention to itself, and had a kind of ache in it that appealed to me. I ended this third phrase (measures 5–8) on *re*, keeping the music open and indicating that something else was about to occur.

I now had a balanced structure that produced a rhythmically closed (fragmented) section. It seemed too soon for a chorus, so I continued writing the verse (Ex. 18.04).

Ex. 18.04

During the process of composing measures 4–8, I noticed that all my phrases were front-heavy and, to avoid monotony and to increase the forward thrust, I allowed enough room in my last phrase to contain a back-heavy phrase that begins in measure 8 and continues into measure 9 (Ex. 18.09).

Ex. 18.05 Verse ending

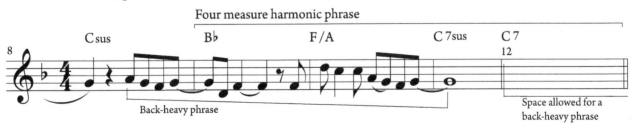

I really liked the new melodic phrase (beginning on the third beat of measure 8) for a couple of reasons: (1) it was an added phrase, unbalancing the verse and giving the verse thrust into the chorus; (2) it ended on the third measure of the four-measure harmonic phrase, allowing me to compose a more substantial back-heavy phrase into my chorus. I didn't love the fact that the section ended on the too-obvious dominant harmony. This was especially troublesome because I heard the next phrase starting on the tonic chord. However, the music for the entire verse seemed to have a quality of innocence or naiveté that made this choice appropriate.

Music for the chorus

Ex. 18.06 Chorus

My first aim in writing a chorus is to create a memorable melody. Feeling inspired, I created a melody that has a memorable rhythm and shape (Ex. 18.06). The minor 6th leap from A to F in measure 13 followed by a descending half step and P5th give this melody a memorable shape, while the syncopations on the anticipated third beat and the anticipated first beat of measure 14 give it a memorable rhythm. I immediately repeated this motive (one of the song's hooks) because this formed an identity element and would possibly become the most memorable part of the song. I liked the pungency of the last note of the hook phrase that ends on a major seventh interval between the A in the melody and B♭ in the bass.

I especially liked the way the melodic phrase and the harmonic phrase did not coincide; this made the whole music—music that sounds simple—interesting (Ex. 18.07).

Ex. 18.07

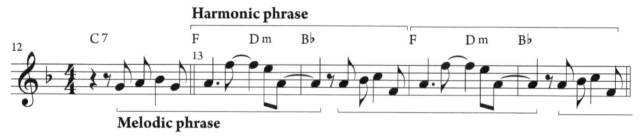

After the first four measures of the chorus's intervallic leaps (measures 13–15), I felt the melody's need to settle in a more conjunct type of movement. I began this new section of the chorus with the same melodic rhythm that began all the other phrases in the chorus, but took the melody to a new place (Ex. 18.08).

Ex. 18.08

The phrase I created is little more than an elaboration on the note G, *re* in the key of F. *Re* plays such an important role in so many songs in setting up *do*, as it does here as well. Measure 19 contains a ♭VII chord that adds some needed tension to the phrase; I especially like the supportable nonchord tones, A, C, and F (marked with asterisks), in the melody pitted against the E♭ in the harmony. I felt the need to add a measure (measure 21) to the phrase structure, a gesture that also increases the tension and focuses the interest in what is about to happen: the title.

The next-to-last phrase of the chorus melody anticipates the final *do*. Having the penultimate phrase end on *do*, but leaving it harmonically and rhythmically open, allows the music to make a kind of soft landing, informing the listener that the section is musically ending (Ex. 18.09).

Ex. 18.09 The two last phrases in the chorus

The first time that the melody moves to *do*, I harmonized it with IV, followed immediately with IVm—which gives this phrase an added poignancy—and the last time the melody moves to *do*, I harmonized it with I^sus that resolves to the I chord. I chose not to close the melody and harmony at the same time; closing both melody and harmony at the same time is avoided because doing so is akin to running into a brick wall. Repeating the melodic phrase also gives some breadth to my last phrase.

I've already alluded to the similarities that exist in various phrases within this song. This song seemed to want to evolve out of itself and I allowed it to do that. Just as a novelist creates characters and then lets them take twists and turns that the author hadn't plotted out beforehand, a song often leads the songwriter to where it wants to go, and it is best to follow along.

There is no exact name for it (although you could say that is a kind of rhythmic and tonal permutation), but there is no denying that the chorus melody in measures 12–13, resembles the verse melody in measures 5–6, yet it is different enough to sound fresh

331

when it arrives. The ability to create contrast within similarity is a basic compositional guideline that can and should be cultivated; it is a way to create interest while unifying the song (Ex. 18.10).

Ex. 18.10 Similarities in verse and chorus melodies

Verse, measures 5, 6

Dream-in's been   a   way   for me ___

Chorus, measures 12, 13

I'm won-d'rin'   if   you   dream   of me

I often write music first. I'm reminded of what Billy Joel said when a Berklee student asked him about his process. He said something like this: "I usually write music first, and once I have finished it, my lyrics have to live up to my music." I believe that is an excellent way to write. But there are many other ways. All of them demand rewriting. Rewriting is writing. This is true whether you are writing a novel, a poem, a symphony, or a song.

Writing the lyric

In order to write a lyric, I need to know what the song is about. As soon as I feel that I have composed the music for a song, or at least a section of a song, I play what I've created over and over again until I hear what my music is saying or at least implying. I sing words—real words or nonsense syllables—to what I've created, listening for the sounds that resonate with the musical gestures. I jot down any lyrics that seem to be a natural fit. The next thing I do is start thinking about a title. Once I have a title, I can begin searching for a concept, and once I have a concept, words can begin to flow with my music. To find the most compelling place for a title, I first look for important landmarks: beginnings of sections and important cadences, especially at the ends of sections.

The music in this song dictated that the title should appear in measures 21–25 because that is where an important cadence occurs. Once I knew where the title should appear, I had to find one that sonically fit my music. Luckily, in the process of writing the music for the verse, I heard the lyrics for the first couple of phrases, an incident that occurred quite naturally and I accepted it as the gift that is was. The lyrics I heard were: "I've been called a dreamer; can't say that I'm not." The opening lines of a song are very important and, if they are right, often guide you to the title.

The opening lyrics allowed me to search for the title line in measures 21–25. The line, "Out of my dream, into my life" emerged. I loved that line because it contained a polarity: "in" and "out" and the implied polarity of dream versus reality. Now that I had a title and a hint of a concept, I had to hone in on who was singing to whom and the actual content. I decided the singer would be a young man who is in love with a girl who hadn't completely committed to him. We hear the singer's thoughts in an internal monologue, a first person narrative that expresses his desire to not simply be dreaming of her, but to actually be with her.

The verse lyric

I now had a concept for the song and took on the task of writing the verse lyric.

The first lines of the verse focused the listener's attention on the singer—the "me"—so I continued in that vein, knowing that the chorus would focus on the singee—the "you"—and the possibility of two of them being together. This early decision is an acknowledgment of the importance of singing a song to someone, not simply to oneself about oneself, but rather, to sing to another—the "you" that in every song is, ultimately, the audience.

In writing a lyric to music, I look for matched phrases because they indicate where rhyme is called for. The ending of the second phrase, the eighth note anticipation of measure 4, and the eighth note anticipation to measure 8 are matched and call for rhyme. I used consonance as well as assonance: "not" and "want" in verse 1 and "smile" and "life" in verse 2 to satisfy the need for these sonic connections (Ex. 18.11).

Ex. 18.11 Verse with lyric

When there is a choice between a word that provides meaning or one that provides a perfect rhyme, I will nearly always choose one that provides meaning and use a word that, although not a perfect rhyme, has some sonic resonance to the word beckoning for it to appear.

Important notes deserve important words and vice versa. I previously mentioned the high E in measure 6 that I described as having an ache in it. Notice the words that show up on that note. In verse one, the line that contains it is "Dreamin's been a **way** for me to find out what I want." In verse two, the line that contains it is "I wouldn't wanna **miss** a day without you in my life." Both of those words: "way" and "miss," in the context of the lyric, reflect the ache that is implied in that note.

Notice the alliteration that shows up in both of those lines: "Dreamin's been a **w**ay for me to find out **w**hat I **w**ant" and "I **w**ouldn't **w**anna **m**iss a day **w**ithout you in **m**y life." These occurrences of alliteration occurred quite naturally; in a sense, they are simply an extension of musical choices.

The chorus lyric

The beginning of the chorus does not contain the title, but it does contain a musical hook and a fairly strong lyric. This area and the ending of the chorus, where the title resides, are two of the most important and memorable areas in the song (Ex. 18.12).

Ex. 18.12 Chorus beginning

I'm won-drin' if **you dream** of **me** ___ The same way that **I dream** of **you** ___

Notice the words that appear on the musically important areas, on first and third beats or the anticipated first and third beats of the first four measures of the chorus: "you," "me," "I," and "you." The high note that appears twice on the anticipated beat 3 receives the important word "dream." There is a significant connection that these two phrases have with each other musically: they mirror each other and, therefore, lyrically ask for parallel construction: "I'm wondrin' if you dream of me, the same way that I dream of you."

There is only one rhyme used in the first chorus: side/life, yet another use of assonance. In the second chorus and in the last chorus, I changed "I want you by my **side**" to "I want you for my **wife**" to reinforce the earnestness of the wish by using the sonic impact of a perfect rhyme, wife/life (Ex. 18.13).

Ex. 18.13

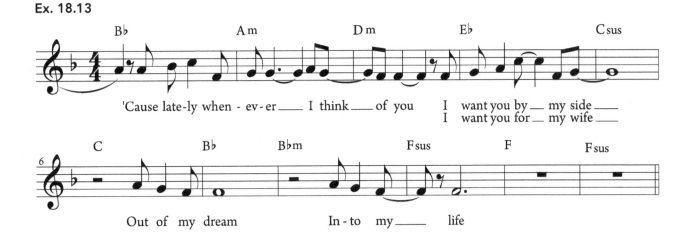

The bridge and coda

I usually save writing the bridge for last, because it is difficult to initially judge whether a song needs a bridge. There is the possibly that an instrumental section should occur instead because either the song may be very wordy or because I've said all I've really wanted to say. So it is best not to waste too much effort on a bridge section until it becomes a necessity. It is also wise to wait because this section can provide a new angle into the song, and it is difficult to know what that is until the other parts are complete.

One consideration in deciding whether a bridge section is needed is the density of the language, the possibility that the listener has been presented with too many words to withstand another barrage of them in yet another section. Since the verse/chorus sections that I had written were not too crowded with words, and the two verses and choruses would not produce as complete a song as one with a bridge, I decided to write one. I began the process of finding something worth singing about that had not been exposed in the two verses I had already written.

Since the title referred to dreams, I imagined what a young person in love would be thinking as he prepared to go to sleep. The answer was obvious; this fellow was obsessing on this girl most of his waking hours, so that's who would be on his mind just before he closed his eyes and drifted off to dreamland. I wrote:

> Each night
> Before I close my eyes
> I imagine how it's gonna be.
> Then I drift off to
> A dream of you
> And I sure do like what I see.

Notice how many rhymes appear in the bridge. Rhyme itself becomes a contrasting device because the verse and chorus sections are almost bereft of rhyme (Ex. 18.14; ▶ AUDIO 18.14).

335

Ex. 18.14 Bridge, instrumental, and coda

Each night, be-fore I close my eyes, I i-mag-ine how it's gon-na be; Then I

drift off to ___ a dream of ___ you, And I sure do like ___ what I see....

Instrumental.........

.... 'Cause late-ly when-ev-er _____ I think ___ of you ___ I

want you for ___ my wife, ___ Out of my dream In—to my

CODA

___ life. Please come out of my dream and in-to my life.

rit.

Out of my dream and in-to my life. ___

One of the main functions of a bridge is to contain contrast. I felt that the music for the bridge had to begin in a tonal area other than the I chord, because both the verse and the chorus sections had begun on that chord. The bridge, therefore, begins on a minor chord, the IIIm. The bridge also contrasts with the verse and the chorus sections by being a balanced section (the eight measures of the body of the bridge and the added one-measure turnaround) instead of the unbalanced twelve measures that both the verse and chorus sections use.

Most bridges that follow a verse/chorus, verse/chorus/bridge format lead immediately back to a vocal chorus. However, I wanted the last lyric idea of the bridge: "Then I drift off to a dream of you, and I sure do like what I see . . . " to psychologically and musically continue for the listener, pulling the listener into the dream itself. So, instead of having the vocal come in at the beginning of the chorus, I inserted an instrumental using the melody and harmony of the chorus, and had the vocal return on the title. I felt that choice was much more evocative and poetic than simply having the entire chorus sung again. This is an example of how form follows function.

I also felt a need to have a coda or extended ending for this song, especially because by employing an instrumental instead of a vocal I had only left the last line of the song for the singer. With the addition of a coda, I had a chance to repeat the title "out of my dream and into my life" in measures 41–48. It is the kind of a deep wish that repeats ad infinitum in the mind of someone in love, and it is the perfect way to end this song.

Conclusion

What should you take away from this excursion into my process?

• Try to create a motive that has the potential to be developed.
• Keep returning to the motive and the materials already written and explore ways to transform them.
• Look to matched phrases for rhyme.
• If you have written music first, look to cadences and beginnings of sections for strong lyric ideas and title placement.
• Create a concept for your song as soon as possible.
• Attempt to sing words to what you've written, initially not concerning yourself with the meaning of the words, but to the sound of the words.
• Important notes in a melodic phrase deserve important words and vice versa.
• Always be aware of balance/imbalance in phrase structure.
• Be aware of the topography of the phrases, where phrases begin and end, how long they are, and how much space you are leaving between them.
• Be especially conscious of back-heavy and front-heavy phrases.
• Contrast one section of your song from another, yet maintain a unity to the entire song.
• Avoid monotony, but don't be afraid to use repetition.
• Write a hook or two if you want your listeners to remember your song.
• Attempt to surprise and delight yourself, and know that in doing so, you'll surprise and delight others.

"Goodbye Again"

Since this too is a song you've never heard before, listen to it before beginning to read about my process of composing it (▶ AUDIO "Goodbye Again" (complete)). Here are verses 1 and 2 and the first part of the chorus to "Goodbye Again" (Ex. 18.15; ▶ AUDIO 18.15).

Ex. 18.15 Verses 1 and 2 and the A section of the chorus, Jack Perricone

I wrote "Goodbye Again" as the result of an assignment I created for my students in Songwriting 1, a course that I teach at the famed Berklee College of Music. The assignment was to write a two- or three-section song with a repeating four-chord progression throughout. Since I have always believed that a teacher must teach by example and since I, up to that time, had not written a song that adhered to a four-chord pattern throughout, I took on the assignment myself.

I based the assignment and my song on one of the most prevalent chord patterns on the pop charts in recent years (Ex. 18.16).

Ex. 18.16 Chord pattern analyzed in two keys

One of the attributes to this chord pattern is its tonal ambiguity. It can be heard in four different keys, the most likely being B♭ Ionian or the G Aeolian mode. (F Mixolydian and E♭ Lydian and are possible but unlikely choices.) The pattern contains three major triads and one minor triad, a distribution that is neither too bright nor too dark.

Music for the verse

I wrote music first and allowed my music to dictate what the lyric was to become. One thing I strove to do was to make my melody as independent from the dictates of the harmony as I could. I chose two main ways of doing this: (1) by metrically and/or rhythmically differentiating the melodic phrase from the harmonic phrase, and (2) by using nonchord tones in the melody (Ex. 18.17).

339

Ex. 18.17 Verse 1

I used nonchord tones (marked with asterisks) almost immediately; notice the amount of nonchord tones throughout, e.g., F, D, and C, three supportable nonchord tones in measure 2. In order to differentiate the melody rhythmically, I began the first melodic phrase on the second beat. The length of the first phrase nearly matches the four-measure harmonic phrase, but it does end soon enough to allow me to begin a back-heavy phrase in measure 4. This gives my second melodic phrase the sought-after independence. This phrase is one of the most interesting in the song; it reaches up to an A, a supportable nonchord tone (♯11) that is set against the tritone, E♭ in the bass. The A does not resolve to the chord tone, G, but moves to another supportable nonchord tone, F. This phrase let me know that this was not going to be a sweet song; there was already a lot of dissonance in it, and this melody/harmony relationship would define the tenor of the song. The next phrase, in measure 8, is a kind of filler; I made a mental note to myself that the lyric taking place there might, like the music, be an afterthought.

The second half of the verse (beginning on measure 9) is nearly a repeat of the first half except for the phrase that begins in the middle of measure 14 and ends on an anticipation of measure 16. This phrase provides a more definite closure to the verse section and sets up expectations for the chorus (Ex. 18.18).

Ex. 18.18 Verse 2

After composing the music to the verses, I felt I had achieved my goal of creating interesting music, one that would inspire a lyric.

Music for the chorus

I began the chorus with a quarter-note pickup that points to the downbeat, making the first beat of the chorus prominent, so that we feel its impact when it arrives. Again, in this song I strove to create a memorable melodic hook using both interesting rhythms and characteristic intervallic leaps. The pickup note begins the chorus with a leap of a major seventh, from B♭ to A, a nonchord tone that immediately resolves to G and descends in a arpeggiated melody that upon reaching B♭, repeats the phrase, but this time with an eighth-note anticipation of the note, A, before the downbeat of measure 18, producing a strong syncopation and a rhythmic displacement that will have consequences in the lyric (Ex. 18.19).

Ex. 18.19 Chorus

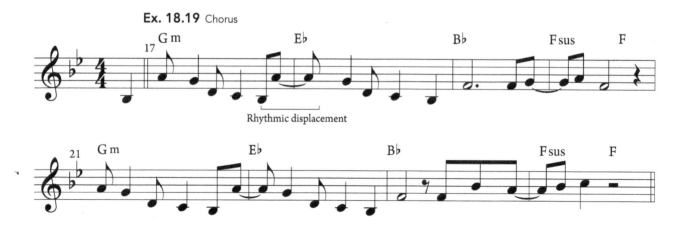

The 2 four-measure melodic phrases in this first section of the chorus nearly coincide with the four-measure harmonic phrases. I considered this a positive, because I wanted to establish a sense of stability and consolidation in the chorus. The third phrase, beginning in measure 21, mainly repeats the first phrase of the chorus except for the last five notes, which ascend in a rather dramatic gesture. Both phrases end open melodically on *fa* and harmonically on ♭VII.

I then proceeded to write a B section to the chorus because I felt that the A section of the chorus was too short to stand alone. It was too short to balance the two verses that preceded it, and I felt that it was not substantial enough to sustain the listener's interest. The B section could also act as a kind of bridge within the chorus and, therefore, provide a needed contrast to the A section (Ex. 18.20; ⊙ AUDIO 18.20).

Ex. 18.20 B section of the chorus and the return of the A section

The choices I made to contrast the B section to the A section of the chorus (measures 25–32) include:

1. Use of the prismatic effect (the two-measure melody that appears in measures 25–26 repeats and receives different harmonies in measures 27–28).
2. A change in the tessitura: The tessitura of the B section is much lower than that of the A section of the chorus.
3. A change in the phrase lengths from two measures to four measures.
4. The phrases now begin on the second beat as opposed to the pickup note to the first beat that occurred at the beginning of the chorus.
5. There is an increased sense of excitement, because syncopation is more prominent and the groove changes to double-time.

In measure 33, I return to the A section of the chorus, but this time in a truncated form of only four measures. I truncated the A section to last for only four measures, because it would have grown monotonous if I had included the entire eight measures. The chorus itself is a miniature version of the AABA form found in the songs of the *Great American Songbook.*

The chorus completed, I spent some time thinking of what a return to the verse section needed and the effect it would have on my listener. I decided to write an instrumental interlude in order to break from the repeated chord pattern by creating a fresh sound. It would have been nice because of the challenge presented to strictly adhere to the same chord progression throughout the entire piece, but I felt the need for a surprise in the song here, so that when the second verse entered it would sound fresh and welcoming.

I changed just one chord—the first chord in this section, from Gm to Am—but my, what a difference it makes! The E♮, the first melody note in this section and a member of the A minor chord, forms a tritone to B♭, the stable third of the key. Another reason the A minor chord works so well is that it is a chord often found in G minor and is characteristic of G Dorian—but it packs a wallop here because it is totally foreign in the tonal environment of this song, which has been in G Aeolian until this point. The melodic sequence I created is made up of a chromatic melodic step progression: E♮, E♭, D and C (Ex. 18.21; ⊙ AUDIO 18.21).

Ex. 18.21 Instrumental interlude

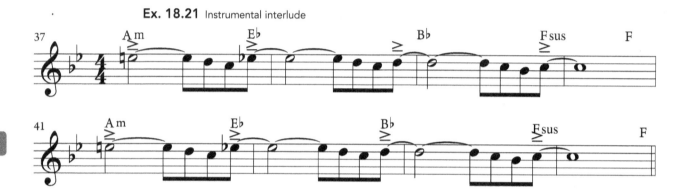

This is all the music in the song; there is no bridge. The interlude provides the needed contrasting element that the bridge would have provided.

The lyrics for "Goodbye Again"

The melodic materials I created did not make use of the many tonal possibilities implicit in the chord pattern. Instead, I had centered the entire music for this song in G minor, producing a soundscape that is rather dark and foreboding. This inspired both the concept and the title. The title "Goodbye Again" occurred to me as I played the first phrase in the chorus. It sang well, but what did it mean? Initially, I had no idea.

After spending some time with this title, I realized that it could refer to a recurring nightmare that would bring a lost lover back, time and again, to the person he had abandoned. The person having the recurring nightmare, who is obsessed with this loss, would deliver the song. I pictured a young woman waking, not just once but every night, with the same nightmarish image ingrained in her mind, an idée fixe. She wishes to get rid of her lover's image but at the same time, while he is with her in her dreams, she wants to be with him. I liked this concept because it was unique and because it really fit the character of the music. I also acknowledged the universality of the feeling, one that I, and I'm sure many others, have experienced.

Prosody in "Goodbye Again"

Since the music itself conjured up the lyric's nightmarish scenario, it guided me in all my lyrical choices. Here are some other factors that led to the creation of the lyrics:

- Each of the phrases that occur in obvious cadencing positions (measure 4, 8, 12, and 16) end open. This, in conjunction with the dissonant minor-keyed melody, inspired a lyric that reverberates with the feeling of being abandoned.
- The melodic phrases within measures 1–8 are unmatched, and don't demand rhyme. However, I do use rhyme: "then," "again," "end" and "then," to tie these disparate musical phrases together. The chorus even resonates with the "en" sound with "Goodbye again," and "plans."
- In the beginning of the chorus, measures 17–20, I especially like the setting of the repetition of the word "goodbye." The first time the title is heard, the first syllable of the word is stressed: **good**-bye. But by beginning the second phrase with "good" placed on the fourth beat of the measure, the second syllable, "bye," falls on the anticipated downbeat of the next measure, highlighting the word in the following way: "good-**bye**" instead of "**good**-bye, causing the repetition of the word to be both more interesting and forceful. The word "goodbye" appears three times in consecutive phrases, the third time sustaining the note attached to "bye," reinforcing not only the word but also the feeling the word generates (Ex. 18.22).

Ex. 18.22 Title displacement

The B section of the chorus intensifies the listener's experience by detailing what occurs in the room between the singer and her ghostly lover, rendering a nearly visceral experience. This section of the chorus lyrics is changed in the second chorus to allow for more variety and to supply more information to the listener (Ex. 18.23).

Ex. 18.23 The B section of the chorus

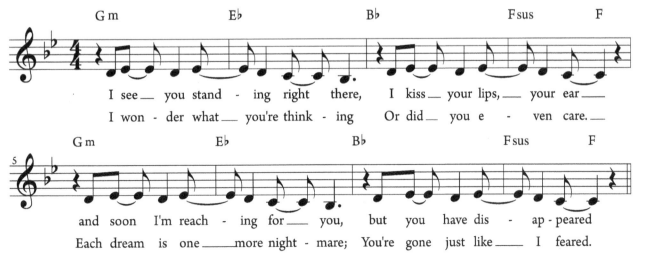

343

The instrumental interlude was created after I had completed the lyrics for the first verse and chorus and is meant to be a kind of a tumultuous aftershock, a reverberant resonance of what has just occurred.

At the end of the song, I chose to repeat the chorus and the instrumental interlude because I felt that it was one of the highpoints of the music and would leave the listeners with the sound of nightmarish fright, highlighting the concept of the song (Ex. 18.24).

Ex. 18.24 The end of the song

Summary

Every song has its own personality and demands. The two songs presented in this chapter are good examples of this. When writing "Goodbye Again" I was more concerned about contrasting each section of the song than in trying to develop melodic ideas, the main focus in writing "Out Of My Dream." The driving forces in both songs were *concept* and *prosody*. If you are intent on making your words and music magnify the meaning of your song, you are bound to find the process that will work for you in completing the song.

Here are some general thoughts and recommendations on writing:

- Write every day. Writing lots of songs and combining that activity with a deep study of songwriting technique and song analysis can allow you to use rational knowledge when needed while staying in in touch with your intuitive self—where the best songs reside.
- The deeper your knowledge of songwriting techniques is, the better are your chances of finishing your songs. The rational knowledge you gain through the study of songwriting techniques, once accomplished and totally assimilated, will function as both a backup for and a participant in your creative efforts.
- Put your feelings in the driver's seat. This may seem contradictory to what you may be thinking I've been teaching, but it is not. The mind can be a horrible back-seat driver. When you create, tell the critic and that highly knowledgeable songwriter you've become to take a rest. It is a great feeling and a great confidence builder, however, to know that you have a storehouse of songwriting techniques to call on if needed—so call on your mind when you really need it so that you can get back in the flow.
- As often as possible, reaffirm that you are a creative being. Remind yourself of this and give yourself permission and encouragement to create because it does take both an effort and an openness to create and we tend to escape from creative endeavor by filling our time with mundane tasks.
- Always strive to write simply and interestingly.

AFTERWORD

Songwriting is a strongly intuitive process as well as a craft. In this book I have concentrated on the craft, because craft can be taught. But in writing this book I've tried to be ever mindful that craft alone is not enough to produce an exceptional song. I am in awe of immensely talented writers such as Irving Berlin, Joni Mitchell, Elton John, Paul McCartney, Billy Joel, Stevie Wonder, Carole King, and Paul Simon, because they have demonstrated throughout their long careers how both their craft and their intuition have guided them into producing masterful songs.

The creative process is extremely complex. It mainly involves consciousness, abstract thought, imagination, the truth, and being open to the moment. In order to produce something of value in any creative endeavor, you must have the desire and will to do so, along with the tools and techniques that allow you to fully express yourself. You may choose to rely completely on your intuition, and that is perfectly understandable. If your mind houses the technical information you need, that information can be put on "standby" in case your intuition momentarily fails you. It is also possible for your rational mind to be in complete alignment with your emotions, your body, and your spirit and to fully participate in the creative process—and if it is, your creative powers increase exponentially. It is this alignment that causes the intuitive moment!

If I have provided you with songwriting tools and techniques, along with musical insight into the ways those tools and techniques can be used, then I will have fulfilled the purpose of this book.

Jack Perricone, 2016

SONGS

351

353

357

"Love Song" Sara Bareilles 79
Copyright © 2006 Sony/ATV Music Publishing LLC and Tiny Bear Music (ASCAP)
All Rights Administered by Sony/ATV Music Publishing LLC, 8 Music Square West,
Nashville, TN 37203

"Love Train" Kenny Gamble, Leon Huff 137
Copyright © 1973, 1982 Warner- Tamerlane Publishing Corp.
All Rights Administered by Warner-Tamerlane Publishing Corp.

"Lucy In The Sky" John Lennon, Paul McCartney 216
Copyright © 1967 Northern Songs Limited
All rights administered by Blackwood Music Inc. under license from ATV Music (Maclen)

"Lush Life" Billy Strayhorn 255
Copyright © 1949 (Renewed) by Music Sales Corporation and Tempo Music, Inc.
All rights administered by Music Sales Corporation (ASCAP)

"Man In The Mirror" Siedah Garrett, Glen Ballard 9
Copyright © 1987 by MCA Music Publishing, Yellowbrick Road Music, Universal Music Corporation, and
Aerostation Corporation

"Maria" Music by Leonard Bernstein, Lyrics by Stephen Sondheim 145
Copyright © 1957 by Leonard Bernstein and Stephen Sondheim

"Mrs. Robinson" Paul Simon 84
Copyright © 1968 Paul Simon (BMI)

"My Life" Billy Joel 187
Copyright © 1978 Impulsive Music
All rights controlled and administered by April Music Inc.

"My Little Town" Paul Simon 166–167
Copyright © 1975 Paul Simon (BMI)

"(You Make Me Feel Like) A Natural Woman" Music by Carole King, Lyrics by Gerry Goffin
199
Copyright ©1967 by Screen Gems- Columbia Music, Inc.

"Need You Now" Hillary Scott, Charles Kelley, Dave Heywood, Josh Kear 65
Copyright © 2009 EMI Foray Music, Hillary Dawn Songs, Warner- Tamerlane
Publishing Corp., Radiobullets Publishing, Dwhaywood Music, Year of the Dog Music,
and Darth Buddha
All rights for Hillary Dawn Songs controlled and administered by EMI Foray Music
All rights for Radiobullets Publishing and Dwhaywood Music administered
by Warner- Tamerlane Publishing Corp.

"Neither One Of Us" Jim Weatherly 230
Copyright © 1971 Polygram International Publishing, Inc.

"Next To Me" Emeli Sandé, Harry Crazy, Hugo Chegwin, Anup Paul 15
Copyright © 2012 Stellar Songs, Ltd., Sony/ATV Music Publishing UK, Ltd., Naughty
Words, Ltd., and Anup Paul Publishing Designee. All rights for Stellar Songs, Ltd., in
the U.S. and Canada controlled and administered by EMI Blackwood Music Inc.
All rights for Sony/ATV Music Publishing UK Limited And Naughty Words Limited administered by Sony/
ATV Music Publishing LLC, 8 Music Square West, Nashville, TN 37203

"1913 Massacre" 181–182
Copyright © 1961 (renewed) Sanga Music Inc., New York, NY.

"Norwegian Wood" John Lennon, Paul McCartney 171
Copyright ©1965 Northern Songs, Ltd.
All rights administered by Blackwood Music Inc. under license from ATV Music (Maclen)

"Oh, My Darling Clementine" 55
Public domain

359

"She Loves You" John Lennon, Paul McCartney   121

"Since U Been Gone" Luke Gottwald, Max Martin   219

"Sing a Simple Song" Sly Stone   135

"Slow Dancing In a Burning Room" John Mayer   295

"Slow Turning" John Hiatt   224

"Smells Like Teen Spirit" Kurt Cobain, Dave Grohl, Chris Novoselic   220

"Sober" P!nk, Nate Hills, Kara DioGuardi, Marcella Araica   67

"Somebody Loves Me" Music by George Gershwin, Lyrics by Ira Gershwin   125

"Somebody That I Used To Know" Wally De Backer, Luiz Bonfa   282

"Someone Like You" Adele Adkins, Dan Wilson 291 Copyright © 2010, 2011 Universal Music Publishing LTD., Chrysalis Music and Sugar Lake Music

"Someone To Watch Over Me" Music by George Gershwin, Lyrics by Ira Gershwin   117

"Sometimes I'm Happy" Victor Youmans, Irving Caesar   29

"The Way You Do The Things You Do" William "Smokey" Robinson, Robert Rogers   35, 218
Copyright © 1964 (renewed 1992, 2000) 1979 Jobete Music Co., Inc.
All rights controlled and administered by EMI April Music, Inc.

"We Are Never Ever Getting Back Together" Taylor Swift, Max Martin, Shellback   311
Copyright © 2012 Sony/ ATV Music Publishing, LLC, Taylor Swift Music, and MXM Music AB
All rights on behalf of Sony/ATV Music Publishing LLC and Taylor Swift Music administered by Sony /ATV
Music Publishing LLC, 8 Music Square West, Nashville TN 37203. All rights on behalf of MXM Music AB
administered by Kobalt Songs Music Publishing

"We Are The World" Michael Jackson, Lionel Ritchie   227
Copyright © 1985 by Brockman Music, Brenda Richie Publishing and Mijac Music
All Rights on behalf Mijac Music administered by Sony/ATV Music Publishing LLC, 424 Church Street,
Suite 1200, Nashville, TN 37219

"We Are Young" Nate Ruess, Andrew Dost, Jack Antonoff, Jeffrey Bhasker   190
Copyright © 2012 WB Music Corp., FBR Music, Bearvon Music, Sony/ATV Music Publishing LLC, Way
Above Music, Rough Art and Shira Lee Lawrence Rick Music, Sony/ATV Songs,
LLC and Way Above Music
All rights on behalf of FBR Music and Bearvon Music administered by WB Music Corp.

"What Do You Mean?" Justin Bieber, Jason Boyd, Mason Levy   281
Copyright © 2015 Universal Music Corp., Bieber Time Publishing, Poo Bz Publishing, Inc.,
Hitco South, Artist Publishing Group West and Mason Levy Productions
All rights for Bieber Time Publishing administered by Universal Music Corp.
All rights for Poo Bz Publishing Inc. and Hitco South Administered by BMG Rights
Management (US) LLC
All rights for Artist Publishing Group West and Mason Levy Productions administered
by WB Music Corp.

"What Goes Around Comes Around" Justin Timberlake, Timberland, Tim Mosley,
Nate Hills   320-321
Copyright © 2006 by Zomba Enterprises, Inc., Tennman Tunes, WB Music Corp.,
Virginia Beach Music, W.B.M. Music Corp., and Danjahandz Muzik, Zomba Music
Publishers Limited, Warner Chappell Music
All rights on behalf of Virginia Beach Music administered by WBMusic Corp.
All rights on behalf of Danjahandz Muzik administered by W.B. Music Corp.
All rights for Tennman Tunes administered by Zomba Enterprises, Inc.

"What I Wouldn't Do (For The Love Of You)" Music by Jack Perricone, Lyrics
by Denise Utt   304-305
Copyright© 1979 by Twelfth Street Music, Whiffie Music, and Roaring Fork Music

"When A Man Loves A Woman" Calvin Lewis, Andrew Wright   62
Copyright © 1966 (Renewed) Pronto Music, Quincy Music Publishing Co. and Mijac Music
All rights for Pronto Music and Quincy Music Publishing Co administered
by Warner-Tamerlane Publishing Corp.
All rights for Mijac Music administered by Sony/ATV Music Publishing LLC, 8 Music Square West,
Nashville, TN 37203

"When Doves Cry" Prince   321
Copyright © 1984 Controversy Music
All rights controlled and administered by Universal Music Corp.

"When I Fall In Love" Music by Victor Young, Lyrics by Edward Heyman   63
Copyright © 1952 by Victor Young Publications, Inc. Copyright renewed and assigned to Chappell & Co.
and Intersong- USA, Inc.

"When I Was Your Man" Bruno Mars, Philip Lawrence, Ari Levine   250
Copyright © 2012 BMG Gold Songs, Universal Music Corp., Toy Plane Music, Northside Independent Music
Publishing, LLC, Thou Art the Hunger, WB Music Corp.,
Roc Nation Music, Music Fanamenem, and Downtown DMP Songs
All rights on behalf of Thou Art The Hunger administered by Northside Independent Music Publishing LLC.
All rights on behalf of ROC Nation music administered by WB Music Corp. All rights for Downtown DMO
Songs administered by Downtown Music Publishing LLC

Songs

366

APPENDIX: SYMBOLS USED IN THIS BOOK

The movable *do* system, rather than a fixed *do* system, is used in the analysis of techniques examined in this book because it provides you access to tonal relationships in all keys. For example, in the key of C, the tonic note, C, is designated as *do* and the 5th scale degree, G, is designated as *sol*. But in the key of G, because G is the tonic, it is designated as *do*, and C, the 4th scale degree, is designated as *fa*. In the key of B♭, B♭ is *do* and F is *sol*., etc.

The following chart shows all of the diatonic major scales with the designated solfege symbol for each scale degree of each of the major scales.

The text does occasionally reference the syllabic name for the third scale degree of minor scales; it is designated *me*, pronounced "may."

Ex. App_001

Solfege symbols in all major keys
<u>Key</u>

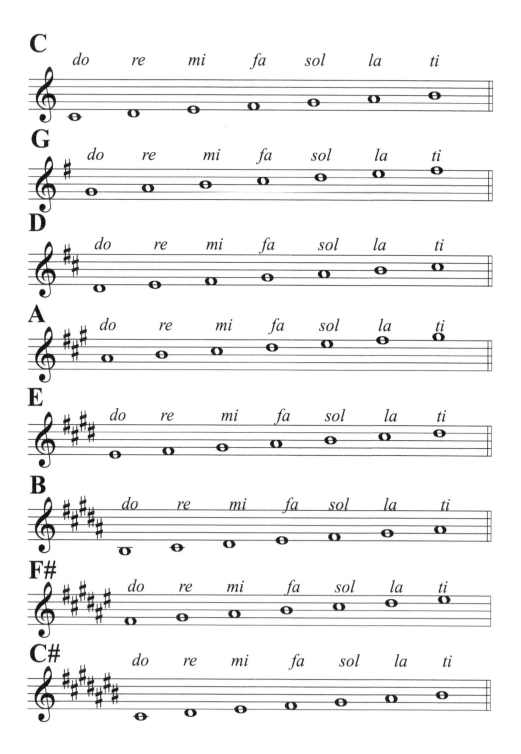

Ex. App_002

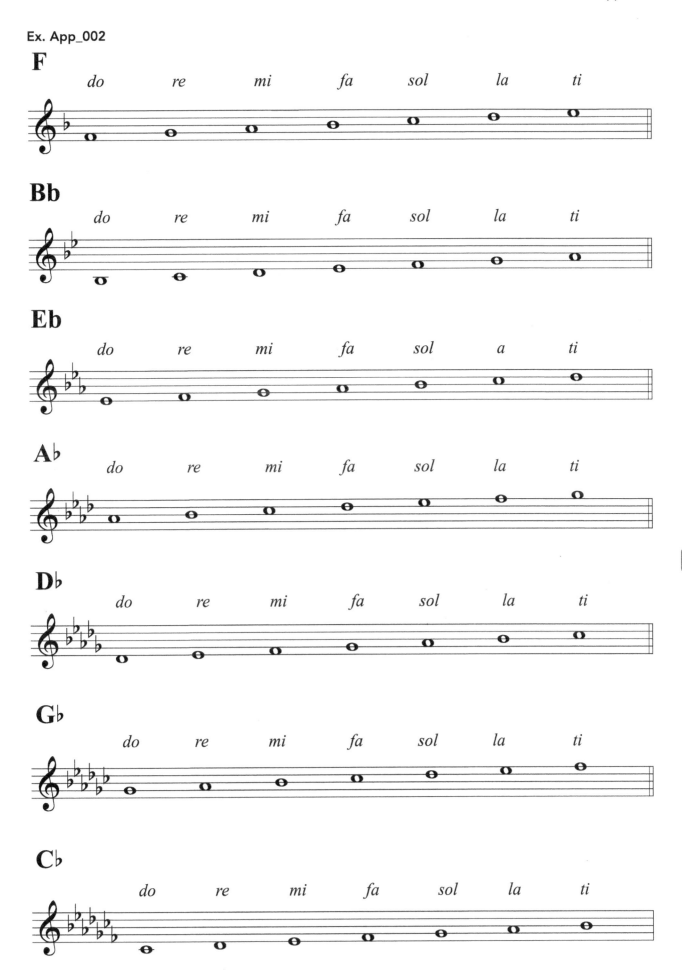

All chromatic notes are given a numerical designation rather than a solfege name, e.g., a G♯ in the key of C is designated as ♯5, not *si*.

Chord analysis symbols correspond to the chord symbols used in popular sheet music. Hence, a Cmaj7 in the key of C is analyzed as Imaj7, a Dm7 is designated as a IIm7, etc. Instead of the arcane symbols used during the baroque era and in classical harmonic analysis, a chord inversion is notated so that it corresponds to the actual chord that appears in a lead sheet or in a vocal piano arrangement. When an inversion appears, the chord analysis designates it with a number under a slash, e.g., in the key of C, a Cmaj7/E, a first inversion of a Cmaj7 chord, is designated as Imaj7/3, indicating that the third of the chord is in the bass; G/F chord in the key of C, a dominant seventh chord with its seventh in the bass, appears as V/7.

Ex. App_003

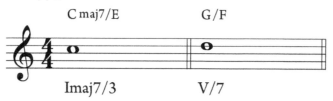

In a minor key, the designation of the scale degrees is based on the way intervals are named, i.e., on the major scale. Hence the minor third is designated ♭3, and the chord built on the 3rd scale degree in minor is designated ♭III. This symbology is used at Berklee College of Music, a college that trains more musicians in jazz and popular music than any other college of music in the world.

Ex. App_004

INDEX